SHRM • BNA Series ⟨6⟩

Managing HR in the Information Age

Editorial Advisory Board

ROBERT L. BERRA, AEP
Senior Vice President
Monsanto Company

CATHERINE DOWNES BOWER
Vice President, Communications and Public Relations
Society for Human Resource Management

STEPHEN J. CARROLL
Professor, Organizational Behavior & Industrial Relations
College of Business & Management
University of Maryland

PHILIP FARISH
Editor
Human Resource Management News

GERALD W. HOLDER, AEP
Senior Vice President (Retired)
Marion Laboratories

EDWARD H. LYONS
Vice President, Technical Services
Society for Human Resource Management

GEORGE T. MILKOVICH
Professor, Personnel & Human Resource Studies
New York State School of Industrial & Labor Relations
Cornell University

MARY GREEN MINER
Publisher, BNA Books
The Bureau of National Affairs, Inc.

RONALD C. PILENZO, SPHR
President
Society for Human Resource Management

JAMES H. WILKINS, JR., SPHR
Director, Personnel Accreditation Institute
Society for Human Resource Management

SHRM ◆ BNA Series ⟨6⟩

Managing HR in the Information Age

Randall S. Schuler
Editor

James Walker
Consulting Editor

The Bureau of National Affairs, Inc., Washington, D.C.

Copyright © 1991
The Bureau of National Affairs, Inc.

Library of Congress Cataloging-in-Publication Data

Managing HR in the information age / Randall S. Schuler, editor ; James Walker, consulting editor.
   p. cm.
   Includes indexes.
   ISBN 0-87179-606-6
   1. Personnel management.   2. Organizational change.
3. Communication in organization.   4. Communication in personnel management.   I. Schuler, Randall S.   II. Walker, James W., 1941-.
HF5549.M31344   1991
658.3—dc20   91-21249
                                                                        CIP

Authorization to photocopy items for internal or personal use, or the internal or personal use of specific clients, is granted by BNA Books for libraries and other users registered with the Copyright Clearance Center (CCC) Transactional Reporting Service, provided that $0.50 per page is paid directly to CCC, 27 Congress St., Salem, MA 01970. 0-87179-606-6/91/$0 + .50.

Published by BNA Books, 1231 25th St., N.W., Washington, D.C. 20037

Printed in the United States of America
International Standard Book Number: 0-87179-606-6

Preface

It has been 15 years since the first volume of the original ASPA Handbook of Personnel and Industrial Relations was published. A great deal has changed in our profession since then. No longer is PAIR (personnel and industrial relations) the accepted acronym for the management of human resources, primarily because our roles and our accountabilities are so different. And just as the acronyms have changed to reflect the evolving role of the human resource professional, so too has the society which represents them.

In late 1989, the members of ASPA, which stood for the American Society for Personnel Administration, adopted a new name: the Society for Human Resource Management, or SHRM. There were three basic reasons for this change: Members were no longer merely administrators, but important players in the corporate hierarchy; member representation had expanded throughout the world; and more and more frequently their titles said human resource management.

Human resource executives have been broadening their horizons and learning new ways to make a bigger contribution to their organizations. So, too, does the focus of this new HRM (human resource management) series indicate the extent to which the field has changed and how pace-setting human resource executives have been reshaping management practice. We have tried to reflect those changes in this new series.

The original series was eight volumes with a heavy emphasis on "how-to-do-it." This new series, comprised of six volumes, focuses more heavily on the why than the how, on strategy and integration rather than the specifics of execution.

The very process we used to develop this series indicates the shift in orientation. Each of the six volumes had a different well-known academician as its editor. These individuals were supported by at least one consulting editor, a senior practitioner in the HRM field whose role was to provide the "real world" perspective so necessary to this kind of project. And the overall series was guided by an editorial advisory board made up of practitioners, academicians, and representatives of BNA and SHRM. Members of the editorial advisory board are listed opposite the title page of this Volume.

Collectively, we struggled through the development of each volume and its chapters, striving to achieve the proper balance between a macro perspective of the profession and an evolutionary approach to the material presented. Our target audience—middle to upper level practitioners and those who aspire to such positions—was a constant presence during all of our discussions.

The six volumes in this series and their key players are:

1. *Human Resource Management: Evolving Roles and Responsibilities* edited by Lee Dyer, professor at Cornell University with Jerry Holder, retired vice president of human resources for Marion Laboratories, as consulting editor. Additional consulting editors included Robert Berra of Monsanto, Leo Contois of Consolidated Foods (retired) and Garth Dimon of Bristol-Meyers.

2. *Human Resource Planning, Employment and Placement* edited by Wayne Cascio, professor at the University of Colorado with Donald Sweet of Hawkins Associates, Inc. as consulting editor.

3. *Compensation and Benefits* edited by Luis R. Gomez-Mejia, professor at the University of Colorado with consulting editors Ray Olsen of TRW and George Milkovich of Cornell University.

4. *Employee and Labor Relations* edited by John Fossum, professor, University of Minnesota, with Jerauld Mattson of International Multifoods as consulting editor.

5. *Developing Human Resources* edited by Kenneth N. Wexley, professor, Michigan State University with John Hinrichs of Management Decision Systems as consulting editor.

6. *Managing Human Resources in the Information Age* with Randall S. Schuler of New York University as editor and James Walker of Walker and Associates as consulting editor.

This new management series reflects the coming of age of human resource management. SHRM is grateful to the individuals whose work is reflected in its pages and proud to mark this professional transition with such an outstanding series.

Ronald C. Pilenzo
Alexandria, VA
June 1990

Introduction

The decade of the 1990s is and promises to continue to be filled with rapid change, challenge, uncertainty, and intense global competition demanding ever higher standards of quality and rates of innovation while at the same time reducing costs. More than ever, there will be a premium on obtaining and utilizing information. For the human resource department, this means scanning the external environment to stay abreast of legal trends, international and national economic activity, social and demographic changes, and technological trends and developments. With this information, the HR department will create scenarios of how these external environmental forces are likely to impact the organization. For example, environmental scanning of work force demographics may indicate that there will be labor shortages of domestic workers but that any shortfalls are likely to be made up by unprecedented flows of immigration. With this and other scenarios from external environmental changes, the HR department will need to craft organizational responses. For these responses to be effective, they will need to be sufficiently anticipated, discussed, and shared with the organization, and then implemented with the full support of the organization.

For the HR department, the decade of the 1990s also means scanning the internal environment to stay abreast of the changes in strategies and directions of the organization, the needs and characteristics of the work force, and the needs of the line managers as they seek to make their organizations more competitive, flexible, adaptable, and focused. With this information, the HR department will also create scenarios as to how the internal environment is likely to affect the organization. These scenarios then will lead the HR department to craft potential responses that will enable the organization to successfully deal with the demands of the highly competitive environment. This may result in the HR department completely restructuring itself so that it can better serve the needs of its customers, particularly the line managers and employees.

As a consequence of the trends and events in the 1990s, the essence of this sixth volume in the SHRM/BNA series on HRM is getting, managing, and using human resource-related information and communications in organizations. Addressed under this general umbrella are topics such as: the sources and types of HR information in external and internal environments; who collects the information and how is it collected; how is the information managed; what are the forms of communication within the organization; what are the ways in which line managers and HR managers can share the information and communication processes; and what effect are the new needs and uses of communication and information having upon the structure of the HR profession, its roles, and the HR department.

Chapter 6.1, "Characteristics of the External Environment: Projections and Implications for HRM," by Randall S. Schuler, includes descriptions of work force demographics, international business conditions, economic and organizational trends, and technological trends and developments as projected for the 1990s. Along with these projections, the author presents several scenarios about their impact and the implications for organizations and their HR responses.

In dealing with the external environment described in the first chapter, organizations can do many things. Chapter 6.2, "Organizational Responses to the External Environment," by Ursula Fairbairn and Michelle M. Joyce, describes two major things organizations can do. They can either act on the environment directly, or they can develop programs within the organization in response to the environment. Development of these programs can be regarded as either reacting to or anticipating changes in the environment. This chapter describes and provides examples of what organizations are doing and can be doing in response to the external environment. These include such issues as working with the community on childcare programs, establishing drug programs, and offering eldercare for employees and their families.

Chapter 6.3, "Internal Information for Managing HR Programs," turns our attention to the HR information needs and sources within the organization. Here, the authors, Michael J. Burke and Gary Kaufman, describe the types, sources, and ways of gathering HR-relevant information that exists within the organization. This chapter is, in essence, a personnel research chapter, but it is written at a more managerial level rather than a technical level. Consequently, the role of HR information (research) in HR decision making is discussed. The purposes of gathering all this information are highlighted and examples of such are provided.

Chapter 6.4, "Communications in Times of Change," by Richard A. Guzzo and Katherine J. Klein, presents the prevalence and understanding of communication processes during times of organizational change. This chapter examines three patterns of communication and information flow in organizations: top-down, bottom-up, and lateral, in relation to four types of organizational change: conversion to computer technology, organizational down sizing, productivity and quality of work life improvement programs, and implementation of employee ownership programs. The goals of this chapter are to develop an understanding of how communication flows can facilitate change in these areas; and to identify some generally useful principles for managing communications during times of organizational change. Because this decade will continue to be filled with change, particularly of the types discussed by the authors, this is a very useful contribution for those responsible for facilitating change.

Chapter 6.5, "HR Information Systems," by Nicholas J. Beutell and Alfred J. Walker, covers issues related to the development, implementation, maintenance, and usage of HRISs in organizations. Issues of privacy and getting the rest of the organization to buy into the system are addressed. This chapter covers some of the technical detail, but is primarily aimed at the managerial and strategic levels.

In Chapter 6.6, "New HRM Roles, Responsibilities, and Structures," Stephen J. Carroll brings us full circle vis-a-vis Volume 1. Issues related to the HR department and HR profession are addressed. These range from the structure of the new HR department to the skills and knowledge required for tomorrow's HR professionals. Along with the "whats" are the "whys" of these changes and examples of companies that are making the changes for the information age of the 1990s. The "whys" refer back to many of the previous chapters in Volumes 1 through 5, thus offering a fine perspective for the entire series of books.

I would like to acknowledge the contributions of several dozen practitioners and academics who met in Washington on several occasions to review and criticize earlier outlines and drafts of this volume. Special thanks go to the authors of the chapters in this volume, both in their excitement about the project and their willingness to improve upon their initial submissions. Their efforts and those of Anne Scott of The Bureau of National Affairs combine to make this a fine volume to conclude the entire series of six volumes.

x   Managing HR in the Information Age

I would also like to thank Mary Miner of The Bureau of National Affairs and Cate Bower and Ron Pilenzo of the Society for Human Resource Management for sponsoring this major project.

Randall S. Schuler
New York City
May 1991

About the Authors

Chapter 6.1

Characteristics of the External Environment: Projections and Implications for HRM

Randall S. Schuler (Ph.D., Michigan State University) is a research professor, Stern School of Business, New York University. His interests are international HRM, organizational innovation, personnel and HRM, entrepreneurship, and the interface of competitive strategy and human resource management. He has authored or edited over 25 books, including *Dimensions of International Human Resource Management, Personnel and Human Resource Management,* 4th ed., *Case Problems in Management and Organizational Behavior,* 4th ed., *Effective Personnel Management,* 3rd ed., *Human Resource Management in the 1980s, Personnel and Human Resource Management Australia,* 2nd ed., and *Managing Job Stress.* In addition, he has contributed over 20 chapters to reading books and has published over 80 articles in professional journals and academic proceedings. Presently, he is on the Editorial Board of *Human Resource Planning, Human Resource Management, Organization Science, HR Reporter, Asia Pacific Human Resource Management,* and *Journal of High Technology Management.* He is a Fellow of the American Psychological Association. He is the recent past Editor of the *Human Resource Planning* journal.

The author is grateful for the permission to use the materials from *Workforce 2000* and *The Two Minute Warning* granted by Bill Johnston and Jack Grayson, respectively.

Chapter 6.2

Organizational Responses to the External Environment

Ursula F. Fairbairn (M.A.T., Harvard University) is the senior vice president–human resources of Union Pacific Corp., based at its corporate headquarters in Bethlehem, PA. Fairbairn has direct responsibility for all HR activities at the corporate level, including compensation, benefits, employee services, employee development, training, manpower planning, and organization. She previously was a corporate personnel executive at IBM.

Michelle M. Joyce (Ph.D., University of Minnesota) is the manufacturing manager for the Networking Systems Line of Business at IBM. She has previously held the positions of assistant to the site general manager, manager of operating and strategic planning for manufacturing, manager of compensation and benefits, and division manager of personnel research responsible for opinion survey administration, organizational development, and special research projects.

The authors are grateful for the guidance and assistance of Dr. James Fairfield-Sonn of Fairfield-Sonn Associates and the University of Hartford and for the invaluable collaboration and support of our colleagues at IBM, Dr. Andrea Goldberg and Ross Williams.

Chapter 6.3

Internal Information for Managing HR Programs

Michael J. Burke (Ph.D., Illinois Institute of Technology) is the director of industrial/organizational psychology and associate professor of human resource management, A.B. Freeman School of Business, Tulane University. He received his B.A. degree from the University of Notre Dame and his M.S. degree from Purdue University. His primary research interests and consulting activities are in the areas of personnel selection and cost/benefit (utility) analysis of HR programs.

Gary Kaufman (Ph.D., University of Tennessee) is the president of Human Resources Consulting Service, a firm that specializes in improving the effectiveness of an organization's human resources. Before starting his own firm, Kaufman managed the personnel research functions at IRS and J.C. Penney Co. He is currently an adjunct faculty member of the Owen Graduate School of Management at Vanderbilt University.

Chapter 6.4

Communication in Times of Change

Richard A. Guzzo (Ph.D., Yale University) is an associate professor of psychology and management at the University of Maryland. Previously he has been affiliated with McGill University and New York University. Guzzo's research and practice focus on team effectiveness, productivity improvement, and the consequences of employers' off-the-job influences. He has published two books and numerous articles and chapters on these subjects.

Katherine J. Klein (Ph.D., University of Texas) is an associate professor in the department of psychology at the University of Maryland at College Park. Her research focuses on the implementation of computerized technologies in the workplace, employee ownership, and levels of analysis issues. She has published numerous articles and chapters on these topics. In addition, she is a co-author (with Corey Rosen and Karen Young) of the book, *Employee Ownership in America*.

Chapter 6.5

HR Information Systems

Nicholas J. Beutell (Ph.D., Stevens Institute of Technology) is a professor of management and the department chair in the W. Paul Stillman School of Business at Seton Hall University. His research interests include work-family issues, HRIS, and global HR strategy.

Alfred J. Walker (M.B.A., Seton Hall University) is a principal with TPF&C in New York City. He is responsible for directing the strategy and planning aspects of the Human Resource Information Management (HRIM) practice. He specializes in the application of computer-based technology to the HR and management functions. This work includes developing requirements for HR systems, assisting clients with project management and systems architecture problems, vendor evaluation, and determining more effective methods of utilizing mainframe and microbased technology in personnel and payroll applications. Recent client engagements have included work with Coca-Cola, IBM, Marriott, Ontario Hydro, Price Waterhouse, Turner, and Xerox. Before joining TPF&C, Walker directed the HR systems work at AT&T for over 17 years. In addition, he was with Alexander & Alexander and Information Science Inc. for five years.

Chapter 6.6

New HRM Roles, Responsibilities, and Structures

Stephen J. Carroll (Ph.D., University of Minnesota) is a professor of human resource management and organizational behavior at the University of Maryland. He is a Fellow of the American Psychological Association and of the Academy of Management. He is a co-author of 11 books, including *Management by Objectives; The Management of Compensation, Performance Appraisal and Review Systems; Management; Managing Organizational Behavior;* and *Cases in Management.* Carroll also is an active researcher, has been on the editorial boards of several journals, and has consulted with a variety of organizations in both the public and private sectors.

Contents

Preface   v

Introduction   vii

6.1 Characteristics of the External Environment: Projections and Implications for HRM   6-1
Randall S. Schuler

Work-Force Demographics   6-2
International Factors   6-17
Economic and Organizational Trends   6-25
Technological Trends and Developments   6-36
The Changing External Environment and the Practice of HRM   6-42

6.2 Organizational Responses to the External Environment   6-50
Ursula Fairbairn
Michelle M. Joyce

Social and Demographic Environment   6-51
Economic and Competitive Environment   6-65
Legal and Regulatory Environment   6-71
HRM and the Environment in the Future   6-78

6.3 Internal Information for Managing HR Programs   6-84
Michael J. Burke
Gary Kaufman

Decision Making   6-84
Establishing Program Goals   6-85

Organizational Design and Position
Management   6-86
Staffing   6-91
Training and Development   6-99
Performance Management   6-107
Compensation and Benefits   6-116
Labor Relations   6-121
Personnel Research   6-129
Summary   6-136

6.4 Communication in Times of Change   6-142
Richard A. Guzzo
Katherine J. Klein

Communication and Organizational Effectiveness   6-142
Organizational Downsizing   6-143
Employee Ownership   6-146
Programs for Quality and Productivity   6-151
The Implementation of Computer Technologies   6-156
Conclusions   6-160

6.5 HR Information Systems   6-167
Nicholas J. Beutell
Alfred J. Walker

HRIS Growth 1970s to Present   6-168
Components of an HRIS   6-171
Selecting and Implementing an HRIS   6-172
HRIS Data Base Concepts   6-180
Data Administration: The Human Resource Information Center (HRIC)   6-183
HRIS Applications and Modules   6-190
Successful HRIS Installations   6-197

6.6 New HRM Roles, Responsibilities, and Structures 6-204
Stephen J. Carroll

Evolution of HRM Roles 6-205
New Focus for Traditional HRM Roles 6-205
HR Managers as Change Agents 6-208
Greater Emphasis on Strategic HRM 6-211
New Orientation Toward HRM Clientele 6-213
Behavioral Requirements of Future HR Managers 6-214
New HRM Structures 6-217
New Staffing Requirements for HR Professionals 6-221
Conclusion 6-222

Author Index 6-229

Subject Index 6-235

6.1
Characteristics of the External Environment: Projections and Implications for HRM

Randall S. Schuler

Today's organizations operate in an increasingly complex environment characterized by rapid change. Social, demographic, economic, and technological shifts all impact on employers and organizational life. Anticipating these changes and preparing organizations to meet the challenges of the future will become a paramount skill for all HR managers.[1]

A major way to attain this capability is through environmental scanning. This process of systematic surveillance and interpretation helps to identify events, elements, and conditions in the environment that have potential relevance and impact for an organization.[2] Environmental scanning encompasses several components or steps: selecting forecasting techniques, forecasting future conditions, identifying and prioritizing major HRM issues, and developing plans that prepare an organization to deal successfully with these issues.

Of the many aspects of the external environment,[3] most organizations and HR managers focus their attention on four major ones: (1) work-force demographics, (2) international conditions, (3) economic and organizational trends, and (4) technological trends and developments. In describing and discussing these aspects of the external environment, this chapter will aim to identify: (1) the type of information to gather from each component of the environment, (2) where HR managers can systematically collect this information,

(3) the current and future (predicted) conditions or characteristics of each component, and (4) the implications this information might have on future HRM practices.

Work-Force Demographics

No area has greater implications for HRM than the characteristics and quality of the population and its important subcomponent, the work force. HR managers increasingly are realizing that past demographic data does not provide good predictions of the future. Work-force homogeneity, high skill levels, and big labor pools are features of another era. Failure to consider workforce availability and quality when planning for organizational growth and development is proving to be—and will increasingly become—fatal. As a result, HR managers must plan for their organizations' future work-force needs.

In addition to planning for the right numbers at the right place and time, HR managers will become more concerned with attracting potential job applicants, training them, and managing a work force of highly diverse employees in terms of their backgrounds, needs, sex, age, country of origin, and values. This section is a start in the direction of addressing this concern. It looks at what is and what is projected to be. It concludes with some implications for HRM.

Population and Labor Force Projections

With a U.S. population of 250 million today, most projections indicate that the rate of population growth will slow, increasing to just over 300 million in the year 2080. While the most aggressive projections forecast that the U.S. population will reach slightly over 500 million by the year 2080, the least aggressive growth scenario predicts the population in that year will be just under 300 million.[4] These projections differ rather dramatically and illustrate the rather speculative nature of forecasts stretching decades into the future. As a result, most employers, as well as the analyses in this chapter, concentrate on population projections for only the next 10 to 15 years.

Reduced Population and Labor Force Growth

By the year 2000, the U.S. population will reach 275 million, a 15 percent increase from the 240 million U.S. residents in 1985.[5] This rate of gain, approximately one percent per year during the 1980s and three-fourths of one percent per year during the 1990s, is well below the average for the last two decades. At this rate, the U.S. population will grow more slowly than at any time in the nation's history, except for during the Great Depression. The most conservative assumptions (low fertility, high death rates, and low immigration) project even smaller gains, with the population climbing to only about 256 million by the year 2000, or seven percent increase. With opposite assumptions, the population could reach 281 million, a gain of 18 percent.

Changes in immigration present the greatest uncertainties in any population forecast. The U.S. Bureau of the Census assumes that immigration during the balance of the century will match the rate of legal immigration during the recent past: 450,000 per year. At this rate, immigrants and their offspring will comprise a little more than one-fourth of the U.S. population gain. However, if the estimated rate of legal and illegal immigration over the past 15 years continues unchanged, immigration would add 750,000 persons per year to the population and would account for almost half of the net gain.

Slower population growth will be mirrored by reduced growth of the labor force. During the 1990s, the labor force will expand by about 22 percent, from 115 million to 141 million. This increase of 26 million stands in contrast to the labor force increase of 42 million that occurred during the 1980s. Like the general population, the labor force will be increasing at a slower rate during the 1990s than at any time since the 1930s.

Some of these projections are more stable than others. Changes in birth and death rates will not significantly affect projected labor force growth, since these statistics pertain mainly to children and the elderly. However, immigration and changes in labor force participation could have large impacts. For example, a strong economy could pull more workers into the labor market or international unrest could swell the number of illegal aliens seeking jobs. Using the highest rates of immigration projected by the Bureau of Labor Statistics, the U.S. labor force would reach 147 million in 2000. On the other hand, a weak economy, growing desires for early retirement, renewed emphasis on child care by stay-at-home parents, or drastic border-closing legislation could all reduce the size of the labor force. This scenario could cause the labor force to rise to a mere 129 million. In other words, the work force could increase by as little as 12 percent, the slowest rate in the country's history, or by as much as 28 percent, almost as fast as during the 1970s.

In addition to aggregate population and work-force projections, changes in household characteristics can impact organizations and HR planning. At present, almost half of U.S. households have dual wage earners. The size of this group, as well as the number of homes headed by single women, is expected to increase. As a result, working-age individuals will face more time pressure, both at home and at work. How that pressure will affect the efficiency of home and work life remains unknown, but it clearly will increase the need for high-quality child care:[6]

> The evidence is slowly and steadily growing that present warehousing arrangements, with children's earlier entry into nursery school or extended day care, is not good for children, in two ways. The present arrangements on a statistical basis almost surely reduce the level of intelligence. Secondly, group activity creates other-directed, rather than autonomous, independent young people and adults. The work of Robert Zajonc at the University of Michigan makes it unequivocally clear that the child is the enemy of the child when it comes to intellectual development. When you put these kids in collective arrangements earlier and longer, you incur, albeit statistically, a decrement in the average IQ in their environment. In other words, the company of other children provides less intellectual stimulation than that of adults. As this becomes more widely known, you can anticipate that organizations will be forced to accommodate in new ways. What may be the implications when 20 percent of the people in an organization are bringing a kid to work every day?

Other family-related issues are covered in the section below on males and females in the work force.

Age Characteristics of the Labor Pool

The diminishing growth rate of the total population and the work force has dramatic bearing on the age profile of the labor pool. American industry currently faces a shrinking supply of young workers. After more than two decades of growth, the nation's population between ages 16 and 24 has peaked:[7]

Between 1976 and 1980, the labor force grew an average of 2.8 percent, but between 1991 and 1995, the rate of growth will drop to 1.1 percent. Additionally, while over 3 million people joined the labor force in 1978, under 2 million people are projected to enter the labor force each year from 1987 to 1995.

People aged 25 to 54 will constitute a greater percentage of the labor force, increasing from 61 percent in 1975 to 73 percent in 1995. Comparatively, the proportion of younger people (aged 16 to 24) and older people (aged 55 and over) will decline from 24 percent in 1975 to 16 percent in 1995, and from 15 percent to 11 percent, respectively. Between 1984 and 1995, 21.6 million people aged 25-54 will enter the labor force, while the number of workers aged 16 to 24, and 55 and over, will decline by 2.7 million and .8 million, respectively.

Some firms already are facing increased labor shortages and have developed innovative recruitment practices so as not to go understaffed. For example, Pizza Hut leases a van to shuttle in workers from Paramus, NJ to Jersey City, a community about 15 miles away:[8]

> The tactic, new to Pizza Hut, addresses a growing problem called "geographic mismatch" as many new jobs are created in suburbs situated for from pools of the unemployed. As the labor supply generally tightens, mismatch is prompting some employers—nobody seems to know how many—to subsidize or provide transportation for low-paid workers.

This practice may prove competitively successful for individual businesses, but for industries which depend on young people to staff entry-level positions, fierce competition may necessitate the development of labor substitutes. The result could be even lower levels of service in some industries, such as fast food.

Graying of the Work Force

As the work force gets older, so does the entire population. Life expectancies are predicted to increase through the year 2000. Increased longevity, combined with the passage of the Baby Boom generation and its progeny, will result in an increasingly older population. This trend has implications not only for Social Security, but also for private pension programs, especially those offering defined benefits.

Other population projections indicate that the first decade of the twenty-first century will mark the graying of the work force, with a 42 percent increase in the 55 to 64 age category between 2000 and 2010. The population of persons ages 45 to 64 is expected to increase from 43.6 million in 1980 to 72.9 million in 2010, while the age 65 and older population is projected to grow from 24.5 million in 1980 to 42.8 million in 2010.[9]

The large increase in middle-aged workers may collide with corporate efforts to reduce middle management or to reduce vulnerability to demographic noncompetitiveness. Because a large share of the skills and productivity of older workers reflect the specialized needs of a particular firm, older workers who lose jobs will have difficulty finding new jobs that match their previous salaries. A turbulent economy in which many firms expand and contract in response to market conditions will prove especially difficult for middle-aged and older workers. As a result, the long-standing pattern of increasing earnings until retirement may be substantially altered. In addition, an aging population may cause many industries that depend on young people for market growth to retrench. Of these industries, higher education, household furnishing, and rental housing construction could feel the greatest impact.

On balance, the aging work force may produce favorable effects in the early 1990s, but this trend could turn strongly negative by the turn of the century, as aging pushes the huge Baby Boom generation into its fifties.

Women in the Work Force

Ever since employers began looking to replace soldiers during World War II, women have been entering the work force in dramatic and increasing numbers. In 1948, about 30 percent of women were working outside the home; by 1988, this statistic had reached over 50 percent. From a different perspective, less than one-third of the 1948 work force consisted of women; by 1985, women made up 44 percent of the labor market.[10]

This trend is expected to continue during the 1990s. By the year 2000, women will make up approximately 50 percent of the work force, and 61 percent of all women will hold down a job outside the home. In addition, women will comprise about three-fifths of the new entrants into the labor force between 1990 and 2000.

The flood of women entering the work force has been driven by powerful social and economic trends. One of the biggest forces has been changed attitudes about the American family. As late as 1957, only 33 percent of married women worked outside the home, compared to 80 percent of single women and 65 percent of divorced and

Characteristics of the External Environment   6-7

separated women combined.[11] But in the early 1960s, the status quo began to change. Women attained higher levels of education; social values began to shift; and the seeds of the women's movement began to take root. By 1987, the labor participation rate for married women more than doubled to 68 percent, while the rate for formerly married women rose to 70 percent, and the participation rate of single women stayed at 80 percent.[12]

Changing attitudes about marriage also have affected workforce composition. Married men are no longer the mainstay of the working population. With people marrying later, single women are working longer and are less likely to leave the work force when they do get married. Divorce rates have risen, and formerly married women constitute more than half the growth rate among women workers since 1970.[13]

Not only are working wives now commonly accepted, so are working mothers. A big decline in the birth rate during the 1960s led to an influx of women of childbearing age into the American work force. Participation rates surged well into the 1970s and now 76 percent of working women are in their childbearing years. In addition, the fastest-growing segment of the national work force is women with children younger than age 6.[14] By 1987, mothers were returning to work after giving birth sooner than ever before:[15]

> About three-fifths of mothers whose youngest child was between toddler age and first grade were working or looking for work, with little difference for individual ages of 2 to 5 years. Ten years earlier, (in 1977), comparable participation rates ranged from 42 percent for those with 2-year-olds to 51 percent for those with 5 year-olds, while in 1982, participation ranged from 52 percent for those with 2-year-olds to 57 percent for those with 5-year-olds.
>
> About 53 percent of children under age 6 had mothers who were in the labor force in 1987, including 50 percent of those 1 year old and younger. In 1977, the proportions were 38 percent for all children under 6, and 31 percent for the youngest group. Five years ago, the proportions were 46 percent and 42 percent, respectively. Overall, three-fifths (60.2 percent) of the nation's children under 18 are now in families where the mother is working or looking for work, as compared with 55 percent in 1982 and 48 percent in 1977.

Slow economic growth has also made two earners a necessity for many families striving for a middle-class life-style. Technology has simplified housework while society has redefined the role of women to include paid employment as the norm for most. Yet, women continue to be concentrated in traditionally female occupations that pay less than men's jobs. In 1980, 32 percent of all women were in jobs where more than 90 percent of the incumbents were female. As of 1983, the wages of women working full-time averaged only 66 percent of what men earned, up only 4 percentage points from the figure in 1967.

Some signs, however, indicate that these patterns may change substantially over the next 10 years. While women are entering and re-entering the labor force in greater numbers and greater rates, their exit rate is likely to remain low. During the 1990s, 50 percent more men than women are expected to leave the labor force. As a result, 63 percent of labor force growth is expected to be women and female entrance into typically male-dominated jobs is likely to accelerate.

The influx of women into higher education may create new occupational and wage patterns. Women are a rapidly increasing share of advanced education.[16] In 1983, women constituted 45 percent of those receiving accounting degrees, 36 percent of new lawyers, 36 percent of computer science majors, and 42 percent of business majors. These proportions appear likely to rise even further over the next decade. Moreover, while women's wages relative to men's have shown little improvement over the past two decades, the pattern of the last five years is more upward, with relative wages gaining five percentage points in five years. One Rand study projects that women's wages will equal 74 percent of men's by the year 2000. Nonetheless, this wage disparity will continue to put pressure on families and companies. Compensation practices and pay equity will continue to offer opportunities for firms to attract younger females into the work force.

Minorities in the Work Force

Over the next decade, blacks, Hispanics, and other minorities will make up a large share of the expansion of the labor force. Between 1990 and 2000, nonwhites will comprise 29 percent of the net additions to the work force, forming more than 15 percent of the work force in the year 2000.[17]

Black women will account for the largest share of the increase in the non-white labor force. By the year 2000, black women will outnumber black men in the work force, a striking contrast to the pattern among whites, where men outnumber women by almost three to two.

By almost every measure of employment, labor-force participation, earnings, and education, black and Hispanic minorities suffer much greater disadvantages than white. Compounding these statistical indices are the extensively analyzed and debated indications of social disadvantage, such as poor performance in schools, greater dependence on welfare, greater incidence of broken families and children born to unmarried mothers, and higher rates of criminal arrest.

Two particularly disturbing trends in the patterns of disadvantage among minorities are the declines in male labor-force participation and the related increase in the numbers of female household heads. From 1970 to 1984, for example, the proportion of prime-age black men in the labor force dropped from 79 percent to 74 percent, while the proportion of black families headed by women rose from 29 to 43 percent. This trend stands in contrast to Hispanic workers:[18]

> The labor force participation rate for Hispanics is very similar to that of whites. In 1985, the labor force participation rate for the overall population was 64.8 percent, compared to 65 percent for whites, 62.9 percent for blacks, and 64.6 percent for Hispanics. Hispanic men have higher labor force participation rates than white or black men. Age distribution, however, affects the labor force participation rate, the Council notes. Hispanic men, as a population, are younger than non-Hispanics, and they are more likely to leave school early and join the labor force. Young adult men, explains the report, tend to have higher labor force participation rates than older men, thus boosting the participation rate for adult Hispanic men. However, Hispanic women have lower labor force participation rates than white or black women.

Immigrants in the Work Force

The number of immigrants in the work force is expected to grow dramatically over the next 10 years. Table 1 shows the projected percentage increase in the work force between 1985 and 2000, with immigrants representing a significant net addition.

This trend reflects a significant increase in immigrant population. Even with a more restrictive immigration law, approximately 600,000 legal and illegal immigrants a year are projected to enter the United States throughout the balance of the century. Two-thirds or more of working-age immigrants are likely to join the labor force, bringing skills and a willingness to accept jobs that others leave vacant. In the South and West, where these workers are concentrated, immigrants are likely to reshape local economies dramatically, promoting faster economic growth and labor surpluses.[19]

Table 1

Entrants into the Labor Force
1985-2000

	1985 Labor Force	Net New Workers, 1985-2000
Total	115,461,000	25,000,000
Native White Men	47%	15%
Native White Women	36%	42%
Native Non-white Men	5%	7%
Native Non-white Women	5%	13%
Immigrant Men	4%	13%
Immigrant Women	3%	9%

Source: Reprinted with permission from W.B. Johnston, *Workforce 2000*. Indianapolis: Hudson Institute, xxi, 1987.

Skill Levels in the Projected Work Force

While the younger labor pool shrinks and unfilled jobs increase, black teenagers still have a 35 percent unemployment rate and the jobless rate for blacks generally is more than twice that of whites. The Hispanic unemployment rate is approximately 30 percent higher than that of whites. These dismal statistics in part reflect an overall decline in the skill level of labor entrants:[20]

- Illiteracy among minority students is as high as 40 percent. By the year 2000, minorities will make up a majority of the school-age population in 10 states.

- On standardized tests between 1983 and 1986, American high school seniors came in last in biology among students from 13 countries, including Hungary and Singapore. They were 11th in chemistry and ninth in physics.

- In all, 84 percent of the 23,000 people who took an exam of entry-level jobs at New York Telephone in 1988 failed.

In addition to these numbers, approximately 30 percent of the current work force is functionally illiterate. In Japan, the illiteracy rate in the work force is less than 5 percent.

Employers have begun to feel the impact of this skill deficit. New York's "Chemical Bank must interview 40 applicants to find one who can be successfully trained as a teller. And IBM Corp. discovered after installing millions of dollars worth of fancy computer in its Burlington (VT.) factories that it had to teach high-school algebra to thousands of workers before they could run them."[21]

The Conference Board surveyed 130 large companies and 64 percent listed education as their primary community-relations concern, ahead of local economic development.[22] David Kearns, Xerox's former chairman and CEO, has said "the American work force is running out of qualified people. If current demographic and economic trends continue, American business will have to hire a million new workers a year who can't read, write, or count. Teaching them how, and absorbing the lost productivity while they're learning, will cost industry $25 billion a year for as long as it takes."[23] Donald Davis, Chairman of Stanley Works, observes: "The cost of incompetence in U.S. industry is higher than any of us realizes. You can't quantify it, but it shows up in missed opportunities, in bad decisions, and other ways. It's all around us."[24]

Illiteracy is but a symptom of the larger problem afflicting the U.S. economy. The $150 billion yearly trade deficit and a foreign debt of half a trillion dollars reflect the inability of a large percentage of the American work force to compete effectively in an integrated world economy. "Much of the success of Japan stems from the fact that its blue-collar workers can interpret advanced mathematics, read complex engineering blueprints, and perform sophisticated tasks on the factory floor far better than blue collars in the United States," says Merry I. White, professor of comparative sociology at Boston University and author of *The Japanese Educational Challenge*.[25]

Employee Values

Stagnating productivity rates are often attributed to the decline or disappearance of the work ethic. According to some commentators, however, the work ethic has not disappeared. People still value work, but the type of work that interests them has changed. They want challenging jobs that provide them with freedom to make decisions. In general, employees do not seek or desire rapid promotions, especially when they involve geographic transfers, but workers do seek influence and control.

According to a recent study comparing the work values of employees over 40 years old with those under 40:[26]

- Members of the older generation, products of the World War II era, accept authority, while employees from the younger generation, who grew up during the Vietnam war, do not trust authority.

- While members of the older generation see work as a duty and a vehicle for financial support, those of the younger generation think work should be fun and a place to meet other young people.

- Employees who are over 40 believe that experience is the necessary road to promotion, and are willing to spend time in an "apprenticeship," with the expectation of reward for that effort. Younger employees, on the other hand, believe that people should advance just as quickly as their competence permits.

- "Fairness" for the older generation means treating people equally; for the younger generation, it means allowing people to be different.

These values tend to reflect the contrasting concerns of Baby Boomers and their working parents. Their parents, and even some older baby boomers (remember this group ranges in age from approximately 30 to 45), tend to value job security, employment security, and income security. Because this older group usually is less mobile, organizations need to target training and retraining not just at the entry-level worker but at this older worker as well.

One value that seems to cut across employee age groups is the desire for ownership:[27]

> The new buzzword in employee motivation is "ownership," which can mean either an equity share or just a worker's sense that he counts. Says Harvard Business School Professor J. Richard Hackman: "If you want me to care, then I want to be treated like an owner and have some real voice in where we're going." The concept grows out of the "employee involvement" of the 1980s, which got off to a shaky start with quality circles that never amounted to much, then grew stronger as workers were brought into decision-making. Rochester Products in Coopersville, Michigan, which makes fuel injectors for GM, solicits advice from workers on who should be promoted to supervisor. The company also asks them to help evaluate potential suppliers.

Ownership goes a step further by seeking to put employees in the shoes of entrepreneurs. Xerox, 3M, and Honeywell, help finance startups by employees who have promising ideas in return for minority share. Alfred West, founder and chairman of SEI Corp., a $123-million-a-year financial services company in Wayne, Pennsylvania, is planning a more radical experiment with his 1,100 workers. He intends to divide his company into entrepreneurial units, each led by a so-called champion who has been particularly effective in promoting whatever the unit does. West will give each group of employees a 20 percent interest in their unit. After a suitable period, he will invite an investment bank to put a price on the unit. Then West will pay members for their 20 percent. If the unit flops, the members get nothing beyond their salaries. Says West: "I'm an entrepreneur, and I want more people like that here."

Workers also place significant emphasis on individual values of liberty, freedom, and privacy. These values have received more attention and analysis due to employers' attempts to deal with the increasing drug usage of employees and job applicants. While the Employee Polygraph Protection Act of 1988 offered individuals some protection for privacy and due process, the issue has not been settled. Workplace substance use and abuse does not appear to be on the decline, and similar privacy concerns exist regarding AIDS. Thus, it appears as if employers will need to continue addressing both these issues throughout the 1990s.

Implications for HRM

While some HRM implications of these demographic characteristics have already been noted, two topics merit further discussion: (1) training and development, and (2) managing workforce diversity.

Training and Development

With increasing illiteracy among future and current employees, organizations will face an imperative to get involved training and retraining. Some organizations already have begun offer programs for youths and minorities. The exact type of help varies dramatically.

Businesses have a wealth of management and financial expertise which can help schools to improve administrative procedures. They can advise principals on school management and assist in financial planning. Businesses can also provide literacy volunteers.

Time Inc., among other companies, brings disadvantaged students to the company headquarters in New York City to receive weekly tutoring in reading by employees in their offices. Several corporations are providing gifts of much-needed equipment and teacher training. Honeywell Inc., sponsors a summer Teacher Academy, where Minnesota high school math and science teachers team with researchers to develop class projects.[28]

General Electric (GE) has invested $1 million in a program in a poor, black, rural area of Lowndes County (AL) where it operates a $700 million plastics plant.[29] The program partly pays for tutoring sessions given by the faculty of Tuskegee Institute for students in secondary school. In addition, GE has recently initiated a $20 million program which proposes to double the number of students from inner city public schools entering college by the year 2000.[30] Arizona State University, armed with a $100,000 grant from AT&T, has focused on female Hispanic students. This novel program is trying to change the Hispanic cultural pattern which discourages college for women. Teams of mothers and their teenage daughters are brought to the college campus to impress them with the need for college training and to help the young females become eligible for entrance.[31]

Business leaders in Dallas have set up a "I Have a Dream Foundation" to reward kids who stay in school with college tuition aid. In 1982, members of Boston's Private Industry Council launched the Boston Compact, an agreement signed with the Boston school system, which pledged to recruit 200 companies willing to give priority hiring status to graduates of Boston's 17 high schools. The schools, in turn, agreed to specific targets for better attendance, improved math and reading competence, and reduced dropout rates. More than 600 companies currently participate and in 1987, the program provided 1,007 full-time jobs as well as 3,010 summer jobs. Ninety-three percent of all graduates have gone on to higher education, a job, or the military. The results are impressive, given that Boston has a 74 percent minority student population.[32]

In terms of internal practices, firms will need to hire minorities in greater numbers as the pool of competent white males shrinks. Employee testing can help organizations identify specific skill areas that need remedial attention. In all likelihood, training and development programs will have to provide not only job-specific skills but basic reading, writing, communication, and math skills. Employers essentially will have to do the job that public education has not done.[33]

When four New York City banks tried to fill 250 entry-level teller jobs last summer, they found only 100 qualified applicants. The banks' problem raises a compelling question: Aside from teaching the three R's, how can schools best prepare students for the workplace? American Express and Shearson Lehman Hutton think they have an answer. In 1982, working with the New York City Public schools, they began the Academy of Finance, a two-year program for juniors and seniors that combines classroom instruction with on-the-job experience. In addition to their regular course loads, Academy students take classes in economics and finance, and attend seminars that stress good work habits, such as dressing neatly and being on time. Between their junior and senior years they work as paid interns at financial services firms.

Managing Work-Force Diversity

The radical demographic changes in the work force also mean that businesses will need to develop competence in managing very diverse employees. "Successful organizations will react to diversity as the important business issue it is by implementing proactive, strategic human resource planning. Short-term strategies designed to circumvent the situation will keep an organization from effectively positioning itself in tomorrow's world of cultural, gender, and lifestyle diversity."[34] Top corporate management will need to educate line managers on the two goals of "diversity competence": productivity growth and market share expansion, both domestically and internationally.

Most HR managers will need to focus on 10 key areas in managing diversity:[35]

- *Recruitment.* HR managers will have to make a concerted effort to find quality minority hires by improved college relations programs.
- *Career Development.* Programs should expose those minority and female employees with high potential to the same key developmental jobs that have led traditionally to senior positions for their white, male counterparts.
- *Diversity Training for Managers.* Such training should address stereotypes and cultural differences which interfere with the full participation of all employees in the workplace.
- *Diversity Training for Employees.* Employees may need instruction to understand the corporate culture requirements for success in the firm and the career choices open to them.

- *Upward Mobility.* Efforts should be made to break the "invisible ceiling" and increase the number of minorities and women in upper management through mentors and executive appointment.

- *Diverse Input and Feedback.* HR managers should ask minority and female employees themselves what they need rather than ask managers what they think minorities and females need.

- *Self-Help.* Employers should encourage networking and the development of support groups among minorities and women.

- *Accountability.* Managers should be held accountable for developing their diverse work forces.

- *Systems Accommodation.* Company practices should develop respect and support for cultural diversity through recognition of different cultural and religious holidays, diet restrictions, and the like.

- *Outreach.* Organizations which support minority organizations and programs will enhance their reputation as multicultural leaders.

Businesses are taking these diversity issues very seriously. Digital Equipment Corporation now has a manager with the title of "Manager of Valuing Differences," while Honeywell Inc. has a "Director of Work-force Diversity," and Avon Products, Inc. has a "Director of Multicultural Planning and Design."[36] At Hewlett-Packard, training sessions teach managers about different cultures and races and about their own gender biases and training needs.[37] Procter & Gamble has implemented "valuing diversity" programs throughout the company. A mentor program, designed to retain black and female managers, was developed at one plant, and one-day workshops on diversity were given to all new employees.[38]

Other organizations look to the employees themselves for guidance on managing diversity. Equitable Life Assurance Society encourages minorities and women to form support groups. These groups periodically meet with Equitable's CEO to discuss problems in the company pertaining to them. Avon has several councils representing various groups, each having a senior manager present at meetings. These councils inform and advise top management.[39]

Characteristics of the External Environment   6-17

Outside sources, too, can help corporations as they grapple with the diversity issue. The American Institute for Managing Diversity at Morehouse College in Atlanta, GA, conducts two-day seminars. Copeland-Griggs Productions of San Francisco, CA has developed a three-part film/video training series, with an accompanying training manual for each part.

International Factors

Several important aspects of the international scene are having and will continue to have a significant impact on HRM. The international factors reviewed here include: a) the world's populations, b) the shape of the world economy and the locations of the world's economic powers, c) worldwide productivity rates, d) worldwide labor costs, and e) organizational structures and shapes to compete in the worldwide marketplace. The following discussion examines each of these factors, along with their implications for HRM.

Worldwide Population Characteristics

Slightly over five billion people currently populate this planet. By the year 2000, the worldwide population is projected to reach around eight billion. At current growth rates, the work force in the third world nations alone will expand by about 700 million over the next 20 years. The bulk of the projected growth in the world population and work force will occur in Asia, which will account for approximately 50 percent of total growth. Between 1990 and 2000, Asia's work force is projected to grow by 244 million, while Europe's is projected to grow by only 6 million.[40]

Even though Asian countries currently have the highest populations, Europe bought almost 20 percent more U.S. exports than Asia in 1988. However, between 1987 and 1988, exports to Europe grew only 1 percent, while those to Asia grew by 22 percent. On the import side, the United States obtained 43 percent from Asia and only 24 percent from Europe in 1988. Because of the lagging economic growth in Africa and Latin America, the major U.S. markets will continue to be Asia and Europe, but Asia will become the more predominant market because of its rapid population growth, superior technology, and efficient organization. The rather wide wage disparity with the United States and Europe will also continue to assist Asia in its rapid development. In fact, the "Little Tigers" (Taiwan, South Korea, Singapore, and Hong Kong), which have the lowest wage rates in Asia (outside China), are expected to have the highest growth rates of any countries in the world over the next five years. Within Europe, France and Italy are expected to be the fastest growers.

Although the world is growing primarily in Asia, English is predicted to emerge as the one true universal language. More than 350 million people worldwide currently speak English, another 400 million use it as a second language, and 350 million have an understanding of it.[41] U.S. corporations, however, still need to respect the vast differences in other cultures and understand the language and customs of other nations. In fact, ignoring these differences will only invite even more international competition in the marketplace and displace U.S. goods and services. The following is an example:[42]

> From 1945 to about 1975, an outstanding global characteristic of American business was the ability to go anywhere in the world and build a chemical plant or a refinery, a fertilizer plant, or a factory. Today, without question, we are bested in doing that by a recent third world country. The Koreans do it better. Why? Suppose you are a Saudi Arabian and you hired an American firm to put up a chemical plant. What happens? They assemble a rag-tag band of global roustabouts. They come into your country. They booze it up. They catcall at the women on the street. They preach their own parochial religion. Every one of those things is an offense to the Moslems. What happens if you call in a Korean team? They come in by the planeload from ditch digger to field superintendent. They do a perfectly satisfactory job. They do not preach Buddhism, they do not booze it up, and they are not caterwauling at the women on the street. The Koreans have discovered what American business either never knew or have forgotten. They discovered the customer.

Economic Conditions

Just as populations have changed over the past and are expected to continue to change over the next 20 years, so are the economic conditions of the world. As shown in Table 2, the U.S. share of markets in several industries declined dramatically between 1970 and 1987.[43]

In a similar fashion, U.S. net international investments went from positive $141 billion in 1981 to negative $368 billion in 1987, making the U.S. the world's largest debtor nation. In 1960 the U.S. world share of GNP was 34 percent; today it is approximately 20 percent. By comparison, Japan's went from 3 percent to 15 per-

Table 2

U.S. Share: Technology Markets

	1970	1987
PHONOGRAPHS	90%	1%
COLOR TV'S	90	10
BALLBEARINGS	88	71
TELEPHONE SETS	99	25
SEMICONDUCTORS	89	64
VCR'S	10	1
AUDIO RECORDERS	40	1

cent during the same period—even though its population base is approximately one half that of the United States. These radical shifts in relative percentages of GNP reflect in large part the differential rates of productivity growth. Compared with Japan and several European nations, the United States has had the slowest productivity growth (in terms of manufacturing) for most of the past 25 years.

Nonetheless, the United States still has the highest level of GNP per employee. This position is predicted to change within the next 20 to 30 years. The various predictions for several major trading partners are shown in Table 3.

Financial Realignment

These rather dramatic changes in the economic position of the United States will be accompanied by a rapid realignment of industrial power and financial ownership in the world. For example, Japan and Germany have 52 percent of bank deposits in comparison to 9 percent for the United States. The bank deposits at the world's largest bank, Dai-Ichi Kangyo of Japan, exceed those of Citibank, Bank of America, Chase, Morgan, and Manufacturer's Hanover combined. Foreign investors have used their relatively newly gained financial positions to invest heavily in the United States. Today foreign investors hold more than $300 billion dollars of U.S. investments, almost the same size of U.S. investments abroad. Companies owned by these foreign investors, which include 19 of the *Fortune* 500 companies, employ about 3 million U.S. workers. Foreign investors own approximately 12 percent of U.S. manufacturing and over 25 percent of the prime office space in Los Angeles.

Table 3

Gross Domestic Production (GDP) Figures and Trends

GDP/EMPLOYEE LEVEL: 1987		GDP/EMPLOYEE GROWTH			
			73-87		79-87
U.S.	$38,896	KOREA	5.3%	KOREA	4.7%
CANADA	37,150	JAPAN	2.9	JAPAN	2.8
ITALY	33,259	FRANCE	2.2	FRANCE	1.9
FRANCE	33,171	GERMANY	2.1	ITALY	1.9
GERMANY	31,546	ITALY	1.8	U.K.	1.8
U.K.	27,508	U.K.	1.6	GERMANY	1.5
JAPAN	27,508	CANADA	1.2	CANADA	1.0
KOREA	13,280	U.S.	0.5	U.S.	0.8

IF GROWTH TRENDS CONTINUE, THESE NATIONS WILL PASS THE U.S. IN GDP/EMPLOYEE LEVEL IN THE INDICATED YEARS

	1973-87 TRENDS		1979-87 TRENDS
CANADA	1994	FRANCE	2002
FRANCE	1997	ITALY	2002
ITALY	2000	JAPAN	2005
GERMANY	2001	BELGIUM	2007
NORWAY	2001	CANADA	2011
BELGIUM	2001	GERMANY	2018
JAPAN	2002	U.K.	2021

Source: Reprinted with permission from J. Grayson, "The Two-Minute Warning." Presentation at ASTD, September 18, 1988.

The Reichmann family of Canada is the largest landlord of property in Manhattan. While it is easy to assume that the largest investor in the U.S. is Japan, actually Japan is second.

Of course, the ability to make such large investments in the United States reflects not only the increasing levels of productivity abroad but also the huge savings rates. In contrast to the United States, where savings as a percentage of personal disposable income is less than 4 percent, in Japan it is 17 percent and in Italy it is 24 percent. The United States consumes significantly more than it produces largely at the consent of foreigners. In return, however, foreigners get to own large shares of the United States, as indicated above.

While the United States benefits from enjoying immediate consumption, it increasingly becomes less able to control its own destiny.[44] The United States already has to pay approximately $25 billion per year in interest payments to foreigners. Furthermore, the value of the U.S. dollar is strongly influenced by the relative balance of payments, and the cost of imports to U.S. consumers is influenced by the value of the dollar. The cost of money to U.S. consumers (such as the interest rates on mortgages) and the cost of capital to business are determined in part by the value of the U.S. dollar and the balance of payments position of the United States. The value of the U.S. dollar also influences U.S. manufacturing. In the early 1980s, the value of the dollar was high, causing U.S. manufacturers to turn to foreign sources for parts. Foreign manufacturers have driven out U.S. companies from textile machinery, ceramic production, and many types of machine tools. Today, Boeing uses about 30 percent imported parts in its U.S.-made planes, versus 2 or 3 percent in 1980.

Some benefits do come from this increased investment in the United States. Where foreigners own manufacturing facilities, they have increased the productivity levels through improved management methods. In 1983, when Japan's Bridgestone took over one of Firestone's failing plants in Tennessee, workers were making only 600 tires per day. By adding a few shifts and retraining the work force, the daily level of output now is over 3,000. Similar improvements have been reported at the NUMMI plant in Fremont, CA, the joint project between Toyota and GM.[45]

The future for this economic reversal of productivity growth and investment is likely to continue for the foreseeable future. The United States shows little sign of changing its purchase of foreign goods (especially those of high quality and high prices) or its rate of personal savings, and foreign investors continue to accumulate U.S. dollars.[46]

> Indeed, many of Europe's biggest players are sitting on mountains of cash. German electronics giant Siemens, with an estimated $12 billion in its treasury could afford to buy almost any U.S. company. At its U.S. subsidiary, Siemens Capital Corp., President Hans W. Decker says he wants to boost sales by $300 million in 1988, to more than $3 billion. Reaching that goal is likely to include some U.S. acquisitions. Swedish auto giant Volvo has $4 billion in cash, and President Pehr G. Gyllenhammar says the company is eyeing targets in the U.S. food industry. "We are looking for big stakes—a major acquisition," Gyllenhammar says. "It won't be too long."

While protectionist sentiments may be tempting, they are, most economists believe, rather short-sighted. Protectionist economic policies could diminish world trade and the ability of the United States to earn foreign currency to pay off its enormous debt. This situation could maintain high interest rates in order to attract foreign investment and further erode the country's ability to determine its own financial and political destiny.

Wage Disputes

To be more successful in world competition, the United States has to face the reality of disparate wage rates. Although U.S. manufacturing workers are no longer the highest paid in the world, its CEOs continue to be. U.S. manufacturing workers are still well paid, compared to the $.25 day pay rate of Chinese workers. Other interesting compensation comparisons are shown in Table 4.

In short, U.S. wage rates have declined relative to Japan's and other nations, but they are still high enough to make it relatively impossible for U.S. firms to compete on the basis of cost. Low wages allow China to compete in almost any area of highly labor-intensive activity. It makes the sale of handcrafted quilts, each of which takes approximately a month of handwork, to U.S. wholesalers at $30 a

Table 4

Comparative Rates of Compensation

CEO Compensation (Total Comp.)		Intl. Compensation Mfg. Production Workers	
U.S.	$391,000	Norway	$17.39
Germany	255,000	W. Germany	16.87
Japan	249,000	U.S.	13.44
U.K.	217,000	France	12.42
France	191,000	Japan	11.14
Italy	166,000	U.K.	8.96
Korea	75,000	Korea	1.79
		Mexico	1.57

Source: TPF&C June 1987; and BLS August 1988 as presented by J. Grayson, September 18, 1988 at ASTD.

piece possible. Japan continues to lose markets in steel and ship building to Korea because of Korea's much lower wage rates. Population growth rates make it likely that huge labor pools will continue to exist, especially in Asia. In addition, the relatively high unemployment rates in Europe show no sign of abating, and the development of Eastern European economies are likely to supply a new source of relatively inexpensive but high-quality workers.

Besides undermining U.S. competitiveness in labor-intensive markets, huge wage disparities also make it hard for U.S. companies to maintain expatriates abroad. In the new Europe of 1992, wage disparities, combined with the lower value of the dollar vis-a-vis its major trading partners, make it very difficult for U.S. multinationals to compete. However, the successes of Ford, IBM, and Dow show that U.S. companies can succeed in these markets, given a lot of hard work over a long period of time. In fact, these companies have been urged to enter European markets before 1992 to ensure themselves a position in the European marketplace. Thus, given the disadvantage of wage disparities, U.S. firms attempting to compete globally need to turn to the strength of its work force: creativity. As one analysis stated:[47]

> The United States can still climb ahead of its competitors if it draws upon its talent and ingenuity. We have the richest mix and the most creativity in the world. We have not yet begun to tap into that vast resource, and if we do, the U.S. will remain atop world competition.

U.S. companies will also need workers capable of turning out high-quality goods and services. However, quality without innovation and creativity, is likely to produce a short-lived competitive advantage. Japanese multinationals have shown that any nation can produce high-quality products, even when local manufacturing traditions and customs do not emphasize high quality. For example, Nissan has succeeded in England despite that country's tradition of hostile union-management relationships by implementing just-in-time inventory systems and egalitarian management principles.

Reorganizing and Restructuring

As economic markets become increasingly global and interconnected, organizations also will need to develop new structures and linkages.[48] U.S. managers will have to shape organizations that can respond quickly to developments abroad. Speed, customization, and agility will become even more imperative virtues of companies.

To achieve these qualities, businesses will need a global organizational structure characterized by a decentralized but coordinated framework.

These changes in organizational structures will bring similar developments in HRM. Personnel managers will need to articulate expatriate, third-country, and host-country policies so as to create a worldwide work force. HR policies will need to make expatriate assignment an attractive option for the best employees to pursue. At the same time, assignments anywhere will have to be seen as vital components of the whole. According to Jerry Junkins, the CEO of Texas Instruments, overseas managers need to look beyond their own fiefdoms to consider the capabilities and needs of the entire company. At Texas Instruments all members of its worldwide management group work together in regular strategy meetings so as to:[49]

> ensure that the company knows enough about its customers' needs to invest in the manufacturing technologies that will satisfy the greatest numbers of buyers, no matter where they come from. The strategy seems to be working: After steep losses in 1985, TI has posted seven consecutive quarters of profit. In the troubled semiconductor business, that counts as a win.

HRM Implications

The creation of more effective worldwide organizational structures is only a first step for companies aiming to compete globally. Businesses also must focus on doing things better within their organizations.[50] Regarding HRM, U.S. corporations will need to adjust and create better policies and practices governing the following areas:

- Quality
- Integrated Operating Systems
- Job Design/Organization Structure
- Accounting Systems/Measurement
- Employment Security
- Compensation and Rewards
- Involvement
- Training, Selection, and Development
- Symbols, Status & Membership

- Union Role
- Integration
- Commitment

Table 5 illustrates exactly what is meant by each of these agenda items.

In more general terms, HR managers should play an active role in preparing their companies for the inevitable worldwide marketplace. HR managers should keep CEOs informed about people-related business issues, such as the need for new organizational structures or new sales force competencies to sell worldwide. All of these aspects of HRM fit quite well with domestic economic and organizational activities described in the following section.

Economic and Organizational Trends

American executives anticipate vast changes in the world and their organizations. Many of the reasons for this anticipation result from the rapidly changing demographic conditions and the fast-paced, highly competitive international marketplace described earlier in this chapter. Executives look at these and other conditions and foresee that the 1990s will be tougher, with companies having to develop and make decisions faster.

As a result, organizations will be adopting more fluid structures that can be altered as conditions change. More than before, companies will live by computers, shaping strategy and structure to fit information technology. Businesses will engage in more mergers, joint ventures, acquisition, downsizings, and development in order to become and stay competitive. And they will be coping with a more demanding work force which is increasingly characterized by its diversity. The higher usage of computers and automation will change the nature of jobs and require more skilled workers at a time when labor is scarce and functional illiteracy is on the rise. The significant implications for HRM of these events and trends are described in detail in this section.

Changing Jobs and Skills Needed

Technological demands and the shift from manufacturing to service and finance industries will reconfigure U.S. occupational

Table 5

Agenda for Adjustment
Priority Items

ACCOUNTING

1. Improve and make visible explicit measures of productivity and quality and incorporate into business plans
2. Revise the accounting system to include P&Q factors

COMPENSATION

1. Create rewards for productivity and quality at *all* levels of the organization
2. Make a larger percentage of compensation variable

INVOLVEMENT

1. Make involvement department & company wide by changing the way information is shared and problems solved
2. Focus on real problems and give people real authority

EMPLOYMENT SECURITY

1. Give 80% of workforce quasi-guaranteed employment security
2. Employ a larger percent of part-time, temporary workers

QUALITY

1. Install "total" quality control: all functions, customers, and vendors, blue and white collar
2. Senior execs personally take quality training and put quality into their own and others reward systems

OPERATING SYSTEMS

1. Create cross-functional design and operating teams
2. Use FMS, CIM, JIT in all functions to degree possible

TRAINING

1. Increase training time by at least 50%; make more OJT
2. Expand and deepen employee recruiting procedures; involve employees in the process of selection

SYMBOLS, STATUS, MEMBERSHIP

1. Remove executive dining rooms, reserved parking spaces, badges
2. Reduce closed office/work spaces; more spaces more common and connected

JOB DESIGN/ORGANIZATION STRUCTURE

1. Reduce and broaden job classifications
2. Reduce management layers drastically and decentralize decision making more

> **Table 5** continued
>
> UNION ROLE
> 1. Involve unions at early stages in change efforts
> 2. Include union officials on involvement and strategy teams
>
> *Source:* Reprinted with permission from J. Grayson and C. O'Dell, *The Two Minute Warning*. New York: The Free Press, 1988.

patterns. The jobs created between now and 2000 will differ substantially from those in existence today. As shown in Figure 1, a number of jobs in the least-skilled job classes will disappear, while high-skilled professions will grow rapidly. While manufacturing employed 21 percent of the workforce in 1985, it is expected to employ only 15 percent in 2000. Employment in the financial industry is expected to go to 7 percent, up from its current level of 6%. Agriculture and construction are also expected to decline in the same time period.[51]

Overall, the skill mix of the economy will move rapidly upscale, with most new jobs demanding more education and higher levels of language, math, and reasoning skills. These occupational changes will present a difficult challenge for the disadvantaged, particularly for black men and Hispanics, who are underrepresented in the faster-growing professions and overrepresented in the shrinking job categories (see Figure 2).

The Winning Organization

Organizations of the year 2000 will be much more global, lean, flat, flexible, fast, customer-oriented, quality-focused, and innovative. Above all, change will become a constant characteristic. Restructuring, retraining, and retooling will become the modus operandi.

In terms of HRM, these changes will bring about more employee involvement and skill utilization. Organizations will have fewer jobs and organizational structures will become leaner and flatter as a result. Job opportunity will exist only for those workers with the requisite skills, or those willing and able to retrain and retool. To satisfy some employee needs for security in the sea of turbulence, organizations will increasingly make use of contract

Figure 1

Black Men and Hispanics Face the Greatest Difficulties in the Emerging Job Market

- ☐ SHARE OF CURRENT JOBS
- ▨ IMPLIED SHARE OF NEW JOBS
- ▩ SHARE OF LABOR FORCE GROWTH

BLACK MEN: 4.9, 3.8, 7.7
BLACK WOMEN: 5.1, 5.6, 12
HISPANICS: 6.4, 5.0, 22

Source: Reprinted with permission from W.B. Johnston, *Workforce 2000*. Indianapolis: Hudson Institute: xxiii, 1987.

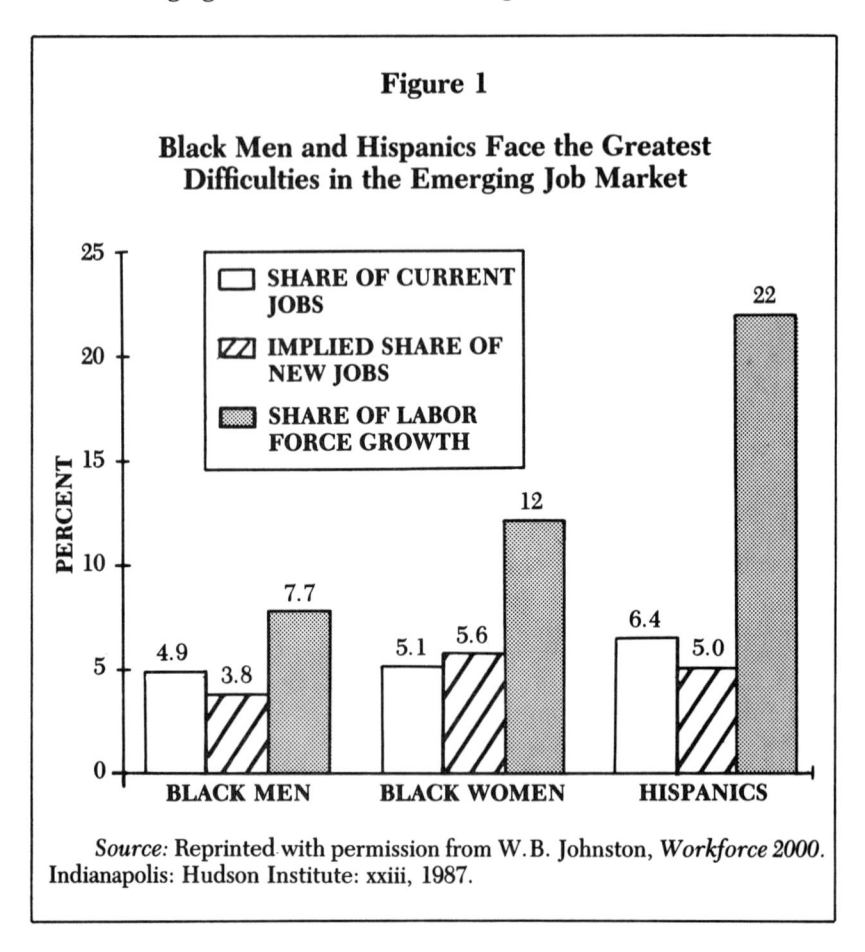

workers. These temporary, at-will workers, who currently comprise about 30 percent of the work force, could grow to as much as 40 percent of the work force in year 2000. This trend may play well with a work force that increasingly needs more flexibility and job security. Figure 3 depicts these organizational changes.[52]

This rising use of contingent workers poses the issue of how and who will pick up the costs of health care and other benefits for these workers. According to Audrey Freedman, an economist with the Conference Board[53]:

> Contingent employees often are used as a "buffer" work force that can be quickly reduced or increased to match business needs, Freedman notes. The technique enhances the job security of a core work force, while reducing the job security of the contingent work

Figure 2

Low Skilled Jobs Are Declining

REPRESENTATIVE	JOBS
Natural Scientists	5.7
Lawyers	5.2
Engineers	5.1
Management	4.4
Teachers	4.2
Technicians	4.1
Marketing and Sales	3.4
Construction	3.2
Administrative	2.9
Service Occupations	2.6
Precision Production	2.5
Farmers	2.3
Transport Workers	2.2
Machine Setters	1.8
Hand Workers	1.7
Helpers and Laborers	1.3

Bar chart (EXISTING JOBS vs NEW JOBS) by SKILL RATING:
- 0.7–1.4: 9, 4
- 1.5–2.4: 31, 23
- 2.5–3.4: 35, 34
- 3.5–4.4: 18, 28
- 4.5–5.4: 5, 11
- 5.5–6.4: 1, 2

Source: W.B. Johnston, 1987. *Workforce 2000.* Indianapolis: Hudson Institute: xxiii.

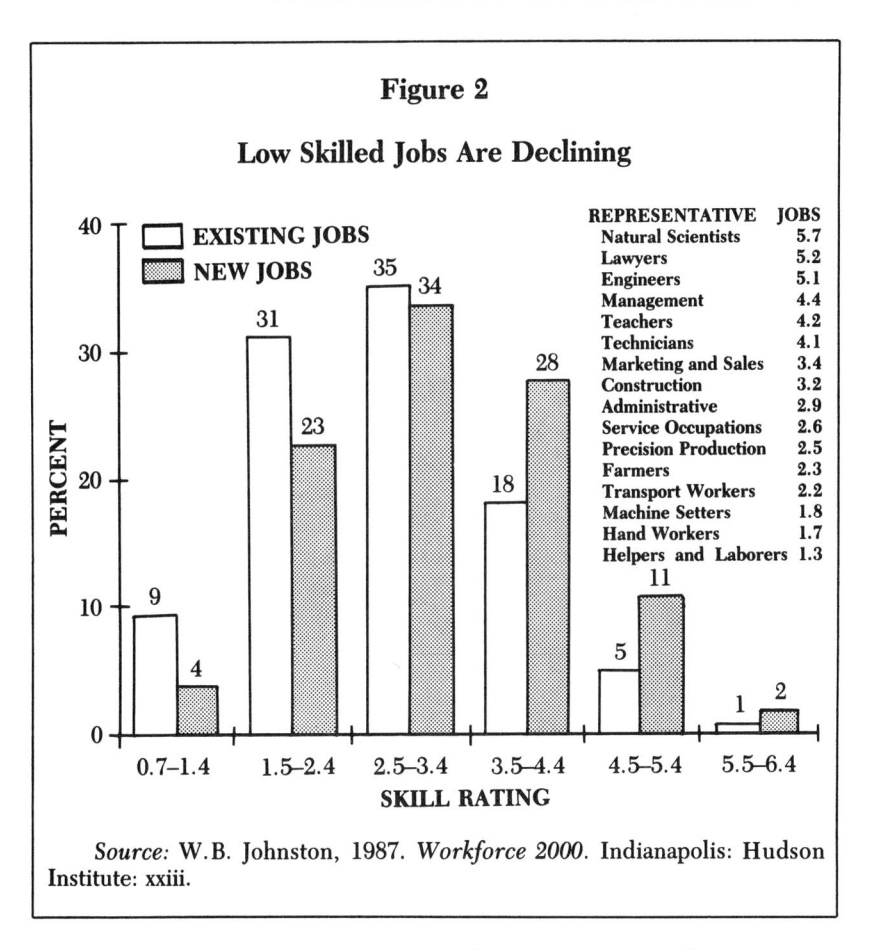

force, Freedman stresses, noting that contingent employees generally receive no pensions, no vacation or holiday pay, and no health benefits. Additionally, there is no obligation to train, promote, or retain contingent employees, whose compensation also is often lower, Freedman observes. This situation is applauded by business strategists concerned with costs because it reduces labor costs per unit of output enormously, Freedman notes.

Downsizing

Eliminating layers of employees will continue to be an important aspect in shaping the winning organization. The most likely targets will be the same ones aimed at in the 1980s: middle managers. Elimination of this group facilitates decentralization, the process so necessary to enhance decision-making speed.

Figure 3

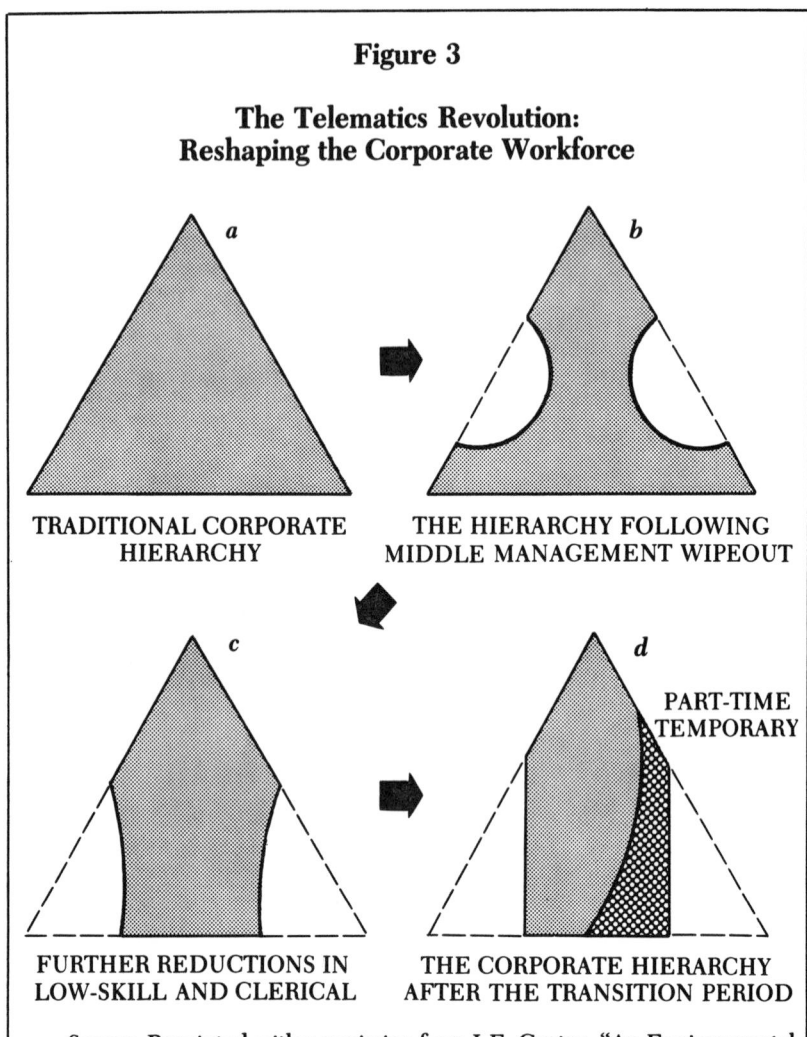

The Telematics Revolution: Reshaping the Corporate Workforce

a TRADITIONAL CORPORATE HIERARCHY

b THE HIERARCHY FOLLOWING MIDDLE MANAGEMENT WIPEOUT

c FURTHER REDUCTIONS IN LOW-SKILL AND CLERICAL

d PART-TIME TEMPORARY — THE CORPORATE HIERARCHY AFTER THE TRANSITION PERIOD

Source: Reprinted with permission from J.F. Coates, "An Environmental Scan: Projecting Future Human Resource Trends." *Human Resource Planning* (Vol. 10, Number 4): 232, 1987.

Downsizing has already happened at some companies, the rather large and global ones. For example:[54]

> IBM has cut its payroll by 16,000 since 1985, mostly through early retirement. The company shifted many remaining workers out of headquarters and manufacturing into marketing and sales. But the company wants to be leaner still. "We haven't done as well as we

should have," says corporate secretary Rich. "We will have to be structured differently in the Nineties."

The major reorganization last January (1987) was a start. The company decentralized into seven largely autonomous business units, including six product lines and one support group to serve the others. The new units, says Rich, no longer have to suffer the "insidious delays of excessive staff reviews." The company was also split into four worldwide geographic regions.

IBM's efforts foreshadow what more and more companies will attempt to do in the 1990s. This trend goes hand in hand with the increasing use of contingent workers and subcontracting. For example, IBM uses Pitney Bowes to run its mail rooms, stockrooms, and reproduction operations. More and more companies are outsourcing their payroll activities to firms such as ADP. However, downsizing alone does not ensure a competitive edge. As a result, many organizations have accompanied these activities with programs to improve quality and facilitate innovation.

Quality-Enhancement

Quality became a catchword in the 1980s in response to customer preferences for quality products, largely supplied by Japan and Germany. Companies such as Xerox, L.L. Bean, and Ford Motor became examples of what quality enhancement means and how the customer responds. Their successes serve as examples as to how quality can be achieved and its importance to survival.

In essence, improving quality is one way of differentiating a product or service. While U.S. firms may have difficulty competing on the basis of cost, many can succeed by improving the quality of their products. In addition, quality enhancement efforts can take a variety of forms, many of which cost little to achieve.

Consider the case of the customer in the typical fast food or retail store. The nature of the good delivered, the hamburger, the pair of pants, are important to the customer, but the smile, the extra effort by the clerk can really make the difference. McDonalds, Disney, and Nordstroms are firms that have capitalized on this premise. For other companies, quality enhancement means changing suppliers. Ford and GM, for example, are establishing closer links with a more limited number of suppliers who can deliver high-quality parts.

Automation is often suggested as a way to improve quality since it removes the unreliable human element out of the process. However, examples such as the NUMMI plant in Fremont, CA and L.L. Bean, demonstrate that state-of-the-art automation is not mandatory. In many cases, enhanced automation is not always a feasible way to go.

Innovation Oriented

One of the most likely means for U.S. firms to compete globally is through the development of new products. Other nations can still copy U.S. products and improve them, but this strategy takes time. The United States has not been a nation to copy and imitate the products of others; it has always centered on the creative-minded individual, the entrepreneur, and the pioneer. Organizations are now recognizing that innovation offers a viable way to differentiate their products and gain a competitive advantage over others.

HRM Implications

The changes described above are likely to spread to more and more U.S. firms during the 1990s. All these efforts to create a winning organization will depend upon significant changes in HRM. For example, downsizing efforts involve outplacement programs, retirement programs, severance pay programs, management succession programs, and better HR planning programs to help reduce the need for further downsizing. Decentralization involves training employees in decision making, instituting new performance appraisals, changing compensation systems, and developing new leadership skills.

Mergers and acquisitions require significant programs in workforce reductions, relations with the communities in which facilities to be closed are located, realignment of reporting relationships, and entire programs to integrate two previously independent and perhaps antagonistic organizations. For HR managers, these times present tremendous opportunities[55]:

> Human resource staff are expected to guide and support company efforts in developing managers as leaders for the new flat, lean, and flexible environment. General Electric believes that teamwork, company-wide perspective, global insight, and customer orientation are critical attributes for its leaders. With fewer managers and fewer management levels, management capabilities are more important. Providing challenging and broadening experiences is the key to developing flexible managers. However, in flat and lean organizations, job rotation and mobility are difficult because there are fewer

managers—and increased time pressures and demands on unit and individual performance. Business units have little slack and have difficulty releasing talented managers for broadening assignments, even temporary ones.

Efforts to enhance quality and innovation may have the most extensive implications for HRM.

In contrast to work-force reductions, efforts to enhance quality and innovation can require a restructuring that will affect a majority of employees and organizational practices and policies. Improving quality and innovation also can come about through many different techniques. HR managers will have to diagnose what is needed and implement a variety of corrective actions. Efforts to enhance quality or innovation also depend upon getting employees to engage in behaviors different from what they have exhibited previously. However, a majority of HR professionals have yet to make these restructuring activities an essential part of their jobs.[56]

Stimulating Innovation

Any program to encourage innovation must start by creating organizational conditions conducive to innovation and entrepreneurial behavior. These conditions can be rather varied. They can be created either formally through official corporate policy or more informally. According to Kanter:[57]

> Innovation [and new venture development] may originate as a deliberate and official decision of the highest levels of management or they may be the more-or-less "spontaneous" creation of mid-level people who take the initiative to solve a problem in new ways or to develop a proposal for change. Of course, highly successful companies allow both, and even official top management decisions to undertake a development effort benefit from the spontaneous creativity of those below.

To encourage as many employees as possible to be innovative, 3M has developed an informal doctrine of allowing employees to bootleg 15 percent of their time to work on their own projects. A less systematic approach is to encourage employees to look at their work in new ways and offer suggestions for new and improved methods or products.[58] Rather than use the term "entrepreneurial behavior," some companies term these efforts "intrapreneurship." Regardless of the name, however, it stimulates innovation, increases competitiveness, and enhances profitability. According to a report by Ameritech, the midwest regional telephone company of AT&T:[59]

"Intrapreneurs added $2 million to Ohio Bell net income," Chicago-based Ameritech said in the report. The Ohio subsidiary's "Enter-Prize" program was set up to encourage intrapreneurs, defined as "employees whose ideas reduce expenses, bring in new revenues or develop new lines of business."

The Dow Chemical Company's new president and chief operating officer, Frank P. Popoff, also has much to say about intrapreneurship.

In Dow's latest quarterly report to stockholders, Mr. Popoff said management's job "is to liberate people to think more entrepreneurially within the organization" by creating a climate in which people can be "change-oriented."

The way to do this is "by avoiding hierarchical organizations and by pushing the decision making down to the lowest levels," he said.

Quality Enhancement Programs

Quality enhancement often means changing production processes in ways that require greater worker involvement and flexibility. At Corning Glass, quality enhancement involves getting employees committed to quality and continual improvement. In addition to issuing policy statements emphasizing the "Total Quality Approach," Corning has followed up with specific HR practices. It has instituted feedback systems, facilitated team work, and made decision making and responsibility a part of everyone's job description.

As job duties change, so too must job classification systems. Brunswick's Mercury Marine division, for example, reduced its number of job classifications from 126 to 12. This change has permitted greater flexibility in the use of production processes and employees. Machine operators also gained greater opportunities to learn more skills. In the Marine division today, machine operators inspect their work and do preventive maintenance in addition to running the machines.[60] As a result of such HR practices, people have become committed to the firm and are willing to give more. In addition to improving quality, these conditions are likely to increase sheer volume of output. By pursuing a quality improvement competitive strategy, L. L. Bean's sales have increased tenfold while the number of permanent employees has grown only fivefold.[61]

Managing the Change Process

Programs to improve quality or stimulate innovation represent important changes for most organizations. Managing these changes

Characteristics of the External Environment 6-35

so as to minimize its potentially traumatic effects on employees is "one of the cutting-edge areas" for HR managers.[62]

The change process, regardless of whether it involves HR quality improvement or automation, benefits from employee communication and participation, modification of the corporate culture, and support from top management. The more extensive the changes, the more people affected, and more parts of the organization significantly altered, the more likely HR practices will change at all levels of the organization. In addition, significant changes will require systematic implementation over time in stages.

Efforts for improving organizations increasingly combine several of the programs described above. HR practices are undergoing modifications based upon strategic changes in organizations, and these strategy shifts are occurring more frequently. More than ever before, organizational change is becoming a fact of life. As a result, employees must adopt a mindset of flexibility and adaptability. Developing this mindset is facilitated by leadership that can skillfully manage transformations and by HR practices that provide retraining and job security.[63]

Besides necessitating new HR initiatives, restructuring can affect many traditional HR activities. According to a recent survey by the Commerce Clearing House and the Society for Human Resource Management, HR involvement is needed to manage a variety of problems that can arise during the restructuring process[64]:

- Decreased employee morale is the most pervasive HR problem for companies undergoing restructuring, with almost 70 percent reporting a deterioration of employee morale.

- Turnover increased in more than 40 percent of the survey companies and employee loyalty decreased by almost the same amount.

- Misinformation and rumors increased in 60.3 percent of companies and were the main problem that hampered effective communication. "More and more, HR managers are also managing communications," said Pilenzo. Involving them early in organizational restructuring can alleviate many morale problems caused by clouded communication or worse, the total lack of communication.

- While integrating compensation and benefits was listed as top or high priority by 40 percent of respondents, 35 percent said that goal was not accomplished.

Technological Trends and Developments

Information technology, office and factory automation, data communications, voice communication, and other technologies are being implemented together faster than ever before. These developments virtually revolutionize the ways we do work and organize. Referred to by some as telematics technologies, they encompass the following:[65]

- mainframe computers and associated information systems,
- microcomputers and word processors,
- networking technologies,
- telecommunications technologies,
- reprography and printing, and
- peripherals.

Table 6 illustrates these telematics technologies in much more detail.

Singly or together, generally together, these technologies are facilitating the following changes within organizations:[66]

- networking—Interdependencies
- control over time and space
- higher productivity/Amplify Human Cognitive Functions
- new extensions of human action
- new levels of efficiency and productivity/energy, materials conserving
- new power to obscure
- new power to centralize and decentralize
- blurring of organizational distinctions
- promotion of monitoring, evaluation, and simulation
- erosion of hierarchical relationships
- shifting power
- shifting authority
- integration

Table 6

Key Clusters of Telematics Technologies

Mainframe computers and associated information systems
—Central data banks
—Artificial intelligence, expert systems, pattern recognition
—CAD/CAM, robotics
—VLSI, VHSIC

Microcomputers and word processors
—Computer graphics
—Spreadsheets
—Software packages

Networking technologies
—LANs
—PBX
—E-Mail
—Fax
—Voice mail

Telecommunications technologies
—800 numbers
—Packet switching
—Fiber optics
—Cable, one- and two-way
—Communication satellites
—Videotex
—Teletext
—Electronic message systems
—Teleconferencing
—Computer conferencing

Reprography and printing
—Printing on demand
—Xerography
—Facsimile
—Holography

Peripherals
—Cellular telephones
—Encryption
—Voice activation
—VCR
—Audio cassettes
—Pattern recognition
—Protocol converters
—Voice recognition
—Video disks
—Speech compression

Source: Reprinted with permission from J.F. Coates, "An Environmental Scan: Projecting Future Human Resource Trends." *Human Resource Planning* (Vol. 10, Number 4): 234-35, 1987.

- new mischief/vulnerabilities
- promote autonomy/dependency

Improved Customer Service and Quality

Telematics technologies are enabling organizations to shape themselves into winners. They facilitate speed, flexibility, decentralization, and staying in close touch with the customer, as the following example demonstrates:[67]

> How fast is fast enough? The Limited tracks consumer preferences every day through point-of-sale computers. Orders, with facsimile illustrations, are sent by satellite to suppliers around the U.S. and in Hong Kong, South Korea, Singapore, and Sri Lanka. Within days clothing from those distant points begins to collect in Hong Kong. About four times a week a chartered 747 brings it to the company's distribution center in Ohio, where goods are priced and shipped to stores within 48 hours. Says Chairman Leslie Wexner: "That's not fast enough for the Nineties."

Computers can also let customers look inside an organization. Pacific Intermountain Express, a trucking firm, gives customers access to its computers so they can check the status of their shipments. Banks and brokerage firms are also using computers to enable customers to do their business from their homes and offices.

These technologies enable organizations to enhance quality by ensuring better parts and services from their suppliers. Retail chains already are linked with suppliers so that they know the timing and the nature of needed shipments. Technology also facilitates research and development capabilities. All these developments give managers more free time to get to know their companies better:[68]

> Not too far down the road the computer will emerge as a full-fledged management aid, helping to coordinate the daily tasks of administration. The programs to do that, developed after years of studying human behavior, are called groupware. Action Technologies of Emeryville, CA, markets a program named the Coordinator, based on the principle that all managerial interaction can be sorted into "offers," "counteroffers," "commitments," and "requests." The Coordinator keeps track of such transactions, minds deadlines, sends reminders, arranges meetings, and sorts electronic mail. It also lets users organize themselves easily into ad hoc work groups. Coordination Technology, a young company in Trumbull, CT, that will launch its own groupware next year, uses it to manager the temporary groups that form to deal with specific assignments and then dissolve.

Impact of Automation

The telematics technology revolution also has promoted manufacturing advances. These advances include the emerging technologies of robotics; CAD/CAM/CAE; laser and optics; biotechnologies; polymers and alloys; advanced ceramics; and computer-integrated manufacturing.[69]

U.S. manufacturing companies are finally in position to leap into total automation. Although the United States now lags behind Japan and Germany in automation use, many executives predict this situation will change during the 1990s.[70] "We are gathering momentum in the United States today, and as the momentum builds we are going to make quantum leaps in factory automation," according to Joseph Tulkoff, director of manufacturing technology for Lockheed-Georgia Company.

Factory automation will bring increased use of robots. Annual sales of robots are expected to be twenty thousand units by the end of the century, compared with the current rate of five thousand units. Estimates are that by 1995, robots will displace about 4.3 percent of the work force. Although most employees are expected to remain with their current employers, many will need substantial retraining. The costs of this retraining will be offset by lower labor costs, enhanced product quality, fewer defects, and a better flow of materials.[71]

Factories will not be the only workplaces undergoing automation. Almost 80 percent of the white-collar jobs in the United States eventually will be automated, including managers, professionals, and clerical staff. The biggest gains in office productivity are predicted to come from automating the jobs of professionals and managers.[72] According to the consulting firm of Booz Allen & Hamilton, less than half of the $50 billion spent by U.S. business each year for office automation goes for equipment for managers and professionals. Yet the yearly compensation for these groups is nearly double ($550 billion) that of the clerical group. With more office automation for managers and professionals, Booz Allen & Hamilton predicts that U.S. companies can increase their productivity by 15 percent and save up to $125 billion annually by instituting the following technologies:[73]

- ▪ Automated calendars, tickler files, and other forms of equipment can replace the handwritten lists made by business people to keep track of their time and that of others.

- Word and image processors allow managers and professionals to better review and edit their work. Personal computers could reduce the time these individuals spend in making decisions and analyzing data, and audiovisual conferences could replace the face-to-face meeting—and eliminate the accompanying travel time.

- Retrieval-of-information services and electronic mail (the latter a broad term encompassing facsimile, keyboard, and speech or voice-activated mail) could increase productivity and help connect other types of automated tools with each other.

Leaner Organizational Structures

Automation, whether in the factory or the office, has had and will continue to change organizational structures. Because information is instantaneously available, layers of management between the top and first-line management become useless. Automation permits top management to bypass middle managers on their way to the first-line management. This shift in the chain of command in turn can lead to ambiguity in reporting relationships. Other significant relationships and events within the traditional organization structure are also impacted by the telematic technologies:[74]

> Let us assume that a division director puts out some foolish memorandum on Thursday afternoon. What did you do in the old days? You sat around and you groused, and wondered when he was going to retire. Nothing happens. But, when you have got electronic mail, tomorrow morning 17 denunciations may be in his electronic mailbox. And if the fool was stupid enough to put a code on his mailbox to shield himself from his underlings, that young person just hired from the University of Illinois would crack that code for breakfast. There no longer is a mechanism for shielding the superior from the wrath of his underlings. . . .
>
> Other things will happen. Suppose your headquarters is in Chicago and the expert who has the information that you, the VIP, want, is in San Francisco. You are not going to go down, down, down the chain of command, across the country, and up, up, up the chain of command. Electronically you will go right out to the expert, and get what you want. Being 100% American, the last thing you will say as you sign off, is "Charlie, if anything develops, let me know." You have just wiped out the chain of command. Unless Chairlie is a timid fool, if anything develops, he will go directly back to the V.P. Technology is now shifting the priorities in the corporation from where you stand in the hierarchy to what you know.

Thus, the telematics technologies will lead to far more than better products and faster, leaner organizations. Technology will undermine traditional authority structures. Blue-collar workers will become information managers by becoming computer operators at advanced plants. And traditional managers will no longer be needed:[75]

> A few observers believe that computers in the workplace will lead to far more than better information and better products. Shoshana Zuboff, an associate professor at the Harvard business school and author of *In the Age of the Smart Machine*, argues that computerization undermines traditional forms of authority and breaks down barriers between job categories and functions. "You have people doing work which is more abstract, more analytical," says Zuboff. "People not considered managerial in the past are managing information." Zuboff concludes that the role of the managers will have to be redefined in the Nineties. Says she: "Since managers are no longer the guardians of the knowledge base, we do not need the command-control type of executive."

As organizations implement telematics, they will confront increased opportunities to downsize, to decentralize, and to make their internal structures more flexible and responsive. Yet they will also have to be prepared to retrain workers, redesign jobs, and outplace employees, especially managers.

Some observers suggest that telematics will redesign jobs à la Frederick Taylor, in the name of scientific management. Barbara Garson, author of *The Electronic Sweatshop*, expresses concern that the computer's ability to monitor behavior will lead to oppressive control of employees. She also suggests that some fast-food restaurants are using their computer systems to create jobs that virtually remove the need for employees to think and, therefore, to grow on the job. In essence, she sees telematics as leading to the deskilling of jobs. While some may say this change is necessitated by the nature of the work force, others say that it only perpetuates the deskilling of the U.S. work force and thus the eventual decline of U.S. industry.

Although telematics pose significant challenges for HR managers, other characteristics of this revolution must be considered. For instance, work can now go directly to the worker's home via computer, alleviating the need for more day-care services. The ability to have individuals work at home also facilitates the use of subcontractors and contingent employees. As a result, labor costs may drop as individuals could bid for jobs as contingent employees with essentially no benefit packages. However, these arrangements engender new styles of supervision and training, as well as legal implications.

HR managers need to monitor the legal events regarding the utilization of homework activities and limits of liability for worker safety and health.

HRM Implications

The telematics revolution means major change. Organizations need to develop a plan and philosophy that will promote acceptance of and preparation for this technological revolution. The revolution will change the number and types of jobs, skills required, training needs, organizational structures, reporting relationships, and form and style of supervision. Employees will face the pressures of continual obsolescence, the need for continual retraining and adjustment, and the demand for flexibility and willingness to adapt quickly to unpredictable change.

These changes have major implications for every HRM activity. As a result, HR managers need to be involved in the early stages of strategic planning for telematics technology. Because technological change can have such unpredictable effects, HR managers also need to constantly monitor events in the scientific community and in other industries. As for other employees, flexibility and adaptability are the keys for HR managers.

The telematics revolution also will directly impact the HR department itself. Computers can be used for gathering and disseminating organizational survey data, for planning career and HR programs, performing cost-benefit analyses of alternative programs, as well as for preparing payrolls. Personal computers also can enable line managers to do most of the major personnel activities faster and easier than ever before. In other words, HR managers can shift some of the operational personnel activities to line managers and use the time saved to better serve line managers' more strategic and managerial needs.

The Changing External Environment and the Practice of HRM

The external environment has always played a role in how organizations structure and shape themselves. As a result, it has affected how personnel practices were carried out and the position and power of the HR function within organizations. In the 1960s and 1970s, HR managers were expected to have functional expertise in such areas as affirmative action and EEO compliance, and to serve as employee advocates. While functional expertise is still important, today's HR professionals are now expected to work side-by-side with line management on such things as mergers and acquisitions, productivity and quality enhancement efforts. The involvement of HR managers in these activities appears likely to grow:[76]

> The shift from "employee advocate" to "member of the management team" will continue into the 1990s. Human resource professionals will be called upon to think and act like line managers to address people-related business issues. Managers will increasingly expect HR to think and act, and to view human resource activities from a business perspective.
>
> The human resource function will seek to increase its opportunities to contribute to the organization's successful performance. As Robert Galvin, CEO of Motorola, stated at the HRPS Conference, the aim is to "inspire, empower, and enable employees to be more effective."

This shift from employee advocate to member of the management team represents a fundamental change in the organizational status of HR departments. Executives are recognizing that competitiveness demands innovation, high-quality goods and services, a global perspective, flexibility, the latest in telematics technologies, successful management of mergers and acquisitions, and the ability to respond rapidly to the environment and marketplace. All these capacities require a dedicated work force that is integrally tied to the needs and strategies of the business. And because of the predicted changes in the labor supply, the role of HRM as a member of the management team will continue well into the 1990s.

◆

Endnotes

1. Schrenk.
2. Schrenk. See also Coates (1986), Bower and Hallet (1989) and Schuler.
3. For example, see Coates (1986) who identifies 16 trend areas.
4. Coates (1987); Gallup.
5. The following page of projections adapted from Johnston, pp. 76–78.
6. Coates (1987), p. 227.
7. Johnston.
8. *Wall Street Journal*, B2.
9. Doering, Rhodes, and Schuster.
10. Shank.

6-44 Managing HR in the Information Age

11. *Ibid.*
12. *Ibid.*
13. Axel.
14. Ehrlich and S. Garland.
15. *Fair Employment Practices* (1987b), p. 264.
16. Johnston.
17. Adapted from Johnston.
18. *Fair Employment Practices* (1987a), p. 69.
19. Johnston.
20. Perry.
21. Nussbaum.
22. Miller.
23. *Ibid.*
24. *Ibid.*
25. Nussbaum.
26. *Bulletin to Management* (1986).
27. Perry.
28. Ehrlich.
29. Teltsch.
30. *Ibid.*
31. *Ibid.*
32. Miller.
33. Perry.
34. Foster.
35. Copeland.
36. *Ibid.*
37. Nelson-Horchler.
38. Copeland.
39. *Ibid.*; Ramirez.
40. Bacon; Koretz.
41. Fraze (1988a).
42. Coates (1987).
43. Grayson and O'Dell.
44. Koepp; Fierman.
45. Grayson and O'Dell provide evidence for Boeing, Bridgestone and NUMMI.
46. *Business Week* (1988).
47. Fraze (1988b).
48. Kupfer, p. 45.
49. Kirkland, p. 48.
50. Grayson and O'Dell.
51. Levine; Perry.
52. Coates (1987); Peters.
53. *Bulletin to Management* (1985), p. 40.
54. Main, p. 52.
55. Walker.
56. *HR Reporter*, p. 6.
57. Kanter.
58. Schuler and Jackson.
59. Fowler.
60. McComas.
61. Prokesch.
62. *Bulletin to Management*, (1988), p. 3.
63. Tichy and Devanna.
64. *HR Reporter*, October 1989, p. 6.
65. Coates (1987).
66. *Ibid.*
67. Main, p. 50.
68. Dreyfuss.
69. Coates (1987).
70. Kanabayashi.
71. *Ann Arbor Business to Business.*
72. Tarbania.
73. Rendero.
74. Coates (1987).
75. Main, p. 82.
76. Walker (1989), p. 55.

Editor's Note: In addition to the References shown below, there are other significant sources of information and ideas on characteristics of the external environment.

Books

Armstrong, J.S. 1979. *Long-Range Forecasting.* New York: John Wiley & Sons.

Ascher, W. 1978. *Forecasting: An Appraisal for Policy Makers and Planners.* Baltimore: The John Hopkins University Press.

Ayres, R.V. 1969. *Technological Forecasting and Long-Range Planning.* New York: McGraw-Hill.

Beutell, N.J. 1988. "Computers and the Management of Human Resources." In *Personnel and Human Resource Management*, 3rd ed., eds. R.S. Schuler, S.A. Youngblood, and V.L. Huber. St. Paul, MN: West Publishing.

Brown, J.K. 1979. *This Business of Issues: Coping with the Company's Environments*. New York: The Conference Board.

Chase, W.H., ed. 1976. *Corporate Public Issues*. Stamford, CT: IAP.

Davis, S.M. 1987. *Future Perfect*. Reading, MA: Addison-Wesley.

DePree, H. 1986. *Business as Unusual*. Zeeland, MI: Herman Miller.

Didsbury, H.F., Jr., ed. 1985. *The Global Economy: Today Tomorrow and the Transition*. Bethesda, MD: World Future Society.

Dyer, L., ed. 1989. *Human Resource Management Evolving Roles and Responsibilities*. Washington, D.C.: BNA Books.

Hickman, C.R., and M.A. Silva. 1987. *The Future 500*. New York: New American Library.

Hunt, V.D. 1988. *Mechatronics: Japan's Newest Threat*. New York: Chapman and Hall.

Kahn, H., and A. Wiener. 1967. *The Year 2000: A Framework for Speculation on the Next Thirty-Three Years*. New York: MacMillan.

Koxlowski, S. 1988. "Technological Innovation and Strategic HRM: Facing the Challenge of Change." In *Personnel and Human Resource Management*, 4th ed., eds. R.S. Schuler, S.A. Youngblood, and V.L. Huber. St. Paul, MN: West Publishing.

Maccoby, M. 1988. *Why Work*. New York: Simon and Schuster.

Mitroff, I.I. 1987. *Business NOT As Usual*. San Francisco: Jossey-Bass, Inc.

Morrison, J.L., W.L. Renfro, and W.I. Boucher, eds. 1982. *Applying Methods and Techniques of Futures Research*. San Francisco: Jossey-Bass, Inc.

Reich, R.B. 1987. *Tales of a New America*. New York: Vantage Books.

Schodt, F.L. 1988. *Inside the Robot Kingdom: Japan, Mechatronics, and the Coming Robotopia*. New York: Kodanska International.

U.S. Bureau of the Census. 1984. *Population of the United States by Age, Sex, and Race: 1983 to 2080*. Washington, DC: U.S. GPO.

Zuboff, S. 1988. *In the Age of the Smart Machine: The Future of Work and Power*. New York: Basic Books.

Articles
Bergen Record, 1988. "Today, More Matters Than Pay." August, 4: 15.

Bakshian, A., Jr. 1986. "America's Gray Wave of the Future." *Nation's Business* (April): 4.

Bernstein, A., R.W. Anderson, and W. Zellner. 1987. "Help Wanted." *Business Week* (August 10): 48–53.

Brown, J.K. 1987. "Can Ford Stay on Top?" *Business Week* (September 28): 78–86.

Bremmer, B. 1988. "Among Restauranteurs, It's Dog Eat Dog." *Business Week* (January 9): 86.

Garvin, C.C., Jr. 1984. "The Future Has A Mind of Its Own." *The Lamp* 66(1) (Spring): 1–2.

Gelford, S.M. 1988. "The Computer Age Dawns in the Corner Office." *Business Week* (June 27): 84–85.

Godiwalla, Y. 1980. "Environmental Scanning—Does It Help the Chief Executive?" *Long Range Planning* 13(5) (October): 87–99.

Goodstein, M.L. 1988. "Tomorrow's Workforce Today." *Industry Week* (August 15): 41–43.

Harris, P.R., and D.L. Harris. 1983. "Twelve Trends You and Your CEO Should Be Monitoring." *Training and Development Journal* (October): 62–69.

Hegarty, W.H. 1981. "Strategic Planning in the 1980s—Coping with Complex External Forces." *Planning Review* 40: 8–12, 40.

Jain, C. 1987. "Environmental Scanning in U.S. Corporations." *Long Range Planning* 17 (April): 117–128.

Klein, H.E., and W.H. Newman. 1980. "How to Integrate New Environmental Forces into Strategic Planning." *Management Review* 69(7) (July): 40–48.

Kutscher, R.E. 1987. "Overview and Implications of the Projections to 2000." *Monthly Labor Review* (September): 3.

Labich, K. 1988. "The Innovators." *Fortune* (June 6): 50–64.

Linneman, R.E. and H.E. Klein. 1979. "The Use of Multiple Scenarios by U.S. Industrial Companies." *Long Range Planning* 12: 83–90.

Nanus, B. 1981. "The Corporate Futurist." *The World Future Society Bulletin XV* (March-April): 12–14.

Nasar, S. 1988. "Preparing for a New Economy." *Fortune* (September 26): 86–96.

Nelton, S. 1988. "Meet Your New Work Force." *Nation's Business* (July): 14–21.

Owens, E.L. 1987. "Managing the Managers of Tomorrow." *Data Management* (January): 34–35.

Pearce, J.A., II, B.L. Chapman, and F.R. David. 1982. "Environmental Scanning for Small and Growing Firms." *Journal of Small Business Management* (July): 27–34.

Rice, M.F. 1986. "America's New Jobs." *American Demographics* (February): 36.

Schuler, R.S., and I.C. MacMillan. 1984. "Gaining Competitive Advantage through HRM Practices." *Human Resource Management* (Fall): 240–52.

Sherwood, J.J. 1988. "Creating Work Cultures with Competitive Advantage." *Organizational Dynamics* (Winter): 4–27.

Weiner, E. 1976. "Future Scanning for Trade Groups and Companies." *Harvard Business Review* 54(5) (September/October): 14, 174–176.

Zentner, R.D. 1982a. "Forecasting Emerging Issues." Presented at the Fourth General Assembly of the World Future Society. July.

———. 1982b. "Scenarios, Past, Present and Future." *Long Range Planning* 15(3): 12–20.

———. 1984. "Forecasting Public Issues." *The Futurist* 18(3) (June): 25–29.

◆

References

Ann Arbor Business to Business. 1985. "Robots Create Changes in the Work Force." October: 9.

Axel, H. 1985. "Corporations and Families: Changing Practices and Perspectives." *The Conference Board Report No. 868*: 1.

Bacon, K.H. 1988. "Population and Power Preparing for Change." *Wall Street Journal* (June 8): 1.

Bower, C.D., and J.J. Hallet. 1989. "Issues Management at ASPA." *Personnel Administrator* (January): 40–43.

Bulletin to Management. 1985. "Employment Security News and Views." August 1: 40.

———. 1986. "Work Attitudes: Study Reveals Generation Gap." October 2: 326.

———. 1988. "Effective Strategies for Managing Change." July 14: 3.

Business Week. 1987. "Can Ford Stay on Top?" September 28: 78–86.

———. 1988. "A Cash-Rich Europe Finds the U.S. Ripe for Picking." January 15: 48–49.

Coates, J.F. 1986. *Issues Management.* Mt. Airy, MD: Lomond Publications.

———. 1987. "An Environmental Scan: Projecting Future Human Resource Trends." *Human Resource Planning* 10(4): 219–89.

Copeland, L. 1988. "Valuing Diversity, Part 2: Pioneers and Champions of Change." *Personnel* (July): 48.

Doering, M., S.R. Rhodes, and M. Schuster. 1983. *The Aging Worker: A Compilation and Analysis of the Literature.* New York: Sage.

Dreyfuss, J. 1988. "Catching the Computer Wave." *Fortune* (September 26): 78–82.

Ehrlich, E. 1988. "Business Is Becoming a Substitute Teacher." *Business Week* (September 19): 134–135.

Ehrlich, E., and S.B. Garland. 1988. "It's Time to Put Our Money Where Our Future Is." *Business Week* (September 19): 113.

Fair Employment Practices. 1987a. "Hispanics: A Growing Part of the Workforce." June 11: 69.

———. 1987b. "Female Labor Participation Rates." Sept. 3: 264.

———. 1988. "Facing the Future: Economists Warn of the Workers' Skill Gap." May 12: 60.

Fierman, J. 1988. "The Selling of America (Cont'd)." *Fortune* (May 23): 54–64.

Foster, B.P. 1988. "Workforce Diversity and Business." *Training and Development Journal* (April): 39.

Fowler, E. 1988. "Careers in Corporate Intrapreneurship." *The New York Times* (Sept. 13):D-12.

Fraze, J. 1988a. "Changing Times, Changing Values." *Personnel Administrator* (March): 66–69.

———. 1988b. "Focus on Changes, Not Control, Futurist Advises." *Resource* (March): 1, 4.

Gallup, G., Jr. 1984. *Forecast 2000*. New York: Simon and Schuster.

Grayson, T., and C. O'Dell. 1988. *Two Minute Warning*. New York: The Free Press.

HR Reporter. 1989. "HR: An Oft-Missing Partner in Reorganizing." October: 6.

Johnston, W.B. 1987. *Workforce 2000*. Indianapolis: Hudson Institute.

Kanabayashi, M. 1981. "A March of the Robots." *Wall Street Journal* (November 24): 1.

Kanter, R.M. 1985. "Supporting Innovation and Venture Development in Established Companies." *Journal of Business Venturing* (Winter): 47–60.

Kirkland, R.I., Jr. 1988. "Entering a New Age of Boundless Competition." *Fortune* (March 14): 40–48.

Koepp, S. 1987. "Fighting the Urge to Splurge." *Time* (December 14): 56–61.

Koretz, G. 1988. "Why Asia Looms Large in the U.S. Trade Picture." *Business Week* (July 18): 16.

Kupfer, A. 1988. "Managing Now for the 1990s." *Fortune* (September 26): 44–47.

Levine, J. 1988. "Help Wanted." *Incentive* (August): 54–62.

Main, J. 1988. "The Winning Organization." *Fortune* (September 26): 50–56.

McComas, M. 1986. "Cutting Costs Without Killing the Business." *Fortune* (October 13): 76.

Miller, W.H. 1988. "Employers Wrestle with 'Dumb' Kids." *Industry Week* (July 4): 47.

Nelson-Horchler, J. 1988. "Demographics Deliver a Warning." *Industry Week* (April 18): 58.

Nussbaum, B. 1988. "Needed: Human Capital." *Business Week* (September 19): 100–103.

Perry, N. 1988. "Saving the Schools: How Business Can Help." *Fortune* (November 7): 42–52.

Peters, T. 1988. "The Destruction of Hierarchy." *Industry Week* (August 15): 33–35.

Prokesch, S.E. 1985. "Bean Meshes Man, Machine." *The New York Times* (December 23): 19, 21.

Ramirez, A. 1989. "Making Better Use of Older Workers." *Fortune* (January 30): 179–187.

Rendero, T. 1981. "Want to Boost Managerial Productivity and Cut Costs? Try Automation." *Personnel* (March-April): 39–40.

Schrenk, L.P. 1989. "Environmental Scanning." In *Human Resource Management: Evolving Roles and Responsibilities*, ed. L. Dyer. Washington, D.C.: BNA Books.

Schuler, R.S. 1989. "Scanning the Environment: Planning for Human Resource Management and Organizational Change." *Human Resource Planning* (December): 257–276.

Schuler, R.S., and S.E. Jackson. 1987. "Linking Competitive Strategies with Human Resource Management Practices." *Academy of Management Executive* (August): 207–219.

Shank, S.E. 1988. "Women and the Labor Market: the Link Grows Stronger." *Monthly Labor Review* (March): 7.

Tarbania, D.L. 1984. "Automation in the Office: Users Expand Its Role at All Levels." *AMA Forum* (November): 29–30.

Teltsch, K. 1988. "Business Sees Aid to Schools As a Net Gain." *The New York Times* (December 4): 1.

Tichy, N.M., and M.A. Devanna. 1986. *The Transformational Leader*. New York: John Wiley & Sons.

Walker, J.W. 1988. "Managing Human Resource in Flat, Lean and Flexible Organizations: Trends for the 1990s. *Human Resource Planning* 11(2): 124–132.

Wall Street Journal. 1988. "Labor Letter." December 30: B2.

6.2

Organizational Responses to the External Environment

Ursula Fairbairn
Michelle M. Joyce

In the present business environment, U.S. organizations must recruit, manage, and motivate a working population that is more diverse, better educated, and more demanding than ever before in industrial history.[1] At the same time, corporations confront numerous legislative and regulatory constraints ranging across a wide spectrum of social, political, and economic issues. They have to contend with a complex global economy in which large foreign industrial organizations and domestic rivals compete vigorously for a share of the rich U.S. market. They have had to adapt to dramatic shifts in the techniques and technologies of manufacturing, marketing, service, transportation, and communications.[2]

Competitive success in this environment puts a special premium on flexibility: the ability to anticipate and prepare for change, as well as to react to day-to-day problems. An organization's human resources—the right number of people with the right skills, knowledge, and motivation to respond to competitive challenges—are crucial to its success. As a result, HR managers must thoroughly understand not only their own business and the professional personnel discipline, but also the major external environmental issues that face modern corporations—demographic and social, economic and competitive, legal and regulatory forces.[3]

Environmental factors affect individual corporations in varying degrees.[4] A chemical manufacturer will have special concern about health and safety matters. A mail-order house may have little interest in smokestack pollution but a great deal of concern about day care. Other variations reflect differences in the size, geographic location, and profit or non-profit status of organizations. Large corporations, in particular, must deal with issues in the external environment on many fronts and with many constituencies. Nonetheless, small, non-profit, and public organizations also must address many of the same environmental influences.[5]

This chapter will examine three groups of factors in the external environment that have profoundly influenced the evolution of the HR function over the past 20 years. These external forces include social and demographic changes; the economic and competitive environment; and the legal and regulatory arena.

Social and Demographic Environment

From 1970 to 1985, the U.S. population grew by 17 percent, from 205 million to 239 million people. Over that same period, the civilian work force grew by 29 percent, from 82 million to 106 million. As a result of this remarkable expansion, participation in the work force rose from 60 percent to 64 percent.[6]

Two factors largely account for the growth of the labor force during this period. First, the economy expanded vigorously, creating millions of new job opportunities. Second, a flood of women entered the work force to seek both economic betterment and personal fulfillment. Even among mothers with children under the age of six, two-thirds are working.[7]

Other forces contributing to the growth of the labor force include a vast contingent of part-time workers encompassing 6 million men and 13 million women.[8] Underlying this phenomenon is the two-income family, now perceived as a commonplace fact of life.[9] Another key change concerns the age of the U.S. population, which climbed from a median age of 28.0 years in 1970 to 31.5 in 1985.[10]

Finally, educational factors have affected the labor force. In a increasingly technological society, the need for technically degreed college graduates has increased to the point where employers may face difficulty recruiting sufficient numbers of qualified candidates—a serious long-term issue for U.S. competitiveness. Between 1970 and 1985, the number of Americans with four or more years of college grew from 10.7 percent to 19.4 percent. However, the median educational attainment increased only from 12.1 years to 12.6 years with over one-third of 14- to 24-year-olds never finishing high school.

Given these social and demographic trends, the HR function must adapt to meet the needs and expectations of a changing work force.[11] Employers have to design programs for widely diverse populations: single heads of households who have child-care responsibilities, traditional families with one breadwinner, two-career families, part-timers, the advance degreed, and the functionally illiterate.[12] The following discussion examines these efforts in closer detail.

Child Care

To meet the need for child care, employers have implemented many different programs. Some companies have created their own child-care facilities at the worksite. Others have bought spaces from outside child-care centers and resold these slots to employees at a reduced price. Coupons good for discounts on child-care costs are another approach. Some companies provide employees with free professional child-care referral services, utilizing a network of social-service agencies across the country.[13] Two different programs to address employees' child-care needs are described below.

Child-Care Programs at Merck Corporation

Long before child care gained national attention, the Merck Corporation recognized the evolving importance of this issue. Merck's initial foray into child care came about in 1978 when a senior research manager faced losing a highly valued assistant due to maternity. The expectant mother had told her manager that she would not return to work after the birth of her child unless she could find quality child care.

This discussion prompted formation of a task force which conducted a survey among employees at Merck's Rahway, NJ facility. The survey revealed sufficient interest in child care that Merck concluded it should act to fill this employee need. Since the community lacked organizations to fill this need, the company provided seed money so an ad hoc employee group could establish a program, hire appropriate staff, and underwrite an initial facility lease.

These efforts led to the establishment of an Employee Center for Young Children. The success of the Rahway program stimulated employee interest in creating a similar facility at Merck's West Point facility. At the second location, community services were available to meet employee needs, and Merck arranged for employees to receive preferential enrollment in the program.

Both programs have proved very successful and have extensive waiting lists at present. The payback for Merck has been a reduction—from seven months to four months—in the average length of maternity leave. In addition, these programs have helped Merck's image and its recruitment of young professionals. Merck currently is helping to fund expansion of the programs at both locations.

Transamerica Life's Supercare for Kids

In April 1986, Transamerica Life companies initiated a unique child-care program called Supercare for Kids. Supercare is a daily care facility for mildly ill children. Transamerica Life estimates that it lost between $150,000 to $180,000 annually because of employees' absences to care for sick children. Together with the California Medical Center in Los Angeles, Transamerica developed a program to provide this service to employees.

When a child registered with the program becomes sick on a workday, the parent calls the Supercare Hotline, describes the symptoms, and then takes the child to the facility. The care service accepts only children with mild illnesses; highly contagious diseases, such as chicken pox and measles, are not handled. Employees pay a nominal fee for each use of the service, while Transamerica Life pays the monthly program registration cost.

Elder Care and Other Care Programs

Securing elder care is another frequent need of employees. Unavailability of such services can lead to absenteeism, lowered productivity, and even depression in employees who are caring for aged family members. Since elder care is a relatively new benefit area, companies are proceeding cautiously in implementing it.[14] The following cases describe two different approaches to providing elder care for employees.

Elder Care at Wang Laboratories

In 1984, Wang Laboratories, in cooperation with Elder Services of Merrimack Valley, Inc., launched a three-year demonstration project to assist working family members with the care of aging relatives. In addition, the project sought to gather data about the effect of work life on employees' ability to give elder care. This opportunity allowed Wang to support an effort with potentially far-reaching social benefits and to get a better understanding of the cost factors employees may face in the future as they and their relatives age.

Wang's support involved arranging access to its employee population and contributing staff time and office space that is funded by the U.S. Department of Health and Human Services. The project included an exploratory study that surveyed Wang employees to identify those caring for older family members and to analyze the effect of elder care on employees' attitudes and productivity.

A case manager from an elder services agency visited employees' relatives, assessed their needs, and identified appropriate service plans. Families also received recommendations as to the most appropriate funding source for these services, ranging from Medicaid or state Home Care to the program's newly established dependent care account. A special consideration identified through the project involved the high number of Wang employees of Asian descent. The study found that a number of these employees' elderly relatives felt disenfranchised from the Asian social and cultural context. In response, Elder Services designed group activities which were very well attended.

By the time the project ended in August 1987, 50 referrals had been given to employees who responded to program publicity; nine employees and their relatives actually enrolled in the program. Despite the low enrollment figures, Wang believes the pilot project provided useful information on employees' current needs for adult dependent care and helped to raise the company's consciousness on the issue. Wang is currently adopting a flexible benefits program that will include adult dependent care as one of its options.

IBM's Child- and Elder-Care Referral Services

IBM's concern for employees' families includes both child and elder care. In July 1984, IBM implemented its nationwide Child Care Referral Services. Through this initiative, the firm hoped to offer standardized, high-quality services to its U.S. employees and to stimulate a better supply of day-care facilities near company locations.

Available to IBM's 265,000 U.S. employees, retirees, and their spouses, the program utilizes a network of 200 community-based resource and referral organizations managed by Work/Family Directions, an outside vendor. Services offered include clarification of needs, consumer education, information, and referrals to child-care providers with openings.

In 1988, IBM implemented a similar Elder Care Referral Service. The elder-care initiative was prompted in part by a 1986 work-life study which indicated that 30 percent of IBM employees bear some responsibility for older relatives, including 8 percent who have elderly dependents and 4 percent who have elderly resident dependents. The program provides employees who have relatives ages 60 or older with personalized consultation, consumer education, information, and referrals. Work/Family Directions directs the program via a network of 175 community-based consultation and referral organizations with expertise in gerontology and elder care.

Since its inception, the Child Care Referral Service has helped more than 21,000 IBM employees seeking care for 26,000 children. IBM hopes to report similarly positive results for the Elder Care Referral Service. The company is currently considering additional family-life programs, such as parenting seminars.

Flexible Work Schedules

Part-time or flexible work schedules have proven useful in meeting the needs of single parents and dual-career families. These schedules also fit the plans of older workers who would like to ease into retirement,[15] and of part-time workers who are just interested in earning extra money.

The part-time work force has unique demographics. Part-time employees typically are younger (ages 16 to 24) or older (over age 65) than full-time workers. A higher percentage of part-timers work in the retail trade and service industries, and part-time employees are more likely to have schedules other than a regular day-time shift. Two-thirds are women, most of whom are married, while male part-timers tend to be single. Individuals who work multiple jobs made up 5.4 percent of the work force in 1985—the highest level in 20 years. About 80 percent of men who hold multiple jobs work full time on their primary jobs, compared to 60 percent of women.

Companies find that options like flexible starting times, part-time work, flexible work schedules, and job sharing can achieve cost savings, productivity gains, and a more flexible work force.[16] Alternative work schedules have proven especially beneficial in filling positions which are difficult to staff or which are not needed on a full-time basis. Flexible work schedules also match the requirements of companies that need around-the-clock staffing, such as the food service and health-care industries. Job sharing, the least used of alternative work schedules, is considered to be particularly useful in decreasing layoffs and improving cyclical productivity.

In general, employees have reacted positively to these new arrangements. A 1984 study of alternative work schedules by the General Accounting Office found that participants reported improved morale, higher levels of commitment, and increased productivity.[17] An emerging issue facing companies attempting to implement flexible work schedules concerns the extent to which part-time workers should participate in the benefits programs available to full-time employees.

As noted above, alternative schedules appeal to older workers who wish to ease into retirement. Taking advantage of this pool of experienced workers calls for a new level of planning on the part of personnel staffs.[18] However, the effort can produce a source of reliable, competent, and productive temporary employees at savings relative to fees charged by temporary agencies. One successful program targeting the semi-retired is described below.

Travelers' Retiree Job Bank

In 1979, senior executives of the Travelers Companies decided to take a leadership role in coping with some of the problems of aging. This decision launched the Older Americans Program, which in turn led to the creation of Traveler's Retiree Job Bank.

The Job Bank, which allows retirees to work up to 960 hours per year, serves the needs of both the corporation and the retirees. Retirees work in temporary positions during peak periods, fill in for employees absent due to illness, personal leave or vacation, and handle jobs left vacant by delays in hiring new employees. In addition, continuing part-time job-share positions are available. About 700 retirees currently work in departments throughout the company.

The program has enabled Travelers to hire from a population that has proven to be reliable, competent, and productive. Given retirees' familiarity with the business, the company needs to spend minimal time on orientation. Retirees are paid at the midpoint of the salary range for the position in which they work, which often amounts to less than the fees charged by temporary agencies. At present, Travelers estimates that the job bank program saves the company over $1 million a year.

For retirees, the job bank provides an opportunity to earn extra income and to remain in the work force. Although more than 85 percent of Travelers' employees ages 55 or older had indicated an interest in working part-time after retirement, the program receives more requests for services than it has retirees available. As a result, Travelers has expanded the job bank to include recruiting retirees of other companies.

Medical Care

The growing diversity of the working population reflects parallel changes in life-styles. In general, a "revolution of rising expectations" has taken place. Greater numbers of employees have come to expect—or even to take for granted—such new benefits as health management, physical fitness, and smoking cessation programs. As a result, HR managers are called upon to weigh the value of each proposed new benefit area against its estimated cost.[19]

Along with the needs for family care and alternative work schedules, quality of life issues, such as wellness, physical fitness, and drug and alcohol problems have generated new HRM initiatives. One driving force for these initiatives is the skyrocketing cost of medical care. The average per capita cost for health care rose to $1,721 in 1985. For employers, health-related issues include the direct costs of medical benefits as well as the indirect costs of absenteeism, replacement, training, productivity losses, and lowered morale.[20] In contrast, wellness programs can be initiated at relatively low cost and produce returns ranging from $5 to $14 for every dollar spent.

As a result, organizations have begun to experiment with a variety of programs designed to enhance employees' well-being. The number of company-sponsored employee assistance programs (EAPs) has grown from 5,000 in 1979 to 12,000 in 1987.[21] EAPs have been shown to lower insurance premiums and substantially reduce productivity losses due to health-related problems.

EAPs which help employees deal with drug and alcohol problems have proven to be the most cost-effective type of program. The lost productivity associated with drug and alcohol abuse costs employers an estimated $176 billion, while the cost of testing for and treatment of drug addiction runs to some $2 billion. Other high-return initiatives are stop-smoking clinics and screening programs to detect medical risks and prescribe prevention.

As the following Johnson and Johnson example demonstrates, wellness programs can produce substantial reductions in health-care costs and improved health for the work force.[22]

Johnson and Johnson's Live for Life Program

Johnson and Johnson, which has built a reputation on products that treat the ills of America, extended this health consciousness to its own employees through a worksite wellness program initiated in 1978. Live for Life provides a comprehensive management system to improve employees' health and to contain company health-care costs.

Live for Life rests upon two assumptions: (1) life-style practices (such as diet, smoking, exercise, and so on) contribute substantially to an individual's health status, and (2) healthy life-styles can be successfully promoted in the work setting. Designed to encourage voluntary adoption of healthy habits, the program includes a health profile system, which assesses employees' health status; action programs, which offer behavior-change courses in seven health-risk areas; and a health promotion marketing system, which provides ongoing educational and promotional activities that foster high-participation levels.

Benefits derived from the program to date include healthier employees, lower health-care costs, and improved morale among employees. In addition, a recent study, funded by Johnson and Johnson and published in the Journal of the American Medical Association, reported that the Live for Life program halved employee hospital costs, which account for up to two-thirds of the company's total health benefit expenses. Live for Life is currently available to 33,850 Johnson and Johnson employees at 75 domestic and overseas locations. The company is also marketing the program to other corporations through a subsidiary, Johnson and Johnson Health Management, Inc.

Education and Training to Meet Corporate Needs

The need for a stronger education base among the U.S. working population is universally acknowledged. Despite demanding recruitment requirements, American businesses this year will have to hire more than one million entry-level workers who are virtually unable to read, write, or count. By some estimates, as many as 72 million Americans lack the reading skills needed to fill out a job application, write a check, or even read a poison warning label.[23]

Training these individuals and absorbing their lost productivity may cost as much as $25 billion.[24] In addition, the rapid pace of technological change promises to create higher training costs. In many areas, an employees' knowledge base can become obsolete in as little as five years. The very nature of work, from manufacturing to service industries, has become more complex and demands a higher level of training.

In response to this educational deficit and the need for updated technological skills,[25] some companies have set up extensive and complex in-house educational programs. Employer-provided education programs offer the means to keep pace with the specialized needs of customers and the growing requirements for technical training and management development. Other organizations have developed an evolving partnership role with external educational institutions.[26] Descriptions of some of these initiatives follow.

Employee and Customer Education at IBM

IBM's emphasis on education began more than a quarter century before the advent of the computer age. In 1933, IBM President Thomas J. Watson Sr. opened the company's first dedicated education and training center adjoining the IBM manufacturing plant at Endicott, NY. Given the company's parallel commitments to technological change and full employment, the need for ongoing training and retraining became fundamental to IBM's way of life.

On average, more than 18,000 IBM employees worldwide leave their regular job assignments each workday to participate in some type of education or training class. Management training at all levels amounts to at least 40 hours a year per person. Educational activities range from the technical to the professional, from marketing and service courses to seminars for senior managers.

Educational techniques vary widely. IBM offers formal classes, traditional lectures, and individual learning modules utilizing books, audiovisual tapes, or interactive computer-based programs. A satellite network broadcasts lectures to employees at a number of IBM laboratories and manufacturing locations. The IBM Management Development Center, located at corporate headquarters in Armonk, NY, provides training for all new and middle-level managers. Technical and professional employees may attend classes at IBM's state-of-the-art Corporate Education Center at Thornwood, NY. The center includes 250 bedrooms to accommodate students from distant IBM locations.

Marketing and customer education, based in Atlanta and Dallas, targets customers as well as IBM's sales force and branch office administration staffs. Employee programs include training to qualify new people for their jobs and to enhance the skills of experienced IBMers. Customers are offered a broad range of product education through IBM technical education centers in major cities worldwide.

The marketing and customer education operation also oversees some 150 learning centers in branch offices throughout the United States. In these centers, both employees and customers can participate in self-paced study and computer-based training programs. Today, more than 40 percent of IBM's service education has been converted to interactive, computer-based training. By eliminating the need for travel, this cost-effective approach keeps IBM's large service organization available to respond promptly to customers' needs.

Motorola's Training and Education Center

As one of America's industrial leaders, Motorola faces increasing international competition in markets that did not even exist a few years earlier. Corporate growth and development in this high-tech world, Motorola believes, still depend on people. To improve the productivity and performance of both employees and the organization, the company established the Motorola Training and Education Center (MTEC).

The centerpiece of Motorola's educational thrust is the Chicago-area Galvin Center. The center, which opened in 1986 at a cost of $8.5 million, serves up to 4,800 students annually. In addition, Motorola commits a set percentage—1.5 percent in 1985—of its annual payroll for training and education. As a result, an estimated 3 million hours of training a year are given to Motorola 90,000 employees worldwide.

MTEC offers to both employees and selected vendors training as well as education-related products and services designed to support Motorola's business objectives. However, the center must compete with other vendors that offer training to each business sector of the company. As a result, MTEC strives to offer performance-based training aimed at the right people at the right time.

Programs and services available from MTEC include the following: research and development services to design new training efforts; planning and evaluation programs; regional training consultants throughout the world; functional training managers; professional course designers; seminar delivery services; development services for professional staff; and, residential programs for senior executives and key manufacturing managers.

MTEC has provided Motorola with a demonstrable return on its training investment. The "Total Quality Improvement" programs have saved more than $5.2 million in two years at three Florida facilities. The "Sales Call Dimensions" program for salespeople has generated increases of 30 percent in overall orders, 79 percent in orders from new customers, and 27 percent in profits resulting from higher productivity. In 1986, the American Society for Training and Development selected Motorola as the recipient of the society's annual award for excellence in HR development. MTEC has recently broadened its focus to include training in such areas as the management of change and the effective management of technology.

AETNA's Institute for Corporate Education

Since AETNA is an insurance and financial service institution that produces no tangible product, its success depends on the quality of service provided to clients. AETNA's Institute for Corporate Education, which opened in 1984, aims to help the company achieve its business objectives by ensuring quality services. Training programs are designed to give employees and producers the skills, knowledge, and attitudes necessary to grow in their present position, to compete for broader responsibilities, and to improve AETNA's overall productivity and profitability.

Operating with an annual budget of the $15.8 million, the institute has several distinctive features. First, the institute pursues its mission by continually conducting experiments on new and established training technologies, such as interactive video, educational television, teleconferencing, telepresentation, and computer-based instruction. Second, new courses are developed through a systematic methodology, called the "Learning Design Model," which includes numerous quality-assurance checks. Third, most of the institute's programs are conducted at or from its new $26 million Educational Center. By consolidating operations under one roof, the center has enhanced the institute's service delivery.

Some interesting aspects of the Educational Center include the following: closed-circuit television which allows students to review the day's work or to prepare for the next day by dialing up videotaped lectures; a fitness center run in conjunction with AETNA's wellness program; a Corporate Information Center which houses the company's former library collection along with 200 databases that employees can scan and print out bibliographies and abstracts of articles.

At present, the institute provides 60,000 student days of instruction each year. While most of this instruction takes place at the Educational Center, satellite connections to field offices in eight cities offer additional educational and training opportunities. Future plans include expansion of direct satellite broadcasts to field sites, implementation of an "Effective Business Skills" curriculum to address basic academic deficiencies, and introduction of a core curriculum for upper management.

Education and Training to Address Societal Needs

Today's U.S. high schools are turning out 700,000 functionally illiterate students each year, while a similar number of students drop out. In addition to tackling their own education and training needs, corporations are beginning to help school systems cope with this grave national problem. Some companies have offered the services of current and retired employees to educational institutions; many other cooperative ventures have been undertaken. Four examples of such initiatives are given below.

IBM's Technical Academic Career Program

Piloted by IBM in the 1984-1985 academic year, the Technical Academic Career Program helps colleges and universities to fill critical faculty and administrative positions within engineering and science programs. It supplies this assistance by making available newly retired IBM professionals who possess the qualifications and desire to teach in technical disciplines as a second career.

For selection into the program, IBM management looks for employees who are eligible to retire and have technical background in such fields as engineering, physical science, computer science, or information systems. In addition, individuals must possess the skills necessary for an academic position and the profesional characteristics that would appropriately represesnt IBM.

To participate, a school must offer an IBM employee a full-time position with a minimum two-year salary of $30,000 or more. IBM pays participating employees 35 percent of their final IBM salary for two years, plus retirement benefits. If relocation is required, the company also provides a fixed sum of $15,000 to cover moving costs.

The program is now available to all IBM business units with technical personnel. In 1986 and 1987, 35 employees accepted teaching positions as part of this program. IBM anticipates that substantial numbers of employees will continue to elect to retire into a teaching career through the program.

Arthur D. Little's Management Education Institute

The Management Education Institute is the educational component of the international management consulting and research firm of Arthur D. Little, Inc. The institute, chartered in 1971, is an autonomous educational institution, but relies on Arthur D. Little for human, physical, and financial resources. In return for this support, the institute adapts its curricula to reflect changes in Arthur D. Little's marketplace.

Accredited by the New England Association of Schools and Colleges, the institute offers a master's of science in management program and a number of shorter management education programs focusing on special areas. The master's program, an 11-month intensive program, offers an effective educational option to promising managers at sponsoring international corporations, governments, and national enterprises. Unlike other educational programs, the institute approaches management problems from an international perspective that takes into account cultural, regional, and political differences. This approach, and the institute's curriculum and faculty, draws heavily upon the experience and expertise supplied by Arthur D. Little's consulting efforts.

The institute receives 200 to 250 applications each year, from which it selects 60 to 75 individuals for the master's program. Since its creation, the institute has attracted participants from industries and governments in more than 100 countries throughout the world. Virtually all of its alumni have returned to work in their own countries, lending a far-reaching impact to the institute's efforts.

Xerox's Institute for Research on Learning

Xerox has invested $5 million to establish the Institute for Research on Learning, a non-profit organization dedicated to seeking ways to train the so-called untrainable—the million-plus entry-level workers who lack basic reading, writing, and arithmetic skills.

The institute is associated with Xerox's Palo Alto Research Center and the University of California's Graduate School of Education at Berkeley. Through the use of new computers and artificial intelligence, institute researchers study how people learn and think, thereby creating more effective ways to train the work force of tomorrow.

Given that the institute only opened in 1986, research results are not yet ready for public release, and evaluation of the venture at this point would be premature. Xerox is actively seeking other companies and organizations to collaborate in the institute.

Educational Enhancement Efforts at BellSouth

BellSouth Corporation established the BellSouth Foundation in 1986 with the goal of improving the quality of education in the Southeast. BellSouth's efforts reflect its belief that prosperity and social vitality depend on a region's schools.

The foundation's first grants, totaling $1.63 million, were awarded in August 1987 to six programs aimed at improving elementary, secondary, and higher education in the Southeast. The results of these programs are not yet available, but BellSouth hopes its lead will prompt other companies to invest their employees' special talents and resource in community schools.

As a technological company, BellSouth obviously benefits from an educated work force, but it derives a broader benefit as well from its effort. BellSouth's success is directly linked to the economies of the nine Southeastern states. Through funding and personal involvement, BellSouth seeks to acts as a catalyst to attract resources that will enhance the overall prosperity of the states in which it operates.

Economic and Competitive Environment

One of the most noteworthy shifts in U.S. business development over the past two decades involves a trend toward bigness. The total assets of Citicorp and Exxon—an estimated $143 billion in 1985—are equal to the combined assets of all 10 million individual proprietorships in the United States. The 800 leading manufacturing, transportation, utilities, finance, and retail firms employ about as many Americans as the combined work forces of 15 million or so proprietorships, partnerships, and smaller corporations.[27]

This trend toward bigness stems from three principal factors, each with overtones for HRM:

- Technological advances. Major advances in computer technology, satellite communications, and robotic automation have greatly reduced the costs of mass production.[28]

- Mergers and acquisitions. During the 1980s, mergers and acquisitions accelerated in both number and size. In the first half of the decade, 62 Fortune 500 corporations underwent takeovers; costs associated with the 3,000 mergers in 1985 ran to more than $200 billion.[29] All these mergers and acquisitions required difficult HR decisions about redeployment, reassignment, retraining, outplacement, staff consolidations, and retirement incentive programs.

- Economic fluctuations. The normal ups and downs of the business cycle over the past decade accounted for the demise of many smaller companies which lacked the resources to weather bad times. As economic pressures have intensified, success in the competition for world markets rests largely on strategies developed by multinational companies.

These three factors also interact to affect the overall economy. The extent and timing of technological change can play a critical role in determining the national economic future, as the case of Japan demonstrates. When the value of the yen doubled during a three-year period, Japanese industries managed to slash production costs by accelerating their very effective factory automation program. If Japanese businesses had chosen instead to double product prices, as denominated in dollars, to bring in the same number of yen, they would have priced themselves out of the lucrative U.S. market.

In the United States, the growth in federal budget deficits and sharp decline in the value of the dollar have profoundly altered some fundamental economic attitudes. As confidence in the future of the national economy wanes, resistance to large-scale capital investment and financial instability increase. For an organization to succeed in this unpredictable environment, it must have a quality work force with the flexibility to respond to changing conditions.

Improving Productivity

U.S. productivity has suffered over the past decade, growing by only 1 percent a year, compared to Germany's 3 percent and Japan's 4 percent growth rates.[30] Reasons posited for this poor showing include the gradual shift from a manufacturing to a service economy, where productivity gains are harder to achieve; the twin problems of extractive industries, namely, depletion of natural resources and the costs of safety and pollution-control measures; and the well-touted weaknesses of American management—short-term planning, bureaucracy, and widespread overstaffing.

Whatever the reasons, U.S. businesses must take effective steps to increase productivity or see the national standard of living decline.[31] To a degree, the productivity problem has been masked by changes in the labor force—the influx of women and the entry of baby boomers, who tend to marry later and have smaller families.[32] However, the recent growth in service industries, where productivity gains are more difficult to attain, complicates the difficulty.[33]

Improving productivity demands exploiting new technology. It also requires employees to take more responsibility for the quality of their work, rather than rely on inspection by others to identify shortcomings. In addition, companies must know their customers to ensure that their products answer real market needs. Equally important, businesses must take steps to stabilize the U.S. work force and to improve the training of employees.

Few industries have felt the need for productivity improvements as intensely as the auto industry has. While quota restrictions between 1981 and 1985 allowed automakers to plan long-term strategies and make record profits in 1983 and 1984, competition for foreign exports has intensified again. The top three U.S. auto manufacturers will face revenue losses up to $13.5 billion—and forced plant closings and layoffs—if the overseas market share rises from 25 percent to 40 percent over the next five years.

To meet the challenges of international competition, rising customer expectations, and the need for technological innovation, automakers need to adopt innovative strategies. They also need to involve all employees in these efforts. The following example shows how Ford is attempting to reach this goal. By improving cooperation between the United Auto Workers (UAW) and the company, Ford hopes to achieve the quality that would make it a more secure place to work.[34]

Employee Involvement at Ford

In the late 1970s and early 1980s, leaders in the UAW and at Ford recognized the need for management innovations that would improve product quality, customer satisfaction, and employee commitment. The strategy chosen places greater value on the knowledge and experience of Ford employees by bringing the ingenuity of every worker more fully into the managerial and operating processes. Since 1979, employee involvement has become both company policy and a formal understanding with the UAW.

Ford's employee involvement process attempts to create and maintain a work climate in which all employees can achieve individual goals and work satisfaction by directing their energies toward clearly defined company goals. While the company's statement of mission, values, and guiding principles guides the process, all members of management are encouraged to employ the participative methods best suited to their own organizational circumstances. Managers receive assistance from staffers who administer the employee involvement process, as well as financial support, consulting services, and a wide range of education and training programs for themselves and their employees.

While a cause-and-effect relationship between employee involvement and operating results is difficult to establish, Ford has done remarkably well in recent years. The company received back-to-back Motor Trend Car of the Year awards, the first time in history for any motor car division. Ford's 1986 profits topped the Big Three list for the first time since 1924. In addition, a 1986 opinion survey of a cross-section of 3,200 employees found that 90 percent agreed with the statement "what happens to Ford is important to me."

Ford views employee involvement as an evolutionary process, the power and full potential of which has not yet been realized. Projects on work redesign, leadership development, and teamwork improvement are now underway. The spirit of employee involvement and the practices associated with it are expected to provide the basis for continuing success in meeting Ford's current and future challenges.

Handling Overstaffing

Austerity moves, while often traumatic, can prove economically productive. Exxon, for example, eliminated one-third of its service stations and cut its work force by 32 percent between 1980 and 1986, yet managed to increase product sales by one-third during the same period. Despite such success stories, layoffs can have a debilitating effect on employee morale—and productivity as a result—if handled poorly. As layoffs spread over the past decade, companies developed a variety of programs, ranging from job protection agreements to retraining and redeployment, to bolster morale among workers. Descriptions of a few of these efforts follow.

General Motors' Job Opportunity Bank—Security Program

In their 1984 national negotiations, General Motors and the UAW expressed mutual concern over providing employees with job security while reserving the company's ability to compete should the marketplace change. Job security provisions were negotiated under the Job Opportunity Bank—Security (JOBS) programs, which included two special retirement programs: the Voluntary Termination of Employment Program (VTEP) and the JOBS Pension Program.

JOBS virtually guaranteed that no employee with at least one year of service would be laid off for the next six years. The program required establishment of job banks to protect employees from layoffs due to certain corporate decisions, such as introduction of new technology, outsourcing, negotiated productivity improvements, and consolidation and/or transfer of component work. Whenever such a corporate decision created a work-force surplus, an Employee Development Bank would be established to place displaced employees in new assignments. Assignments ranged from training programs to nontraditional positions within or outside the bargaining unit. A national JOBS committee provides policy guidelines, and various GM locations have local JOBS committees that administer the program.

As of September 1987, approximately 12,400 workers had used the program at a cost of $120 million. The program has a cap of $1 billion to cover the period from 1984 to 1990. Current contract negotiations between the UAW and General Motors appear likely to include a job-protection component with a $1.3 billion cap. Under the new agreement, GM will not be able to lay off workers for most reasons other than production cuts due to slow sales.

Stroh's Termination Transition Services

In 1985, Stroh decided to close its Detroit brewery due to the excess capacity that resulted from acquiring the Joseph Schlitz Brewing Company three years earlier. At the same time, Stroh implemented a comprehensive transition services program conceived by the management consulting firm of Jannotta, Bray, and Associates.

The program attempted to address the many needs facing displaced employees while in transition. Severance packages, negotiated with the union for non-management workers and developed by the corporate HR department for management employees, provided income and benefits coverage to terminated employees. In addition, Stroh recognized longer-service employees through special early retirement and/or welfare benefits. Two transition centers, one for hourly and one for salaried employees, offered the support of professional services in a professional environment.

Transition services included the following: (1) orientation meetings where employees completed questionnaires covering their backgrounds, work histories, and job objectives or plans; (2) four- to five-day job search workshops, which included basic remedial education, job identification, resume mailings, and job fairs; and (3) support services, such as retirement planning, credit and/or financial planning, and personal or family counseling.

Of the 1,159 displaced employees, 66 percent participated in the program, and 98 percent of participants found jobs. In addition, 82 percent of salaried employees located jobs at levels equal to or better than their previous positions. By the time the transition centers closed in June 1986, Stroh had achieved its original goal of assisting displaced employees while enhancing its image as a company genuinely concerned about people.

Retraining and Redeployment at IBM

Retraining and redeployment are long-standing key features in IBM's methods of managing people to meet changing business needs. Unlike companies which use layoffs to handle the problem of surplus employees, IBM deals with workload imbalances by offering to retrain and, if necessary, relocate employees to areas of the business where a need exists. IBM is proud—and its employees are acutely aware—that for nearly 50 years, the company has enjoyed full employment without a single layoff.

IBM's resource requirements shift with changing technologies and market conditions, and the company's retraining and redeployment efforts accommodate these shifts. For example, IBM recently determined its most pressing needs lay in four critical areas: programming, engineering, marketing, and systems engineering. To respond to these demands, the company redeployed 21,500 employees in 1986 and 1987. About 8,000 of these employees also received retraining to work as programmers, systems engineers, and marketing representatives. Participating employees were competitively screened and selected before undergoing the requisite formal and on-the-job training for their new assignments. The redeployment effort, which included IBM operations in the United States and several other countries, was centrally managed in each country.

IBM's retraining and deployment program offers three key benefits: It enables IBM to cut costs and improve efficiency; it enhances the skills of experienced employees; and it creates new career opportunities for employees.

Dealing with Takeovers

Takeovers can force companies with modern, progressive HRM practices to develop and implement different strategies to accomplish major cost reductions. Even unsuccessful takeover attempts can have a severe economic impact on an organization. The following cases demonstrate two different strategies utilized to thwart or address the after-effects of a takeover.

Herman Miller's Silver Parachute Plan

Implemented in September 1986, Herman Miller's Silver Parachute Plan is designed to discourage takeover attempts and to provide security for employees who might be adversely affected in the event of a hostile takeover. The plan came about not because of any existing threat, but in anticipation of future hostile situations.

The plan assures generous benefits to all full-time employees who have at least two years of continuous employment at the time of a takeover. Any employee who either is fired or resigns voluntarily within two years of the ownership change is guaranteed severance pay. Depending on seniority, severance pay ranges from one year's salary to two and a half times that amount. The plan also covers all expenses and legal fees if an employee has to sue the acquiring firm to enforce payment.

Herman Miller is one of the first companies in America to adopt such a program. In the current environment of takeover uncertainty, the company believes it must protect the interests of all employees and their families, not just top executives. Regardless of the plan's effectiveness in thwarting takeover, Herman Miller believes the policy has paid off in enhanced employee morale.

Goodyear's Response to a Takeover Attempt

In 1986, Goodyear successfully defended itself against a hostile takeover attempt. In the process, the company incurred a debt of $5.3 billion to buy half its stock. A three-year plan to reduce this debt had severe HR implications, including plant closings, the sale of business units, and a special retirement program. Other actions taken included reducing operating budgets, freezing executive salaries, and restricting hiring.

Goodyear's HRM organization quickly developed and implemented programs to help the 2,000 employees affected by plant closings. Workers received six months notice, supplemental unemployment compensation, and a two-year continuation of medical benefits. Outplacement services and job fairs helped employees to find new jobs. In addition, Goodyear redeployed many workers to other company locations.

Legal and Regulatory Environment

Over the past 25 years, national legislation has gradually introduced a broad range of worker protections that have restricted companies' freedom to structure themselves and manage their employees. Table 1 lists some of the key laws affecting employers.[35]

Table 1
Key Legislation Affecting Employers

DATE	LAW	PROVISIONS
1963	Equal Pay Act	Requires equal pay for men and women doing similar work under similar conditions.
1964	Civil Rights Act	Prohibits discrimination on the basis of race, color, sex, religion or national origin. Amended in 1972 (Title VII).
1967	Age Discrimination Employment Act	Prohibits discrimination in employment based on age. Amended in 1978 and again in 1986.
1970	Consumer Credit Protection Act	Prohibits discharge for garnishment for just one debt.
1970	Occupational Safety and Health Act (OSHA)	Employers in interstate commerce must comply with federal health and safety standards.
1973	Vocational Rehabilitation Act	Government contractors need to take affirmative action to employ and advance qualified handicapped workers.
1974	Employee Retirement Income Security Act (ERISA)	Requires vesting in pension plans, insures pension funds, requires employee communication on pension matters.
1978	Pregnancy Discrimination Act	Amended Civil Rights Act of 1964 to define discrimination on the basis of sex to include discrimination based on pregnancy.
1984	Retirement Equity Act	Amended ERISA to provide fuller protection to spouses with regard to survivor benefits under pension plans.
1986	Tax Reform Act	Granted fuller protection of benefit rights to the majority of employees. Modified other programs, such as IRAs.
1990	Americans with Disabilities Act	Amends and broadens scope of 1973 Vocational Rehabilitation Act.

The impact of complying with these laws, while undoubtedly of societal value, has created, in some cases, significant financial costs. Even the reporting requirements associated with many of these measures are onerous and expensive.[36] In addition, employees have become more aware of their rights under these laws and more willing to sue employers if they feel aggrieved.

As a result, employers, individually or through trade and professional organizations, have begun to monitor legislative initiatives and lobby for legislation that is least harmful and constraining to business objectives.[37] Current social and economic issues that may generate new legal requirements include drug and alcohol abuse on the job, acquired immune deficiency syndrome (AIDS), and trade legislation to enhance the domestic and international competitiveness of selected industries. Many companies have already established HRM programs that anticipate social changes or provide voluntary standards of business conduct well beyond the minimum legal requirements.

Equal Opportunity

While minorities and women are still underrepresented in higher management, many major corporations have initiated programs to ensure continued recruitment and advancement of these groups.[38] A 1985 study of nine large corporations, for example, found that all had made progress by implementing equal opportunity programs more demanding than federal standards require.

Companies with successful equal opportunity programs tend to have the active commitment of top management, establish separate budgets for affirmative action programs, and include equal opportunity in management assessments.[39] In addition, these organizations collaborate with educational institutions and offer special training and development programs to help develop female and minority recruits. The case of Hewlett-Packard demonstrates how collaboration with higher education can facilitate affirmative action efforts.

Student Employment and Educational Development at Hewlett-Packard

Hewlett Packard initiated its Student Employment and Educational Development (SEED) program with three main objectives:

- to recruit qualified students and to provide them with continuous professional experience,
- to build relations by exposing students to Hewlett-Packard, and

- to encourage the participation of women, minorities, and disabled students.

The program offers motivated college students an opportunity to broaden their education and initiate their careers through practical work experience in a sophisticated work environment. Applicants must have completed at least their first year of college and be able to work at least 10 consecutive weeks during the calendar year for their first assignment. Hewlett-Packard manages the program throughout the United States by providing general policies and guidelines; each site can tailor these guidelines to meet its own needs in terms of the number and backgrounds of students hired. Once accepted into the program, each student is treated as a potential Hewlett-Packard employee.

Through SEED, Hewlett-Packard has developed good campus relations across the country. Successful candidates have shown strong academic achievement in pursuit of their technical or business degrees. A significant percentage—23 percent in 1987—of new permanent college hires are alumni of the program.

Safety and Health

State worker's compensation laws, based on the no-fault liability concept, cover some 83 million employees and account for benefits totalling some $19 million annually. Besides providing benefits to injured employees, many states have also developed safety laws to prevent accidents and injuries.

At the national level, the Occupational Safety and Health Act took effect in 1970. This legislation created the Occupational Safety and Health Administration (OSHA) and the National Institute for Occupational Safety and Health to develop and administer safety standards. While OSHA's role in reducing accidents has occasionally generated controversy, the agency has begun working with employers to emphasize "cooperative regulation" based on cost-effective, performance-related standards.[40]

From any viewpoint, industrial accidents are extremely important to management. The associated costs of lost wages, insurance administration, medical expenses, fire losses, and time lost by employees not involved in the accident run to more than $32 billion a year. As a result, some companies are developing innovative approaches to health and safety. The following discussion focuses on the efforts of one company to develop a personal safety program both on and off the job.

DuPont's Personal Safety Programs

The DuPont Company has a long tradition of concern for employees' safety on and off the job, for the needs of the "whole" employee, and for the interests of the surrounding community. These concerns prompted DuPont to develop an educational program to address violent crime and assault prevention.

The Personal Safety Program includes four components: a Personal Safety Meeting, a Rape Prevention Workshop, a Manager's Workshop, and a Facilitator's Workshop. The Personal Safety Meeting, designed for all audiences, aims to increase individual awareness of the potential for physical assault and to provide practical safety tips and techniques. Women who participate in the Rape Prevention Workshop are helped to increase confidence in their abilities to prevent rape and, if unsuccessful in thwarting an attack, to cope with its aftermath. To support the overall intent of the programs, the Manager's Workshop trains supervisors and managers to provide sensitive and informed support to victims of physical assault. The five-day Facilitator's Workshop prepares employees to act as facilitators for the program.

Since its inception in December 1986, approximately 20,000 employees have participated in the program. DuPont benefits from having more secure employees who are better able to direct their attention to business needs. At present, DuPont is considering a new component, targeting male employees, that would concentrate on learning how to deal with an employee who has suffered a physical assault.

AIDS Education

The AIDS epidemic poses another challenge which forward-thinking employers are attempting to meet head on, rather than waiting for legislation. Some 28,000 individuals have died of AIDS since 1981. By 1988, the number of AIDS cases had reached 50,000, a figure projected to rise to over 275,000 by 1991. Since about 90 percent of AIDS cases are working-age adults, every major company in America has or will have employees with this fatal disease.[41]

As a result, organizations have begun to implement programs to address this issue. For example, a group of 36 employers, including IBM, AT&T, Chemical Bank, and Johnson & Johnson, recently endorsed a 10-point "bill of rights" on AIDS in the workplace, based on recommendation by the Citizens Commission on AIDS for New

York City and northern New Jersey. Besides developing policies regarding the treatment of employees who have AIDS, many companies have recognized the need to educate coworkers about the illness.

Communicating about AIDS at Transamerica Life

In 1986, Transamerica Life Company began a series of activities designed to educate employees and the community about AIDS. Increasing awareness of the disease, a desire to provide factual medical information to employees, and an interest in educating the community led to the formation of a task force to determine company strategy. Numerous actions involving both the company and the community have evolved from this task force.

Within the company, a letter from Transamerica's chief executive officer to all employees emphasized that individuals with AIDS would receive normal medical coverage and would be treated with dignity and respect. Each employee also received a copy of the U.S. Surgeon General's report on AIDS. An education program trained managers to answer employee questions about the disease. In addition, a crisis intervention team of medical, legal, and employee assistance program professionals was established to respond within 24 hours whenever fears or rumors about AIDS arose within a department.

To assist the community, Transamerica Life developed a videotape which outlines the steps any company should take when developing a system to address AIDS. They also have issued a pamphlet with facts about AIDS for distribution to employees, police departments, schools, and other community organizations.

These efforts are only a sampling of the actions that Transamerica Life has undertaken to address the AIDS issue. Response by employees and the community has been positive, and Transamerica Life plans to continue its education efforts.

IBM's AIDS Program

In 1985, IBM's corporate medical department formulated an AIDS position statement. Based on the best medical knowledge available and designed to reflect IBM's basic belief in respect for the individual, the statement assured employees with AIDS would be permitted to work if able to do so and would be eligible for all IBM benefits, including medical disability. The position statement also ensured the privacy rights of individuals with AIDS and directed managers to supply necessary support to afflicted employees.

Beyond this policy guidance, the company has developed a three-part strategic framework to deal with AIDS. Employees affected by AIDS receive access to literature through company medical departments and health information centers. To accelerate AIDS prevention, IBM developed a unique video education program, which provides information on health topics that employees can use at home or supply to community organizations. To support external programs to control and cure AIDS, IBM is actively exploring research and education possibilities. In 1986, company contributions to the American Foundation for AIDS Research helped to establish an AIDS virology lab in the Antenucci Research Building at St. Luke's-Roosevelt Hospital.

By helping to explore new approaches and by communicating to employees in a clear and consistent manner, IBM believes that it has played a useful role in addressing the AIDS issues.

Drug Abuse Programs

Drug abuse, a societal problem of mammoth proportions, costs employers an estimated $33 billion in lost productivity alone.[42] Drug abusers have more accidents, higher absenteeism, and higher medical costs than other employees. According to estimates by the National Institute of Drug Abuse, 40 percent of the nation's largest corporations do some type of drug testing. However, several states have passed laws restricting employers' use of drug testing, prompting many major companies to step up efforts to educate lawmakers about the importance of a drug-free workplace.[43]

Applicant Drug Screening at IBM

IBM views a drug-free work environment as vital to its interests, to the quality of its products, to workplace safety, and to employee productivity. The company offers education and rehabilitation programs for employees and their families, and it supports community abuse prevention programs. In addition, IBM has instituted a comprehensive, nationwide applicant drug screening process, with attendant safeguards to ensure accuracy. Any applicant who does not successfully complete the screening process will not receive a job offer from the company.

Since IBM implemented the program in 1984, many states and local jurisdictions have passed legislation regulating employers' screening procedures. Such legislation has caused IBM to modify its national employment process to comply with local strictures, adding both cost and complexity.

Despite theses developments, IBM continues to believe that the screening process serves the best interests of the corporation. As a result, IBM seeks opportunities to comment on and influence proposed legislation during formulation. Its lobbying efforts promote two goals: to protect employers' right to screen and reject applicants for drug use, and to assist in developing responsible safeguards and consistent employment practices across jurisdictions.

HRM and the Environment in the Future

The HRM function is today largely a product of forces in the external environment with which corporate America must deal to survive and prosper. The function is professionally staffed, strategically oriented, and aware of the need to anticipate change through innovative programs. Its mission is to engage in activities that, directly or indirectly, assist management to accomplish organizational objectives.[44]

The future, by nature, is unpredictable, but some aspects of it are already known. The labor force of 2006 is already alive today. By the year 2000, the average age of the U.S. population will be 36, up from an average age of 30 in 1980. Younger workers, those ages 16 to 34, will represent only 38 percent of the work force in 2000, down from 50 percent in 1985. Workers in their middle years, ages 35 to 54, will become a majority: 51 percent, up from 38 percent in 1985. This trend seems likely to continue, as the country is currently experiencing the lowest birth rate in history.

Minority populations are rising. In the year 2000, one in three 18- to 24-year-olds will be black or Hispanic, compared with one in five in 1980. This population, the normal college-age group, will decline in absolute numbers. Unless current high school and college completion rates change dramatically, these population shifts could cause a 20 percent drop in the number of college graduates entering the work force.

In addition, universities currently face declining enrollments in technical disciplines and a shortage of qualified technical faculty. The implications of these dynamics are of concern today. That concern will grow in future years as organizations continue to seek qualified employees to compete in an increasingly technological world with skilled global competitors.

Women's participation in the labor force and changes in family patterns are more difficult to project. If the current trend persists, the future labor force participation of women should increase somewhat, bringing added diversity and continuing pressures for flexible working arrangements.

With a shortage of workers, HR managers will need to devise new and creative approaches to attracting, developing, utilizing, and retaining skilled employees. The increased availability of older workers will offer a resource which employers can cultivate through creative work patterns. The aging of the population and the work force also suggests a continuing need for health and retirement programs. Improvements in health care extending the average life span could increase the costs of medical benefits in the long term. AIDS, if no medical solution is found, also will put enormous pressure, financial and otherwise, on the entire health-care system.

Despite considerable rhetoric advocating reduced government regulation, the pattern of both federal and state government involvement in the affairs of business—with a few notable exceptions, such as the airline industry—has continued almost unabated. This pattern seems unlikely to change. Management will continue to look to HR staffs both to present a business perspective to legislators when new proposals are debated and to manage new regulations if and when they come into force.

Recent economic development in the United States has been characterized by a shift from manufacturing to services, which have historically lagged in productivity improvements. Other economic shifts have caused a sharply falling dollar and a substantial restructuring of many of the nation's largest enterprises. Finally, the burgeoning federal budget deficit has convinced Congress to seek additional sources of funding for new programs. Increasingly, legislators will look to shift many of these costs to employers.

While the consequences of these changes are uncertain, the value of the HRM function will depend on its ability to anticipate and respond to the subtle driving forces of the external environment.[45] These forces have greatest impact on the largest and most visible multinational corporations, but they also affect smaller, public and non-profit institutions. After all, employers large and small draw from a single work force. In a future when skilled workers are likely to be in limited supply, all organizations will have to compete for them.[46]

For the foreseeable future, the HR function will face continuing demands for increased professionalism and for growing expertise in anticipating trends and devising innovative programs to select, recruit, train, and motivate people.[47] The task of training HR staffs to assess the external environment, as well as carry out traditional assignments, will itself become a major challenge.[48]

♦

Notes

1. Angle, Manz and Van de Ven.
2. Miner and Miner.
3. Ling.
4. Nash and Miner.
5. Gerson and Britt.
6. *Statistical Abstracts of the United States*, 1987.
7. Barrett.
8. Mellor.
9. Nardone.
10. Nemirow.
11. Susser.
12. Rappaport.
13. Friedman.
14. Wagel.
15. Bird.
16. Granrose and Applebaum.
17. Saseen.
18. Blair, Piserchia, Wilbur and Crowder.
19. Howard.
20. Stackel.
21. Thorne.
22. Wilbur.
23. Lodge.
24. Pake.
25. Kearns.
26. Eurich.
27. Heilbroner and Thurow.
28. Davis and Frederick.
29. Slater.
30. Berry.
31. Horton.
32. Thurow.
33. Caldwell (1984).
34. Perkins.
35. Sovereign.
36. Heneman, Schwab, Fossum and Dyer.
37. Marcus and Irion.
38. Perryman and Hoffman.
39. Veron-Gerstenfeld and Burke.
40. Narod.
41. Masi.
42. Petersen.
43. Verespej.
44. Schuler, Beutell, and Youngblood.
45. Schuler and MacMillan.
46. Briscoe.
47. Caldwell (1986).
48. Evans.

References

Angle, H.L., C.C. Manz, and A.H. Van de Ven. 1985. "Integrating Human Resource Management and Corporate Strategy: A Preview of the 3M Story." *Human Resource Management* 24 (Spring): 51–68.

Barrett, N.S. 1984. "Part-Time Work Will Increase, Bringing Changes to Social Mores and Standards of Compensation." *Work in the 21st Century.* Alexandria, VA: American Society for Personnel Administration.

Berry, J.M. 1987. "GNP Analysis Shows Threat to U.S. Standard of Living." *Financier* (September): 16–20.

Bird, C. 1984. "Retirement Will Become Obsolete in the Improved Work Scheme of our 21st Century Economy." *Work in the 21st Century* Alexandria, VA: American Society for Personnel Administration.

Blair, S.N., P.V. Piserchia, C.S. Wilbur, and J.H. Crowder. 1986. "A Public Health Intervention Model for Work-Site Health Promotion." *Journal of the American Medical Association* 255 (February): 921–926.

Briscoe, D.E. 1987. "Human Resource Management Has Come of Age." *Personnel Administrator:* 75–77, 80–83.

Caldwell, P. 1984. "Cultivating Human Potential at Ford." *Journal of Business Strategy* 4: 74–77.

―――. 1986. *Human Resources Outlook 1987.* New York: The Conference Board.

Davis, K. and W.C. Frederick. 1984. *Business and Society.* New York: McGraw-Hill.

Evans, P.A.L. 1984. "On the Importance of a Generalist Conception of Human Resource Management: A Cross-National Look." *Human Resources Management* 23 (Winter): 347–363.

Eurich, N.P. 1984. *Corporate Classrooms.* Pittsburgh: Carnegie Foundation.

Friedman, D.A. 1986. "Eldercare: The Employee Benefit of the 1990s?" *Across the Board* 23 (June): 45–51.

Gerson, H.E. and L.P. Britt III. 1984. "Workers Will Have Legal Rights to Jobs through State Courts; Affirmative Action Will Expand." *Work in the 21st Century.* Alexandria, VA: American Society for Personnel Administration.

Granrose, C.S. and E. Applebaum. 1986: "The Efficiency of Temporary Help and Part-Time Employment." *Personnel Administrator* (January): 71–82.

Heilbroner, R.L. and L.C. Thurow. 1987. *Economics Explained.* New York: Simon and Schuster.

Heneman, H.G., III, D.P. Schwab, J.A. Fossum, and L.D. Dyer. 1986. *Personnel/ Human Resource Management,* 3rd ed. Homewood, IL: Richard D. Irwin, Inc.

Horton, S.G. 1984. "People and Productivity." *Industrial Management* (May/June).

Howard, J.S. 1971. "Employee Wellness: It's Good Business." *D&B Reports* (May/June): 34–37.

Kearns, D.T. 1986. "Training the Untrainable." Institute for Research in Learning, address at National Press Club, November.

Ling, C.C. 1965. *The Management of Personnel Relations—History and Origins*. Homewood, IL: Richard D. Irwin, Inc.

Lodge, G.C. 1984. "Educators Must Advocate Holism to Prepare Our Human Resources for the Coming Decentralization." *Work in the 21st Century*, Alexandria, VA: American Society for Personnel Administration.

Mellor, E.F. 1987. "Shift Work and Flexitime: How Prevalent Are They?" *Monthly Labor Review* (November): 26–40.

Marcus, A.A. and M.S. Irion. 1987. "The Continued Growth of the Corporate Public Affairs Function." *Academy of Management EXECUTIVE* (August): 247–250.

Masi, D.A. 1987. "AIDS in the Workplace: What Can Be Done?" *Personnel* (July): 57–60.

Miner, J.B. and M.G. Miner. 1985. *Personnel and Industrial Relations: A Managerial Approach*, 4th ed. New York: MacMillan.

Nardone, T.J. 1986. "Part Time Workers, Who Are They?" *Monthly Labor Review* (February): 13–19.

Narod, S. 1984. "Turnaround at OSHA." *Dun's Business Month* (June): 83–84.

Nash, A.N. and J.B. Miner. 1973. *Personnel and Labor Relations: An Evolutionary Approach*. New York: MacMillan.

Nemirow, M. 1984. "Work Sharing Approaches: Past and Present." *Monthly Labor Review* (September): 34–39.

Pake, G.E. 1986. "Training the Untrainable." Institute for Research in Learning, address at National Press Club, November.

Perkins, D.S. 1987. "What Can CEOs Do for Displaced Workers?" *Harvard Business Review* (November/December): 90–93.

Perryman, W. and C.C. Hoffman. 1986. "Affirmative Action: Past, Present and Future/Reopening the Affirmative Action Debate." *Personnel Administrator* (March): 32–40.

Petersen, D.J. 1987. "The Ins and Outs of Implementing a Successful Drug Testing Program." *Personnel* (October): 52–55.

Rappaport, M. 1984. "ChildCare Comes of Age." *Management World* (November): 30–32.

Saseen, S. 1984. "Part-Time Work and Job Sharing." *The GAO Review* (Spring): 6–13.

Schuler, R.S. and I. MacMillan. 1984. "Gaining Competitive Advantage through Human Resource Management." *Human Resource Management* 23 (Fall): 241–255.

Schuler, R.S., N. Beutell, and S.A. Youngblood. 1989. *Effective Personnel Management*, 2nd ed. St. Paul, MN: West Publishing.

Slater, R. 1987. *The Titans of Takeover*. Englewood Cliffs, NJ: Prentice-Hall.

Sovereign, K.L. 1984. *Personnel Law*. Reston, VA: Reston Publishing.

Stackel, L. 1987. "EAPs in the Work Place." *Employment Relations Today* (Autumn): 289–294.

Susser, P.A. 1986. "Balancing Work Place and Family Concerns." *Employment Relations Today* (Autumn): 245–252.

Thorne, D.R. 1987. "Helping Employees: Guidelines for Establishing an Employee Assistance Program." *Business Insurance* (October 11): 33–34.

Thurow, L.C. 1984. "Jobs Versus Productivity: The EuroAmerican Dilemma." *Technology Review* (October): 4–7.

U.S. Bureau of the Census. 1987. *Statistical Abstracts of the United States*, 107th ed. Washington, DC: Government Printing Office.

Verespej, M.A. 1987. "More Restrictions on Drug Testing." *Industry Week* (September 21): 17–18.

Vernon-Gerstenfeld, S. and E. Burke. 1985. "Affirmative Action in Nine Large Companies: A Field Study." *Personnel* (April): 54–60.

Wagel, W.H. 1987. "Eldercare Assistance for Employees at the Travelers." *Personnel* (October): 4–7.

Wilbur, C.S. 1983. "The Johnson & Johnson Program." *Preventive Medicine* (December 12): 672–681.

6.3

Internal Information for Managing HR Programs

Michael J. Burke
Gary Kaufman

As discussed elsewhere in this volume, information is essential for effective HRM. This chapter focuses on information found within organizations and how to use this material to support sound HR decisions. The purpose of this chapter is to provide a pragmatic, factual foundation on which HR managers can base program decisions. The analysis links the decision-making process to seven common HR program areas and identifies potential information sources for each decision, as well as ways of getting it. The seven HR program areas are (1) organization design and position management; (2) staffing; (3) training and development; (4) performance management; (5) compensation and benefits; (6) labor relations; and (7) personnel research.

Decision Making

Program managers face all kinds of decisions, most of which are specific to the demands of their programs. Elaborating on all of those decisions would be an endless task. However, all program managers must, in some way, face three basic decisions:

- What are the program goals?
- Is the program meeting these goals?
- If the program is not achieving its goals, how does it need to be changed?

Establishing Program Goals

This decision is probably the most important one facing HR program managers. Enormous amounts of time, energy, and money can go to waste when goals are vague or inappropriate. Misfocused incentive compensation programs can make mediocre employees feel rewarded and outstanding employees feel mistreated; poorly designed benefit programs can encourage employees to spend too much on medical care. Ill-conceived employment programs can even recruit the wrong applicants.

Sometimes these inaccurate choices reflect uncaring, indifferent program management; more often, they result from a parochial rather than a strategic perspective. Programs should support an organization in reaching its strategic business goals. In the abstract, everyone agrees with this premise, but in practice, human beings have a tendency to focus on things closer to home. In organizations, this tendency causes a sort of functional short-sightedness, where program administration goals become more important than company goals. As a result, ensuring administrative efficiency crowds out innovation, protecting one's territory replaces cooperative efforts, and following procedures overshadows getting results.

The movement in many well-managed organizations toward strategic operation of the HR function offers one potential solution to this HR problem. A strategic HR operation essentially involves developing a partnership with an organization's strategic planners and linking HR program goals more closely to strategic organizational goals. HR program goals thus include things like higher sales, improved profits, reduced expenses, and greater return on investment. Setting these targets does not mean the personnel staff has to pack up a sample case and start making calls. But HR programs should support an organization's business strategy and goals as directly as possible and HR managers should evaluate program effectiveness against company results. Each of the program areas addressed below is accompanied by examples of strategic program goals, the means or procedures for measuring their achievement, and the questions to raise, as well as information to gather, when diagnosing why a program falls short of its goals.

Assessing Goal Attainment

This decision boils down to the question of whether or not action is required. If program goals are being met, nothing needs to be done. If a program is not meeting its goals, responsible program management requires some corrective action.

Decision-making errors can occur in both situations. Sometimes overactive program managers fix things that are not broken or get impatient and change something before it has had a chance to work. Other errors result from failing to make a change or adjustment when needed. These errors of inaction can come from very different causes. Some program managers are reluctant to admit that anything could be wrong with their program. Other program managers are somewhat lazy, and they really don't want to know how the program is working. Still other managers simply don't know how to gather key evaluative information.

To a limited degree, guidelines in this chapter may help curb impatience and overactivity by enabling managers to determine that things are OK or that change is starting. To a greater degree, this chapter can help managers by making them aware of potential sources of information and how to use this information. The defensive or lazy program manager, however, is essentially a problem that higher management has to address.

Identifying Needed Improvements

In the event that a program needs to be changed, the next decision concerns direction: What should be done? These decisions range from small adjustments, such as revising forms or procedures, to fundamental shifts, such as changing the program's goals. As a rule, this step involves more detailed information gathering and more accurate analysis than the other two decisions.

The cause of a failure is often hard to uncover and nearly always involves the interaction of several factors. In general, program failures come from three areas: the program's concept, its mechanics, or its administration.

Program Concept

Failure can result when the basic idea behind a program is flawed. One common example would be a decision to implement better-quality selection tests when ineffective recruiting is the problem. Or a program to remove an apparent performance deficiency might emphasize training when the real problem is that employees lack the information or tools to perform properly.

Program Mechanics

Mechanical malfunctions occur when the procedures, forms, and processes of a program are inappropriate or do not operate properly. A classic example of poor program mechanics was the merit pay program instituted for the federal civil service. The funding mechanisms initially developed by many government agencies failed to apportion money correctly. As a result, many outstanding performers received smaller pay increases than they would have earned under the previous tenure-based system.

Program Administration

Administration failures arise when users of a program do not implement it. This outcome can result from poor program introduction or poor training in the use of the program. It can come from confusing, overly complex procedures and directions. Finally, administration failures can come from users assigning relatively little importance to the program and ignoring it.

Organizational Design and Position Management

Finding the causes of malfunctioning programs and inventing cures for them can become overwhelmingly complex. The remainder of the chapter will provide assistance with the informational aspects of the process in each of the seven HR program areas. This section addresses the first program area, organizational design and position management.

Establishing OD&PM Program Goals

Organizational design and position management (OD&PM) program managers can choose a variety of approaches to this function. The basic possibilities are defined in Table 1. An OD&PM function could theoretically operate with any combination of these approaches. However, in keeping with a generally strategic approach to HRM, this discussion emphasizes strategic goals and associated actions to achieve those goals, although appropriate references will be made to the other possibilities. Thus, the overall goal for a strategically managed OD&PM unit is to structure human resources so they can best accomplish an organization's goals and mission.

Table 1

Approaches to Organizational Design and Program Management

Traditional. Develops and maintains organizational charts, mission statements, and position descriptions. Strives to keep organization clearly defined and structured.

Strategic. Seeks to create organizational and job structures that facilitate accomplishment of the organization's strategic goals.

Cop. Has review and approval authority over changes to structure, staffing guidelines, and job levels.

Consultant. Advises management about the best ways to structure organizations and work design.

Macro. Attends mostly to an organization's overall structure, mission statements, management role specifications, and functional boundaries.

Micro. Works with the design of jobs (for example, job enlargement or job enrichment) and work unit design (for example, socio-technical systems).

Design. Structures and functions are rationally and functionally designed and then filled with matching human resources.

Evolution. Structures and functions are created by the people doing work. Structures and functions are then formalized by OD&PM to fit what has evolved.

Evaluating OD&PM Programs

The basic evaluative information for OD&PM programs comes from indicators of organizational effectiveness. Some common examples include the following ratios:

- HR costs to total revenue or budget;
- staff HR costs to line HR costs;
- management HR costs to employee HR costs;
- Profit to total revenue;
- HR-associated overhead to total overhead;
- productivity per hour worked;
- quality control data, such as percent of rejects or complaints per customer; and
- return on investment or equity.

These data or their components are usually listed in the operating reports of medium to large organizations and most small organizations. To evaluate effectiveness, a program manager will need to keep historical data to analyze trends. In addition, external comparisons, described more fully elsewhere in this volume, can add a more objective perspective. For example, if productivity per hour is going up but still falls significantly below that of competitors, changes will need to be made. A variety of factors impact organizational results, and program managers will need to look behind the numbers to find out what relevant design factors are contributing to results.

A helpful starting point presumably would involve research into the effects of various organizational designs and structures on such variables as morale, profit, and turnover. Indeed, plenty of research has looked at these variables.[1] Unfortunately, one review of 126 studies on organizational structure concluded, "Future researchers can ignore most of these studies and utilize a completely different approach."[2] While the reviewers noted some potentially promising areas for future research, the bottom line was that the studies failed to produce consistent results.

One reason for this ambiguity appears to reflect the practical difficulties of conducting cross-organization, cross-cultural research. Investigators often have a hard time just getting one organization to cooperate in a survey, much less the 200 to 400 needed for acceptable statistical precision. Furthermore, researchers seldom manage to persuade organizations to do controlled experiments on their own structure. Most managers seem to share the feeling that rearranging an organization's structure is like undergoing major surgery[3]—it should be done rarely and with speed—and not merely for the sake of science.

Another possible explanation for inconsistent research findings is that the basic notion of *a priori* setting up a structure and then putting people in it is backwards. This argument holds that structures should be fluid, temporary arrangements created by the people who perform the work.[4] Thus the people and the task demands determine how work is structured, not organizational theorists or OD&PM staff.

When this latter scenario holds true, the OD&PM function has different tactical goals. Instead of designing work structures, it would facilitate meetings of various work groups as they create their own structure. One work group certainly would involve senior management, whose job would be to set the basic parameters of the organization.[5] This sort of process facilitates management-by-objectives systems because it allows some individuals the freedom necessary to structure their own jobs. However, this evolutionary approach does not change an organization's goals and therefore, the overall strategic goal of OD&PM and the information needed to assess goal attainment remains unchanged.

Improving OD&PM Programs

Some of the diagnostic information for identifying problems with OD&PM programs will vary depending on the way the function chooses to approach its task. For example, the traditional approach would look at such factors as:

- the accuracy of position descriptions, organization charts, and mission statements;
- the responsiveness of the unit to senior management needs;
- the quality of relationships with middle managers; and
- the clarity of structure; that is, whether each job and department has a clearly specified function and whether the relationships among jobs and departments support a smooth, logical work flow

Strategically oriented OD&PM functions look more toward addressing what is causing the organization to fall short of its goals. They gather information such as:

- *Costs.* Are there too many people? Are there too many layers of management? Is the management span of control too small? Are the organization's staff functions too large?
- *Productivity.* Are work processes proceeding smoothly and logically or are people and departments getting in each other's way? Is the staff supporting the line or getting in its way? Are jobs structured so that employees find the work motivating? This means clear goals, variety and challenge, freedom to innovate and an encouragement of a sense of responsibility for the work product.

Some of this information can be obtained from operating reports or through observation. Value judgments of "too many" or "too large" are best made with reference to competitors or similar organizations. Other aspects of effectiveness, such as employees' perceptions of the motivational qualities of their jobs, interunit conflicts, and unclear goals, are best assessed either through detailed interviews or opinion surveys. Examples of some useful interview questions are:

- How challenging do you find your work?
- Does your job make full use of your talents?
- Are you as productive as you can be, or are there things that get in your way? If so, what are they?
- How clear are your work goals?
- How clear are your performance standards?
- If you could change one thing about this organization, what would it be?

Survey questions should include both multiple choices to ensure coverage of relevant factors and open-ended opportunities to allow input on matters that might otherwise get overlooked. Interviewing or surveying managers, in addition to employees, provides a valuable perspective on senior management, corporate structures, and interunit conflict.

Operating data often can have a dramatic impact on senior management, particularly if trends are negative or if the competition is clearly more efficient. These data seem to unfreeze current perspectives and open up opportunities for change. Survey results often offer the best information on promising directions for change.

Finally, the evolutionary approach needs some comment. This approach assumes that the people responsible for the work are the best judges of how it should be done. However, senior managers must first set some basic parameters, such as strategic goals and minimum specifications for major organizational segments. In addition, succeeding levels of management need to do the same to ensure an appropriate meshing of the parts of the organization. This task normally is accomplished through interlocking and somewhat overlapping committees that provide both an overall perspective and an appreciation of how work units need to function together.[6] For example, the production group would include members from engineering and marketing and receive guidance from a higher-level steering committee.

Program managers using the evolutionary approach should analyze committee structure from a logical standpoint: Do the appropriate committees exist and do they have appropriate membership? Establishing appropriate committees is a difficult task and will need readjustment as goals and circumstances change. In addition, program managers should conduct interviews or surveys to see if the committees are functioning as desired. Along with the questions listed above, surveys should include specific questions on the committee process:

- How well is your work design committee functioning?
- What needs to be changed about the work design committee process?
- How helpful has your steering committee been? How could it be more helpful?
- How helpful are the committee members from outside your work group? What could they do to be more helpful?

Although many committees will be able to function without a lot of training or support, others will not. A detailed interview or survey process can help program managers to pinpoint trouble spots and intervene when necessary.

Staffing

Over time, the OD&PM function will often become strategically linked to other HR functions, such as staffing. For instance, anticipated changes in work design or job structure may require staff planning; that is, strategies to ensure the right number and types of employees to best match the new work design. The following discussion examines these and other strategic decisions involving staffing programs.

Establishing Staffing Program Goals

Staffing is the process of attracting, selecting, and placing individuals in jobs. This section will focus on the two primary components of staffing: recruitment and selection. Although emphasis is placed on the management of internal recruitment and selection programs, the linkage between the goals of these programs and an organization's strategic objectives also receives attention.

As noted above, organizational or business strategies are concerned with how to compete in a particular industry or in a specific segment of a product market in order to achieve organizational goals, such as improved profits. At this level, the distinctive competencies and competitive advantages an organization possesses take on great importance. In particular, an organization's basic distinctive competencies are, for the most part, the knowledge, skills, and abilities of its work force.[7] Thus, if an organization decides to introduce a new product, it must ensure that its work force has the necessary knowledge, skills, and abilities to carry out the strategy.

An HR manager is likely to be consulted as to whether an organization can achieve its long-term business goals with the current work force. The basic strategic challenge or goal for the HR manager is to determine the HR requirements, that is, the kind and number of employees needed in the long term. If the current supply of human resources falls short of what is needed to meet these organizational or business objectives, the HR director and program managers will have to devise methods—for example, recruitment programs, specific selection procedures, and training programs—to make up the shortage.

Linking HR demand to appropriate staffing procedures or programs typically involves forecasting the impact of personnel recruitment, selection, training, and transfer programs. The intent of such forecasting should be to produce or select the best mix of internal and external HR programs to meet demand. In many respects, internal HR employment programs resemble external programs. For instance, an internal promotion program, such as AT&T's management assessment center, and an external selection procedure, such as Sears assessment center for prospective sales personnel share identical goals: to match people to jobs. The primary distinction is that an internal HR program operates on the internal labor market, whereas an external program operates on the external labor market.

The overall purpose of internal recruitment, selection, and classification procedures—collectively known as HR allocation systems—is to facilitate or optimize the matching of people to jobs.[8] As a general rule, the better a person-job fit, the higher individual and organizational productivity will be.

Evaluating Internal Recruitment Programs

A program manager who heads the internal recruiting aspect of an HR allocation system must oversee the design and implementation of programs to attract the best candidates from within an organization. Appealing procedures for attracting prospective employees include job posting systems and employee referral programs. Although some of these internal recruiting programs can become complicated, they merit consideration, given their potential for identifying available talent, reducing recruiting costs, and contributing to employee development and/or advancement.

Helpful guidelines have been developed to assist HR program managers in (a) assessing the feasibility of a job posting system, (b) increasing its acceptability, and (c) ensuring the legality of the system.[9] These guidelines outline the information needed by an HR program manager to derive applicant eligibility requirements, outline job requirements, generate employee awareness, establish time restraints, determine policies for notifying supervisors, set up applicant review procedures, and provide applicant feedback.

When evaluating internal recruiting efforts, a program manager will need to address a number of questions. First, how are people responding to notice of a job opening? A basic criterion to examine in answering this question is the response rate—the number of applications received divided by the number of jobs posted or noted as open. In addition, an internal recruiting program manager might consider the percentage of jobs filled through internal recruiting efforts. Internal recruitment programs which generate acceptable response and hire rates are likely to succeed in meeting an organization's mission and long-term goals.[10]

Improving Internal Recruitment Programs

Problems related to internal recruiting response rates may become evident after discussing the program with internal applicants. Interviews or informal discussions with internal applicants can yield valuable information for decision-making purposes. For instance, departmental problems relating to poor supervision, bad interpersonal relationships, or unsafe working environments can generate large numbers of internal applications for openings elsewhere in an organization. On the other hand, if a program attracts too few applications, an internal recruitment manager may need to address several important questions:

- How visible is top-management support for the program?
- Is there a history of rejecting internal candidates in favor of external applicants?
- Do supervisors issue threats about applying for other jobs within the company?

- Does peer pressure discourage employees from applying for other jobs within the company?
- Does the HR department do an adequate job in announcing position openings?
- Does the HR department handle internal applicants appropriately?

If poor response and hire rates are not due to internal recruitment problems, the program concept may need revision. That is, external recruiting efforts may prove appropriate. Over time, filling most jobs from within may lead to "incestuous thinking."[11] In this state of shared experience and values, individuals cease to function as individuals and tend to accept without challenge most of the groups ideas. Group thinking clearly can speed up decision making, but incestuous thinking hinders the creative process essential to maintain a competitive edge. Information gathered from company's past internal and external recruiting experience, its successes and failures, as well as its experience with recruiting sources should assist in guiding present recruiting efforts.

Evaluating Internal Promotion and Selection Programs

Internal promotion and selection is the process of determining which individuals identified by internal recruiting efforts should staff the available positions. From a strategic perspective, careful employee selection is important regardless of the type or phase of a corporate or business strategy.[12] Furthermore, careful employee promotion and selection can assist in gaining and maintaining a company's competitive advantage.[13] Successful companies like Data General, Goldman Sachs, and IBM spend a considerable amount of time when selecting candidates to ensure that the individuals filling the openings "fit" the company. For instance, staffing for IBM's PC project required recruiting and selecting just the right kind of people to fit into an entrepreneurial environment. In contrast, numerous organizations make poor use of their human resources by failing to analyze the work context and job. As a result, such organizations do not anticipate how many, when, and where the employees will be needed.

A unique aspect of using employee selection procedures to help achieve long-term organizational goals concerns the noninterventionist nature of such procedures. Internal selection programs deal with the three primary elements of the work system—people, jobs, and work contexts—as they presently exist (or are projected to exist), with the goal of optimizing the fit among the elements. From a practical standpoint, effective selection strategies require little, if any, systematic organizational change or broad program development. As a result, implementing such strategies typically entails substantially less cost and effort than most interventionist (for example, training or work redesign) strategies.

One organization that replaced an interviewing program with a relatively costly managerial assessment center found that the productivity of its sales managers increased dramatically over and above the costs of the assessment center.[14] Other organizations, such as the Chicago and Northwestern Railroad, AT&T, and the U.S. Employment Service, also have found that valid personnel selection procedures can have substantial impact on the bottom line. These organizations, as well as many others, are forerunners of a movement to translate the immediate goal of most personnel selection programs (namely, appropriately matching of people with jobs) to organizational goals (namely, increased profits and/or percentage increase in output). Although other HR strategies such as training and work design have merit, personnel recruitment and selection strategies can by themselves contribute substantially to individual and organizational productivity.

Evaluating and Choosing a Selection Method

Figure 1 outlines the major steps in the implementation and evaluation of a sound personnel selection program at a typical organization. An essential but often overlooked step in this process is to conduct a job analysis.[15] The job analysis provides the necessary information (such as the tasks and job duties) for developing performance measures, as well as the data (namely, knowledge, skills, and abilities) for determining which selection procedures to develop or adopt.

A key responsibility of an HR program manager is determining whether scores on selection measures do in fact relate to successful job performance. The important question to ask is: What is the relative effectiveness of potential alternative selection procedures in predicting job performance for the job or jobs under consideration? This process of determining the relationship (predictive effectiveness) between scores on selection procedures and job performance is known as that of selection procedure validation.

Figure 1

Typical Steps for Implementing and Evaluating a Personnel Selection Program

```
                    Conduct a job analysis
                   /                      \
                  ↓                        ↓
    Develop job performance      Determine necessary
    measures                     personal characteristics
                                 to perform job
                  │                        ↓
                  │              Develop and/or adopt
                  │              selection procedures
                  │              to assess personal
                  │              characteristics
                  ↓                        ↓
    Measure job performance      Measure personal
                                 characteristics with
                                 selection procedures
                   \                      /
                    ↓                    ↓
                  Assess relationship[a]
                  between selection
                  procedure evaluations
                  and job performance
                  results
                           ↓
                  Assessment Phase:[b]
                  Implement Selection
                  Program
```

[a]The relationship between selection procedure scores and job performance results is most often determined with a current sample of job incumbents.
[b]Follow-up studies (such as fairness analysis, economic utility analysis) are often conducted.

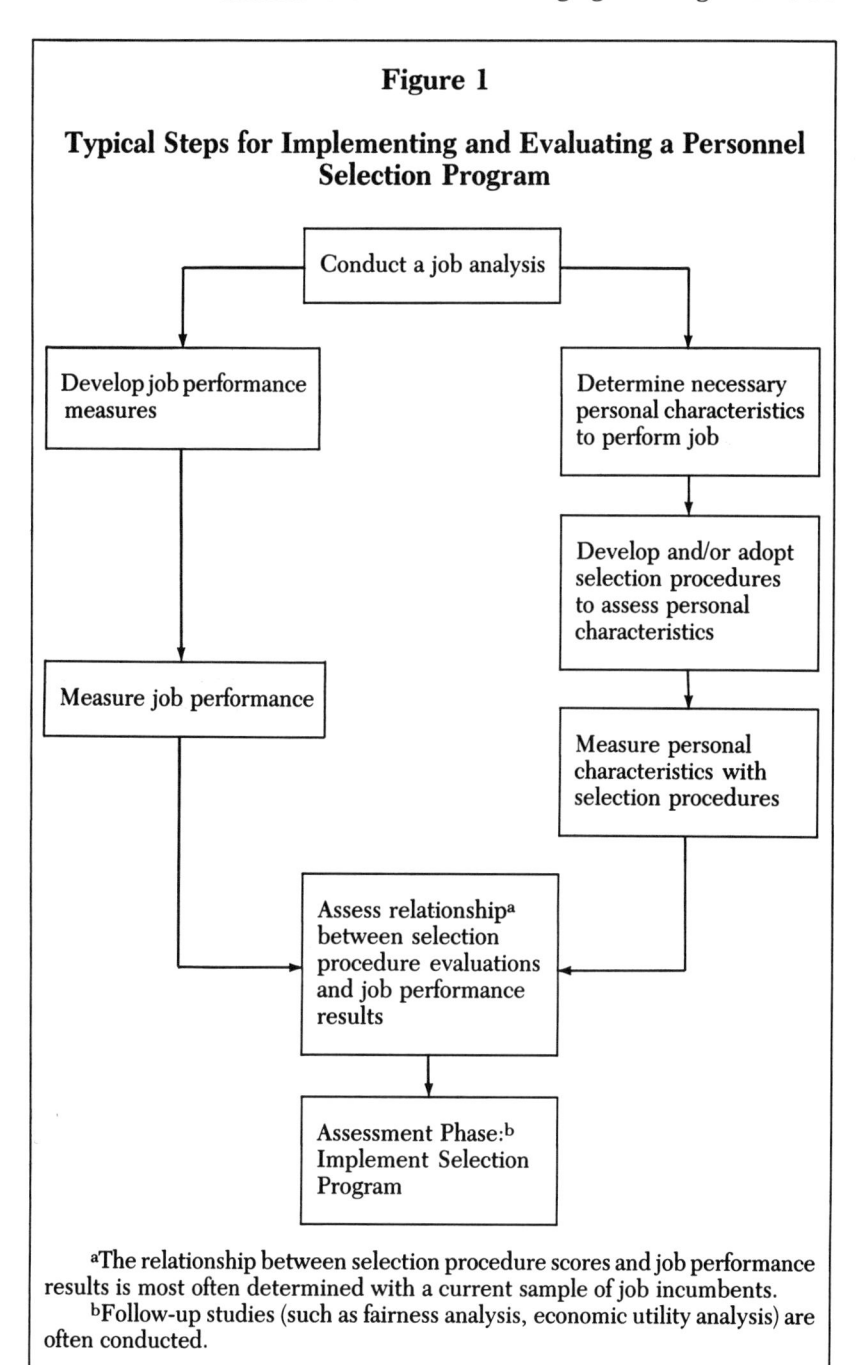

Once program managers have determined that scores on certain selection procedures do or can be expected to relate to job performance, they can determine which specific procedure to recommend for use.[16] Besides internal selection procedure validation efforts, outside research data may assist selection procedure decisions. Validity generalization analysis or meta-analysis makes it possible in some cases for organizations to generalize the predictions associated with certain selection procedures (such as standardized ability tests or interviews) across jobs and organizations.[17] As a result, an HR program manager may not need to carry out an in-house study to validate every selection procedure for every job in each part of the organization. If the jobs for which selection procedures are desired fall into the same classifications as the jobs that made up the validity generalization study, data from the study will suggest which selection procedure is most likely to produce the best predictions of future job performance in the organization.[18] A rapidly growing number of organizations are using the results of these validity generalization studies as the basis for selection programs. Some of these companies include Sears-Roebuck, CIA, Armco Inc., the U.S. Employment Service, along with 13 large petroleum companies and 70 private electric utility companies.

After addressing the question of predictive effectiveness, an HR program manager will need to address several other important questions when choosing or evaluating selection procedures:

- Will the selection procedure adversely affect minorities or females?[19]

- Will selection decisions be improved as a result of adopting a particular selection procedure?

- What is the estimated impact of the selection program on the organization's strategic goals?[20]

At the conclusion of an evaluation of potential alternative selection procedures, HR managers must decide how to communicate the evaluation findings. Some leeway is possible when deciding what to report and how to present the findings, and a number of sources give guidelines on communicating information to different audiences.[21] The essential task of a program manager is to provide the best possible information in understandable terms to HR managers and other personnel who have an interest in the HR program's processes or outcomes.

After deciding on a selection procedure, the organization enters the actual assessment phase. In this phase, the relative emphasis on recruiting, interviewing, using selection tests, and making reference checks will vary from one organization to another, and even from one job to another within the same organization. The type of information gathered at each step also is likely to vary from one organization to another. For instance, one organization may use a selection interview to gauge an applicant's attitudes toward work, while another organization may use an interview to determine whether an applicant's previous work experience provided adequate preparation for the present job. Regardless of the number of steps or types of information gathered, the overall goal of the assessment phase is to obtain the information which will permit an informed judgment on whom to select from the available applicant pool.

Improving Internal Selection and Promotion Programs

Choosing the best applicant for a job can prove difficult even when applicants are current employees within an organization. Although an organization may develop, evaluate, and implement what it believes is a sound selection system, selection errors often occur. An organization invariably will find that an applicant predicted to be successful failed to meet minimum performance standards. On the other hand, employers across the country reject thousands of applicants every year who would have performed above minimum performance standards if hired. The basic fact is that selection procedure predictions are not perfect predictions.

A distressingly common reason for selection errors involves failure to define precisely what an applicant is to do—namely, expected job performance.[22] The more an HR program manager and a line manager know about the job, the greater the probability of accurately predicting job performance will be. As indicated in Figure 1, an essential first step in the selection process is a job analysis—a precise definition of job performance.

Even if a job analysis formed the basis of selection procedure recommendations, the information gathered during the analysis may be flawed. HR program managers may need to address the following diagnostic questions to pinpoint problems:

- Are the sources of the job information credible?
- Was there a description of the general level of skill or knowledge required to perform the job tasks?

- If scales were used to evaluate tasks or knowledge, skills, and abilities (KSAs), do they have acceptable measurement properties?
- Was there a lack of consensus among job experts regarding tasks or KSAs?

Selection error can also result from a lack of precision in assessing applicants.[23] HR program managers should ensure that selection procedures and the assessment process meet professional standards. Some key questions to ask when diagnosing potential problems with selection procedures include the following:

- Was the choice of selection procedure(s) based on the findings of a sound job analysis and/or relevant research?
- Did personal interest or mere familiarity with a selection procedure influence the choice?
- Is the evaluation of applicants minimally dependent on who made the assessment?
- If multiple selection procedures are used, are there appropriate rules for combining the assessments?

Training and Development

The success of an organization depends not only on using validated selection procedures which lead to correct hiring decisions, but also on correctly placing and properly managing these people. As to the management of employees, training to enhance technical and nontechnical skills, to conduct performance appraisals and feedback sessions, and to implement management-by-objectives procedures can play a significant role in maintaining the well-being of an organization.

Establishing Training and Development Program Goals

Similar to personnel selection, training and development aims to improve the fit between employees and their current or future jobs. In a strategic sense, these programs involve identification and development of the knowledge, skills, and abilities needed now and in the future to support organizational and business strategies.

Unfortunately, many organizations do not examine how training and development programs can enhance achievement of long-term organizational objectives. Even fewer are willing to alter business plans with respect to future employee capabilities.[24] For the most part, training activities tend to focus on more immediate individual or organizational needs with little emphasis on developing employee careers to assist in meeting long-term business goals. American businesses spend an estimated $30 billion annually on training and development programs but evaluate less than 10 percent of that amount in terms of its value-adding impact.[25]

Although the overall concern for training is to improve the fit of employees with their current or future jobs, training programs have more specific goals such as:

- removing current or anticipated performance deficiencies,
- increasing employees' self-awareness of their strengths and weaknesses,
- improving decision-making and problem-solving skills,
- increasing employee motivation, and/or
- modifying employee values or attitudes.

For instance, companies like Hershey and IBM strategically attempt to remove performance deficiencies by using down periods to retrain workers rather than lay employees off.[26] Xerox likewise spends approximately $125 million a year in training and retraining, much of which is related to dealing with obsolescence.[27] The important point is that training should be purposeful: A training program should target a more or less specific goal related to an organization's strategic objectives.

Given the need to support immediate and long-term business strategies as well as the potential high cost of training and development, program managers need to ensure that training programs are properly developed and effectively managed. HR managers are going to increasingly face the question: "What is the training's value?"[28] Answering this question requires appropriate evaluation. The following discussion outlines informational needs related to training program evaluation such as whether or not the benefits of training (for example, performance improvement) exceed its cost. At several points, the guidance is prescriptive, and intentionally so. If training program managers can appropriately diagnose training needs, develop and deliver training programs, and evaluate the organizational impact of training programs, they should be able to show that the organization does get its money's worth out of these programs.

Evaluating Training and Development Programs

The first step in establishing a training program that will effectively meet specified goals is to diagnose training needs and choose training programs. The components of training program development and evaluation receive detailed discussion in Volume V of this series. For the present analysis, a training program manager should ask the following three questions when determining training needs:

- Where in the organization is training needed?
- What must a trainee learn or change in order to successfully perform the job?
- Who in the organization needs training and of what kind?

Most training experts would agree that these questions can be answered by detailed analyses of the organization, job, and employee.[29] Despite the value of such detailed analyses, many training program managers will not have such complete information readily available. Nor is it probable that a training program manager will be able to quickly carry out such analyses. However, if an organization is strategically managing its human resources, some type of information bearing on the above three questions probably will be available. Regardless of the quality or availability of this information, HR managers should attempt to address the above questions when determining training needs. Otherwise, a training manager might adopt a program simply because it is well advertised or the "hot ticket" in upgrading skills at other organizations. A "hot ticket" only burns a hole in an organization's pocket.

Program Development

Once training needs are identified, a training program manager should participate in developing training course objectives. The key question in setting course objectives is: What training outcomes will most facilitate an employee becoming an improved performer in the least amount of time? In other words, what should an employee be able to do at the end of training so that only practice stands between the employee and successful performance?[30] Writing course objectives so as to express the behaviors to be trained helps to ensure clarity. A number of sources provide additional assistance in specifying knowledge, skill, and attitudinal course objectives.[31]

After objectives are set, program managers will need to select the training method. Although the method chosen depends on the purpose of the training, traditional methods, such as lecture, work best if supplemented with role playing or practice. Numerous organizations—NASA-Manned Spacecraft Center, General Electric, Imperial Oil of Canada, and Pillsbury Company to name a few—have reported on the effectiveness of various behavioral training strategies for improving job skills. For example, NASA realized an average 10 percent increase in managerial job performance as a result of a behavioral training program involving active participation, feedback, practice, and simulation. Whenever possible, use of a behavioral modeling approach can enhance training.[32]

Besides selecting appropriate training methods, training managers should consider the issues prior to implementing training:

- What should be the size of a training group?
- Is the needed training equipment available?
- What is the available time of participants?
- Is the training room appropriate for participative methods?

These very practical questions are essential to address prior to training. In one organization, a well-designed appraisal feedback training program that used role play led to confusion and frustration because the small size and poor acoustics of the training room could not accommodate simultaneous practice sessions.

Assessing Training Outcomes

Once training is completed, a training program manager will typically address immediately or a short time later whether the training program met its goals. The primary evaluation questions are: Did the trainee learn? And, is there a change in the trainee's on-the-job behavior? The first question addresses whether or not trainees have learned, while the second question is concerned with whether they transfer what they have learned to the job. Table 2 outlines these two primary questions, areas which a program manager might measure to answer those questions, and the sources of internal information to develop these measures.

Evaluation of on-the-job performance changes makes it easier to link training results to an organization's strategic goals.[33] While linking nontechnical training to organizational outcomes has historically proven particularly difficult, this is no longer the case. As in the earlier discussion of meta–analysis, training program managers

Table 2

Training Program Evaluation

What Does the Organization Want to Know?	What Could be Measured?	What Internal Information Might be Looked At?
I. Did the trainee learn?	*Subjective learning*: Principles, facts, attitudes, or skills learned during training or by the end of training as assessed judgmentally.	Statements of opinion, belief or judgment completed by the trainee, trainer, or another observer.
	Objective learning: Principles, facts, attitudes or skills learned during or at the end of training as assessed by objective means.	Standardized knowledge tests. Work sample performance.
II. Is there a change in the trainee's on-the-job behavior?	*Subjective behavior*: Perceived changes in on-the-job behavior.	Judgmental evaluations by trainees, peers, or supervisor.
	Results: Tangible changes in job performance measures.	Quantity and Quality indices. Cost measures. Time measures.

have at their disposal a set of procedures which are equally useful in quantifying the organizational outcomes of technical or nontechnical training. Although these procedures may not always yield exact or even approximate dollar estimates of the value of training, they do provide estimates of other important organizational performance units (for example, number of lives saved at a hospital as a result of hospital management training). At last, some answers to that age-old question, "What is training worth?" are available.

Improving Training Programs

Failure to meet training course objectives can result from a number of factors. One source is failure to articulate training objectives in clear terms. Unclear objectives often lead to evaluating training in terms of a "happiness index," that is, whether trainees enjoyed the training. Without clear training objectives, the training needs assessment, which should have formed the basis of the training program, is flawed. In such cases, employees typically are heard making comments like, "Why is management wasting our time with this training course?"

A related issue arises when training programs do not work because the problem is a nontraining problem. A performance problem which has been attributed to a knowledge or skill deficiency may in fact be a problem of execution.[34] That is, something in the work situation is inhibiting employees from performing tasks that they know how to carry out.

Some questions which might help to determine whether poor performance is a feedback, job design, or reward system problem rather than a training deficiency include:

- Feedback. Do employees know what they are to do? Does the employee know that he or she is not meeting minimum performance standards?
- Job Design. Does the employee have the necessary machines, tools, equipment, or subject matter to perform adequately? Have obstacles which might interfere with effective performance been removed?
- Reward systems. Are there sufficient incentives for performing the work effectively? Have the negative consequences of performing the work effectively been removed?

If the answer to any of these questions is no, training improvements may not address the problem.

Another reason for poor training outcomes concerns program selection and design. If the training program itself is not appropriate, it will not accomplish the desired results. All too often, training program managers and organizational decision makers rely heavily on labels and glorified content descriptions when choosing and judging the probable usefulness of a training program. Training managers would do better to rely on a particular training method (for example, behavioral modeling on lecture with discussion and practice) when evaluating which program might be most effective in improving learning and on-the-job performance.

Other issues to address in the event that training fails to produce the desired results include the following:

- Does management support the training program?
- Are the physical surroundings the proper climate for training?
- Are there factors which might inhibit the carry-over of acquired skills from training to the job?
- Are there role conflicts between the trainer, supervisor, and trainee?
- Does the training program need to be modified for targeted audiences?
- Is the individual delivering the training competent?
- Are the instruments for evaluating training appropriate?
- Should more funds be allocated to improve training delivery?

Performance Management

Performance management, while a relatively new HR function, has begun to replace the traditional performance appraisal function in many organizations. Nearly everyone has some familiarity with performance appraisal. In American culture, performance evaluations start informally in infancy, become formal in school, and occur regularly throughout an individual's working career. In fact, performance appraisal may be the oldest of the personnel management functions. One of the authors even has a copy of a narrative appraisal of army officers that was supposedly written by a general in George Washington's army.

Nearly all medium and large organizations have a structured performance appraisal process with supporting forms, time tables, and training materials. A typical goal of a performance appraisal program is to provide an organization with accurate measurements of performance on a regular basis. The appraisal information then becomes the basis for providing developmental feedback, administering merit pay, justifying promotions, documenting disciplinary actions or terminations, and assessing training needs.

Why change from performance appraisal to performance management? A likely reason for the change is that performance appraisal programs are generally unpopular. Most managers do not like to give candid, accurate appraisals and most employees do not like hearing about their shortcomings.

Appraisals are threatening, stressful events, and even appraisers do all kinds of things to try to make them more comfortable. The head of a large federal agency used to ask one of the authors to change the executive appraisal system every year, never realizing that it was his own discomfort giving appraisals, and not the form, that caused him difficulty. This misconception is a common occurrence. The uncomfortableness and pain come from the evaluative nature of appraisal and the interpersonal interactions, not from the appraisal form or process. The only way to avoid the tension is to avoid the appraisal; unfortunately, this is exactly what many managers do.

The change to performance management also reflects the belief that the primary goal of appraisal—accurate measurement of performance—is unattainable under normal organizational conditions. Ratings and judgments of personnel are impacted by a host of well-documented rating errors, biases, and tendencies.[35] In addition, a recent study documented significant correlations between appraisal ratings and organizational levels, regional locations, line versus staff jobs, age, race, sex, and type of business.[36] Add to this list the effects from the varying styles and standards of individual raters, the resulting measure would leave little room for the contribution of an individual's actual performance!

Identifying Performance Management Program Goals

Before addressing program goals, the distinction between performance management and performance appraisal deserves some discussion. Most performance management systems still contain performance appraisal process; however, performance management appraisals typically emphasize results rather than personal characteristics or behaviors. The overall goal is to maximize organizational performance, and the most direct way to assess an individual's contribution to that performance is through the results the individual achieves. Ratings of personality characteristics and behaviors are still included, but they primarily are used for coaching and development.

Performance management contains two other functions found in traditional appraisal programs: identification of high-potential employees and poor performers. However, both of these "identifications" should lead to management decisions. Unlike traditional appraisal programs, performance management more directly informs and structures decision making. This distinction becomes more clear through the following descriptions of performance management goals:

- Increase motivation.
- Identify *and promote* high-potential employees and managers.
- Identify *and rehabilitate or remove* poorly performing employees and managers.

Evaluating Performance Management Programs

Sources of information and suggestions for collecting information on each of the tactical goals are described below.

Increase Motivation

Motivation is an internal psychological state related to the amount of energy one has and how one chooses to use it. Definitions of motivation vary according to whether the focus is on the amount of energy ("need theories") or how the individual chooses to use the energy ("process theories").[37] Unfortunately, internal psychological states create measurement problems; we can't touch, see, smell, or count motivation. Instead, surrogate measures of behaviors that may reflect motivation are utilized.

A key surrogate measure used to assess motivation is productivity. Most industrial psychologists believe that productivity is the product of ability times motivation (provided other outside factors are constant). Since an individual's or a work group's ability level changes little over the period of a research study, any changes in productivity presumably reflect changes in motivation (provided that the experimenters control outside factors). Program managers can use this same reasoning to look at their organization's productivity levels and determine whether a program has impacted employee motivation. Managers will also have to make sure that ability levels do not change (through, for example, different personnel or a new training class) and that the other outside factors (such as the introduction of new procedures or technology) have not changed.

Another quantitative surrogate measure of motivation is the incidence of organizational withdrawal behaviors, such as tardiness, excessive use of sick leave, and employee-initiated turnover. These organizational withdrawal behaviors provide a reverse index of organizational commitment which contains several motivational components: acceptance of organizational goals, willingness to exert effort on behalf of the organization, and a desire to maintain membership in the organization.

Finally, unit managers can be excellent sources of data on the motivation of their employees. They often observe many of the behavioral signs that indicate motivational level: leaving early, working late, careless mistakes, sluggish performance, grievances, high morale, commitment to organizational goals, and so on. However, HR managers need to adopt a neutral position during the interview or survey because many of the questions can imply criticism, causing supervisors to become defensive and less than candid.

Identify and Promote High-Potential Managers and Employees

Organizations function through people; the better the people, the higher the productivity. Technological changes are currently touted as the productivity boosters of the future. However, organizations with stronger human resources will, in the long run, make better decisions, execute plans more efficiently, and create more innovations than organizations with less talent and motivation.

The best way to get good people is to recruit and hire them. The second best way is by making sure that the most talented and motivated employees and managers are placed in the most demanding positions. Achieving this goal starts with the identification process. If the organization has a formal identification process, what happens to persons who are identified as high potentials? Are they promoted more frequently than other employees? Do they receive special encouragement, support, and training? If the identification process is informal, program directors will need to interview a sample of second- and third-level managers. The interview should ask how they identify and nurture high potentials, as well as obtain some specific examples of people these managers have identified and promoted. By covering the past three years in detail, such interviews should provide a good feel for both quantity and quality of identification efforts.

Another way to identify and evaluate organizational policies toward high-potential employees is to compare turnover among employees at the top one third of the performance distribution versus those at the bottom one third. Despite the appraisal accuracy problems noted above, almost any organization's ratings have enough validity for this sort of group comparison. The ideal is very different rates for the two groups, with the high performers turning over much less often. If the rates are within 5 percent of each other (providing the highest rate is at least 10 percent), the organization is not doing enough to encourage the right people to stay. Organizations which compile potential ratings should perform the same sort of analysis on them.

Finally, attitude surveys are helpful. Everyone watches who gets promoted, and employees form reliable opinions as to what management looks for when making promotion decisions. A question like "What are the main reasons people get promoted in this organization?" will provide good quality data on the organization's perceived promotion policies.

Identify and Rehabilitate or Remove Poor Performers

The other side of nurturing high potentials is doing something about poor performers. All organizations have a distribution of

Internal Information for Managing HR Programs   6-111

performers, some high, most satisfactory, and some low. While the quickest way to upgrade the performance of an organization is to replace poor performers with good or outstanding performers, this is easier said than done. Supervisors do not like to rate their employees "unacceptable" or even "needs improvement," which in turn leads to weaknesses in the documentation needed to support a discharge.

A first type of information to examine in identifying poor performance comes from an organization's probationary program. This program is basically an agreement between a company and an employee that employment during the first year (or six months or 90 days) can be terminated without progressive discipline and a lot of supporting documentation; a kind of "no fault" parting. If the organization has such a program, how much attention is paid to it? Does personnel notify supervisors when an employee's probationary period is nearly up? How many potential performers are eliminated by the program?

The next thing to check is the organization's performance appraisal distribution. Unless the company has mandated a specific distribution, HR managers will need to calculate what percentage of ratings call below the "good" or "satisfactory" level on the rating scale. A distribution with only three percent poor performers is not realistic in any organization. In the event of such a finding, HR managers should examine the process as described in the next section.

Next, look at turnover figures. Unless the organization has recently instituted a layoff or reduction in force, the percentage of employee-initiated turnovers will exceed the percentage of company-initiated turnovers. To some degree, these figures underestimate true company-initiated turnover because employees are often given the chance to resign voluntarily instead of being fired. Although precise guidelines do not exist, reasonable rates of company-initiated turnover would be 10 percent for entry-level employees, 5 percent for positions above entry level, and 3 percent for senior managers and executives. These estimates take into account that even the best selection systems are no more than about 50 percent accurate in predicting individual performance. In addition, experience suggests that even the best, most hard-nosed managers tolerate a residual number of marginal and poor performers.

Finally, an organization's rehabilitation programs can supply useful information. In the vast majority of cases, the early stages of rehabilitation are quite informal—feedback and coaching sessions between employee and supervisor—and seldom leave a trail of data. However, many medium to large companies have a formal "problem employee" program to assist supervisors with employees' drug and alcohol abuse, mental illness, and chronic poor performance. However, mental illness and drug or alcohol abuse generate the same supervisory reluctance to identify as performance problems. As a result, HR managers should check to see the rate of use of the program.

Estimates vary regarding the usage of employee assistance programs. One survey of 100 companies of various sizes reported the following totals for drug or alcohol abuse and mental illness combined: 6.2 percent among production employees, 4.1 percent among office employees, and 3.4 percent among management.[38] Since these data are mostly from company records, they may significantly underestimate the actual figures. In fact, in a recent large-scale U.S. Postal Service study, 10 percent (515 of 5,465) of all eligible job applicants tested positive for illicit drug use at the time of their pre-employment medical examinations.[39] However, expecting to find 10 percent of all employees in a "problem employee" program would be unrealistic; 5 percent is about as good a referral rate as any employer could achieve.

Improving Performance Management Programs

The type of corrective action required will vary depending on which of the three performance management goals a program has failed to meet. The following discussion addresses appropriate revisions for achieving each goal.

Increase Motivation

Despite measurement difficulties, researchers have developed relatively concrete ways to diagnose motivation problems in organizations. Numerous studies confirm that three factors are important for motivation as reflected by individual and group productivity: goal setting, feedback, and incentives. In gathering information about problems in motivation, HR managers should evaluate their programs (or lack of programs) for goal setting, feedback, and incentives against the criteria listed below. For example, check a random sample of employees: Do they have goals? If so, how specific, realistic and challenging are they? Since the effectiveness of each factor depends on how managers and employees perceive it, opinion surveys or interviews are indispensable. Each factor is reviewed below in terms of what to look for in diagnosing and remedying motivation problems.

Goals. Goals provide the direction for motivational energy.[40] The most effective goals are:

- Specific. Write goals in terms of observable behaviors or results. "Do your best" is a poor goal; "increase sales 10 percent" is much better.

- Realistic. The person who is to accomplish the goal must believe that it is within his or her power to reach the goal with reasonable effort.

- Challenging. To get maximum impact, a goal must present a challenge to the employee. If the goal is too easy, the employee will not exert extra effort. If the goal is too hard, the employee will give up.

Feedback. Feedback works in two ways. First, feedback seems to be necessary to learn how to do something. Second, feedback operates as kind of an implicit goal-setting process. Posting last week's sales results makes most employees try to do better. To be effective, feedback should:

- Occur shortly after performance. In learning situations or when correcting problems, employees need constant feedback. For normal operations, weekly or monthly feedback is usually sufficient. Annual appraisal feedback seems to have little impact.

- Offer specifics. The more detailed and concrete the feedback, the better able employees will be at utilizing it.

- Focus on results. "You didn't get this report in on time" is better than "You're getting a bit lazy about deadlines." This latter example gets too much into personality and inspires defensiveness.

Incentives. Most of the research in this area examines nonmonetary performance incentives or motivators. A review of 98 studies reported that financial incentive research produces more inconsistent results than feedback and goal-setting research.[41] Nonetheless, a large number of companies thrive on financial incentives such as piece-work rates, commissions, and bonus payments. Despite conflicting research results, enough evidence exists to suggest that with effective administration, financial incentives are very effective motivators. The conditions for effective administration appear to be:

- Clear connection between the results achieved and the incentive earned.
- Reasonable control over results.
- Equitable compensation for amount of work or contribution.
- Easily understood systems for allocating money.

Identify and Promote High-Potential Managers and Employees

As with motivation, the first step is to examine the organization's programs and procedures, both formal and informal. How are high potentials identified? What sources of information contribute to this decision? How many and what level of managers are involved in the decisions?

Program effectiveness is essentially determined by the quality of promotion decisions. Decision quality is often difficult to assess directly, but the decision-making process can be examined. What is the quality of information used to make promotion decisions? How is the information used? For significant managerial promotions, decisions should involve multiple sources of information and different organizational levels and perspectives. For nonexempt promotions from entry level, clear standards should exist and be applied uniformly. In addition, information beyond current performance should enter into promotional decisions since the next job up the career ladder may require different attributes. For example, everyone is familiar with (and indeed may have worked for) the outstanding technician who, once promoted, made a lousy manager.

Regarding different perspectives, promotions beyond two or three steps above entry level for nonexempt and all managerial personnel are too important to rest on one person's decision. Everyone has blindspots and judgmental quirks that are difficult to change. Good promotional decisions should require at least two people to consider the information and agree on the promotion. For example, at J.C. Penney Co., first- and second-level managers are evaluated and discussed annually in a meeting of their store manager, the district personnel manager, and the district manager. The store manager presents information on operating results, appraisal ratings, and potential for advancement. Then together the managers identify who should be promoted, given developmental transfers, or removed from management. This process leads to promotional decisions that, according to internal opinion surveys, first- and second-level managers regard as fair and job-related.

One final place to look for difficulties involves the incentives given to middle-level managers for development and promotion. Are managers encouraged to provide good people to the rest of the organization? Or do they have an incentive to keep their best people as long as they can? The Internal Revenue Service evaluates all managers on only three criteria: results, development of subordinates, and effectiveness in promoting equal employment opportunities. Middle and senior managers who consistently provide well-developed managerial talent to the organization seem to play a strong role in contributing to the IRS's reputation as the best-managed federal agency.

Identify and Rehabilitate or Remove Poor Performers

Reluctance to identify poor performers is one of the most common problems. Analyze what happens to managers when they identify a poor performer. Are they given an endless documentation process and advised to give the employee yet "another chance"? Do employee relations specialists and attorneys second-guess managers' judgments? Does the organization have a problem employee program to provide support and professional assistance? Do unwritten organizational norms operate for or against acting on poor performers? If identification of poor performers creates too many negative outcomes, supervisors will simply bide their time until they can transfer problem employees to other units.

In evaluating programs to address poor performance, the best place to start is the probationary period. No organization should go without a probationary employment program. The program should also receive appropriate support. Are supervisors notified and given the right forms to complete prior to the expiration of the probationary period? Are the procedures straightforward and efficient? Do higher-level managers advise their subordinate managers to make appropriate use of the program? One good way to encourage this practice is to collect statistics on the occurence of non-probationary versus probationary terminations. A memo citing these figures and comparing the costs associated with each type of termination may pressure managers into taking the program more seriously.

In organizations that have problem employee programs, HR managers should conduct a similar analysis of the forces that contribute to program use and disuse. Supervisors often will avoid contacting the problem employee program even when they have solid evidence of problems like alcoholism, for fear that a referral will end the employee's career. They may not realize that their inaction only facilitates the progression of the problem. Another area to check involves the interaction of the program's professional staff with managers. These issues are very sensitive and need to be handled promptly, supportively, and very discretely. Finally, check the program's success rates. Success rates above 50 percent have been reported for some organizational programs.[42]

Compensation and Benefits

Most compensation and benefits administrators would agree with the statement: "People work for rewards." Although stated succinctly, this sentence implies a great deal. That is, people come to work, perform work, and stay at work when the rewards from work are fair and acceptable. Compensation and benefit systems are fundamental tools for motivating individuals to engage in these behaviors. Once again, an organization's strategic and business objectives, in addition to its labor markets and competition, play major roles in shaping the compensation and benefit systems.

Identifying Compensation and Benefit Program Goals

Table 3 lists some of the broad goals of an organization's compensation and benefit systems. The systems must meet each goal to a reasonable degree in order to attract (get people to come to work), motivate (get people to perform work effectively), and retain effective employees (get good performers to stay).

Table 3

Broad Goals of Organizational Compensation and Benefit Systems

Goal	Description
Adequate	Having employees perceive that the organization's pay and coverage of valued benefits are adequate.
Equitable	Having employees perceive that the organization compensation and benefit practices are fair.
Motivating	Structuring and administering compensation and benefits so as to motivate high levels of performance.
Competitive	Creating a compensation and benefit system that is competitive within relevant labor markets.
Efficient	Structuring and administering compensation and benefits in an effective manner.

Although many compensation managers and senior management recognize the need to keep hourly wages and salaries adequate, equitable, competitive, and linked to performance, few give the same attention to achieving these goals in benefit programs. This neglect is ironic considering that benefits typically comprise 35-40 percent of total payroll costs in the United States. Furthermore, benefit practices and services are likely to have a substantial impact on the adequacy and efficiency goals noted in Table 3. It doesn't take a genius to figure out the impact of overly high deductibles, unreasonable required employee contributions, insurance carrier inefficiency, or benefit-staff ineffectiveness on an organization's long-term employment goals.

Although the broad goals in Table 3 may shape the compensation and benefit systems, compensation program managers are responsible for achieving more specific goals with respect to particular programs. For instance, a compensation manager may handle implementing a job evaluation program to meet one or more of the following goals:

- To establish a systematic structure of jobs based on their worth to the organization.

- To develop a pay structure that is internally equitable.
- To provide a basis for negotiating pay rates when management is engaged in collective bargaining with unions.
- To develop a base for an individual incentive compensation program, a gainsharing program, or a profit sharing program.

In addition, compensation and benefit program managers are often engaged in various efforts to improve the administrative aspects of compensation and benefit programs.

Evaluating Compensation and Benefit Programs

A primary means for gathering internal information to evaluate compensation and benefit programs is an employee survey. Since the focus of this chapter concerns internal information, salary surveys will not enter the discussion. Some of the following general survey questions can help to determine if the compensation and benefit programs are meeting goals:

- Do the internal labor market demands exceed what is being provided? That is, are the absolute levels of compensation and benefits adequate?
- Are there perceptions of internal inequity among employees?
- Are the compensation and benefit communications informative?
- Are the employee compensation and benefit programs structured and administered in an effective fashion?

When surveying employees on these issues, compensation managers should attend to factors concerning the scope, methods, and procedure involved.[43] That is, a program manager may need to focus on only one of the above questions, in a particular job group, using a predeveloped questionnaire. In other cases, a survey may need to include several questions addressed to all employees and use a combination of methods, such as a mailed questionnaire and telephone survey.

Although a number of national and local consulting firms offer compensation and benefit survey services, a compensation manager may initially consider the possibility of in-house survey development, administration, and analysis. Staff training and computer facilities are two areas to examine when considering whether internal personnel should conduct the survey. Does the organization have qualified individuals who can develop, administer, analyze, and communicate the results of a survey? Does it have the necessary computer facilities and software to produce the desired results? Regardless of whether the survey is conducted by internal personnel or external consultants, respondent anonymity should be insured so as to obtain valid and meaningful results.

Employee opinion or attitude questionnaires have become increasingly popular tools for evaluating flexible benefit programs. Flexible benefit plans vary greatly, but all provide employees with some choices in the types and amounts of benefits and services they receive. While flexible benefit plans share the goals of most other compensation and benefit programs, they often have additional goals, such as to respond to a changing work force, cut costs, and improve employee understanding of benefits. Some notable examples of flexible benefit plans include the true "cafeteria plans" (where the employee can select the application of company dollars) at TRW and the Educational Testing Service.

When evaluating the extent to which a benefit program has achieved particular goals, program managers may find it helpful to assess employee perceptions of "adequacy" and "value." A program may offer either very adequate or very inadequate coverage of valued benefits, or it may adequately cover benefits of little value, or have some other combination of coverage characteristics. An employer should have answers to the question: How adequate are the coverages of valued (preferred) benefits? Compensation and benefit managers should keep in mind that employee preferences may change considerably over a relatively short time.[44]

In addition, compensation and benefit program managers may want to address the following types of questions when evaluating a benefit plan with internal surveys:

- Do employees perceive that the benefits offered are competitive with other similar organizations?
- Are the deductibles for various benefits perceived as reasonable?
- Are employees satisfied with the processing of claims by benefit carriers?
- Are the benefit communications useful?

- Does the benefit office provide sound advice to employees?
- Are the organization's benefit policies consistent?

Program costs are other important areas to assess when evaluating compensation and benefits. Program managers have a number of quantitative cost issues to consider, and indices are available to assist this process.[45] However, cost indices, as well as survey data, should form only one part of a composite picture to judge the effectiveness of a compensation and benefit system in meeting strategic organizational goals. As one author noted, the final analysis should proceed along these lines:[46]

> The compensation system has a purpose which is quite far-reaching, important, and complex. To achieve its mission, it must establish and maintain a structure, and we can audit whether or not it is attending to that responsibility. The second task for compensation is to service the needs of the organization with a minimum of exceptions to the system. We can track system utilization to see how well it is operating against preset standards and goals. Since creation of pay equity is a fundamental mission, we can look at the results of the use of the system to determine if pay is being properly distributed across all groups. We can also measure the cost of wages and salaries and check to see if it is within acceptable ranges. Finally, we can measure employee attitudes toward the pay and performance appraisal system. By evaluating how well the organization is doing across this wide range of indices, we can make a judgment as to the effectiveness of the compensation department.

Improving Compensation and Benefit Programs

To diagnose compensation and benefit program problems, program managers can supplement quantitative indices with input from staffing program managers and personnel researchers. A few examples of questions which staffers and researchers might assist in answering are:

- Are people turning down job interviews or job offers for more money at another organization? Answers may be found in recruitment interviews or follow-up telephone surveys.
- Are employees leaving due to unfair incentive programs? Answers to such types of problems could be found in employee surveys or in exit interviews.[47]
- Are managers or employees having difficulty implementing or participating in a compensation or benefit program

because they do not understand it? Surveys and interviews may assist in identifying these problems of communications or personnel training.

- Are there administrative problems related to costing and communicating employee benefits when a flexible benefit plan is in place? Considering that people have widely varying and frequently changing needs, a potential minefield in flexible benefit plans is program administration. Employee surveys as well as interviews with human resource information specialists may be beneficial in diagnosing administration problems.

In sum, diagnosing compensation and benefit program problems can become complex. Nonetheless, the primary problems often can be identified with quantitative indices or employee surveys. Compensation and benefit program managers must have such mechanisms in place to evaluate goal attainment and identify problems. Otherwise, the program may do little to assist in the recruitment, motivation, and retention of valued employees.

Labor Relations

The function of labor relations originated from management's desire to counter growing unionization. In 1842, *Commonwealth v. Hunt* legalized the employees' right to join a union, and, in the industrial expansion following the Civil War, union membership grew rapidly. The appeal of unions lay in their ability to obtain increased pay, safer working conditions, and shorter hours for workers. To take away some of this appeal, several companies created positions called "social" or "welfare secretaries" to act as employee representatives and advocates on issues of working conditions, employee medical care, housing, education facilities, and the like.[48]

Although this effort apparently did little to slow the growth of unionization, the function of the welfare secretary was not abandoned. Instead it grew and evolved in many organizations into the first labor relations/employee relations functions. Today, organizations use labor relations to meet employees needs so as to motivate and retain valued employees, as well as to ensure an uninterrupted and efficient delivery of services or production of goods. The following discussion emphasizes the strategic management of labor relations, where the goal is to establish a union-management relationship which leads to productivity improvements.

Identifying Labor Relations Goals

Labor relations and its non-union counterpart, employee relations, can have a variety of orientations. If employees are unionized, labor relations becomes management's representative and advisor in dealing with the union. Labor relations handles negotiations, grievances, and formal communications with the union. Specific tactics will differ from organization to organization depending on the relationship that exists. In some organizations, management attempts to combat and control the union at every opportunity (for example, the Federal Aviation Administration or Texas Air). At the other extreme, management accepts the union as a partner and strives to develop a cooperative relationship that will meet both management and union needs (for example, Ford's Quality of Work relationship with the United Auto Workers).

As for employee relations, this function advises management on relations with employees and serves as a spokesman for employee needs on issues ranging from complaints about supervision, pay, and benefits to concerns about working conditions. Many employee relations functions have a goal similar to that of the early welfare secretaries: to look out for employee needs so they will not want to join a union.

With so many possible approaches to labor relations and employee relations, the present discussion will need to be limited to the strategic management of the labor relations function. Most program managers, however, should find that the information and analysis needed to make decisions about their programs is much the same as that needed to manage a strategic labor relations program.

The overall strategic goals of labor relations concern aspects of the organization's goals that are impacted by the relationship between management and the union(s). In particular, strategic labor relations management aims to create and maintain a union-management relationship that minimizes costs and improves productivity.

Evaluating Labor Relations Programs

The basic information for evaluating the success of a labor relations program comes from data on organizational costs and productivity. However, this information needs to be refined in order to reflect the contribution of the union-management relationship.

Program Costs

Calculating program costs proves somewhat easier than estimating productivity outcomes. Some key areas to examine for costs include the following:

- *Negotiations:* Program managers need to develop and keep historical records tracking the direct expenses involved in preparing and holding negotiations and the indirect costs of time lost from more productive activities. The personnel research function or a statistical consultant can help with analyzing these records to differentiate between true cost trends and irrelevant factors, such as unintentional, year-to-year changes in how indirect expenses are estimated or escalations in costs caused by inflation.

- *Grievances.* One point concerning grievances is clear: Grievances cost money and the amount increases rapidly with the level of the grievance.

- *Inefficient work rules.* Work rules designed for earlier technologies and contractual provisions that restrict who can do what work in what manner can be very expensive. Unfortunately, cost information can be difficult to obtain because the organization probably will not have data on how productive it would be without the work rule. Time and motion studies or comparisons with similar organizations that do not have a particular rule will often yield workable estimates.

- *Pay or benefits exceeding the market or industry norm.* Sometimes management will settle strikes by allowing labor costs to increase above what the market asks or above what competitors are paying. As in the case of U.S. Steel, such concessions can cause a company to become non-competitive. Once again, program managers should use caution in analyzing cost data, especially when obtained via surveys, since figures from different time periods can easily get mixed up. A helpful tactic is to pick some arbitrary year and then make inflation adjustments in order to have comparable figures.

Productivity Outcomes

Assessing the impact of labor relations activities on productivity requires use of indirect measures. The overall productivity or efficiency of an organization or how well it is accomplishing its mission presumably reflects labor productivity. Specific measures will vary depending on what the organization produces or provides; however, some basic kinds of records will be available in nearly every organization:

- volume of products or services;
- overhead costs;
- sales or budget;
- profits;
- quality control data, such as amount of scrap or redone work;
- hours worked; and
- payroll costs.

In analyzing these data, ratios of the various numbers, such as amount of product per hour worked, can prove useful. These ratios have the advantage of producing meaningful information across organizations, time periods, and different economic conditions. Some common ratios include the following:

- profit divided by total revenue or sales,
- quality control rejects divided by total production,
- costs divided by amount of product or service (cost per unit), and
- product or service produced divided by hours worked (hourly productivity).

A number of factors besides the labor-management relationship can influence these numbers, including changes in processes, technology, managerial staff, the economy, and unemployment rates. A labor relations program manager will need to do some investigating in order to isolate the labor relations impact. One common factor to look for is union-controlled productivity rates. Sometimes the formal contract will set these rates and at other times informal work rules may reinforce a certain standard of productivity. In one large, unionized data transcription operation, employees averaged about 6000 key strokes per hour and were paid a straight salary. At a comparable nonunion operation with incentive pay, data transcribers had to reach 12,000 key strokes and the operation averaged 18,000 key strokes per hour. This kind of information should alert a strategic program manager to the potential for a substantial productivity improvement.

Another common indicator to assess the impact of labor relations on productivity is employee commitment to organizational goals. With poor management-union relationships, managers will have one goal and employees will have another, sometimes contradictory, goal. Management says, "Work faster!" and the union and employees say, "Work slower!" These situations can offer enormous potential for productivity gains through improvements in the union-management relationship.

One of the best ways to determine what underlies productivity numbers is to call a few experienced line managers. They can often tell what the numbers reflect in areas that are directly impacted by poor union-management relationships.

Improving Labor Relations Programs

The goals of labor relations programs are to minimize costs and improve productivity. However, words like "minimize" and "improve," create open-ended goals. To make these broad goals more tangible, program managers should take the following actions:

- Set more specific, tactical goals for each year. Examples include "reduce the number of third-step grievances by 10 percent" or "determine potential productivity gains from elimination of (some) work rule."

- Make use of relative standards. Look for things like labor costs trending down and HR-related productivity trending up. Also look at competitors. Is your company one of the low-cost producers of your product or service?

If the organization is not meeting these tactical goals, or if cost and productivity figures are not improving or are not competitive, it is time to start gathering information to find out what is going on.

Program Costs

In the cost area, the first step is to break the data into components. For negotiating costs, look separately at things like preparation time, size of negotiating teams, complexity of issues, and the nature of the union-management relationship at the time of each negotiation. A mediating factor to take into account is the economic condition at the time of negotiation. If unemployment is down and economic growth is up, unions will normally feel they have a stronger bargaining position and negotiations will be more expensive. With high unemployment and difficult business conditions, management usually has the upper hand. Adjust data for uncontrollable factors and identify the factors that you can control to bring costs down.

Helpful information can come from the bargaining histories for recent contracts with other employers. These bargaining histories provide ideas for more efficient ways to try to structure the next negotiations. Finally, consider the possibility that the union also may want to control costs and favor cooperative efforts.

Grievance costs should be analyzed for emerging patterns. For example, a cluster of grievances may highlight an underlying issue that should be resolved at a higher level. In other cases, one or two units may generate a disproportionate number of grievances. This situation often signals a poor relationship between a local manager and union steward. Finally, look to see if formal procedures can be streamlined in a way that would benefit both parties.

Similar analyses should examine the costs of strikes, work slowdowns, work rules, and pay and benefits. Unfortunately, no quick formulas or analytic procedures will show the "true" causes of high costs. Program managers simply have to do enough work to isolate the labor relations components among the masses of cost information available.

Productivity Outcomes

In the productivity area, this same advice applies. Figure out what factors produce the data and then isolate relevant causes that program revisions can impact. The work done on work rules and pay and benefit costs should help here.

Opinion surveys are another measurement technique that can provide information on the union-management relationship and how it impacts productivity and costs. Opinion surveys only reflect people's perceptions, which may differ from reality. However, people's perceptions influence their decisions about how much support they will give the organization and how hard they will work.

Getting accurate information from a survey is a demanding, technically complicated task requiring professional assistance. A program manager will need to get the right sample, create unambiguous questions, and have a well-managed administration. Someone from personnel research or an outside consultant can help in properly carrying out these tasks. Even a do-it-yourself survey will provide data, but is poses the danger that poor-quality data will be used to make decisions.

What questions should the survey include? Direct questions about the union-management relationship or how hard employees feel that they work typically fail to provide useful information. Instead, a good survey will cover such topics as:

- Commitment. Do employees and managers understand the organization's goals? Do they have confidence in its leadership? How optimistic are they about the future of the organization?

- Supervisory relationships. How clear are the supervisor's performance standards? How accurate was the last performance appraisal? What happens when an employee does particularly good work? How much time does the supervisor spend working with individual employees during an average week? What are the most important factors in getting a promotion?

- Barriers to productivity. What do employees feel keeps them from being as productive as they would like to be? What suggestions do employees have for improving productivity? What do employees like most/least about their jobs?

Whan analyzing survey results, program managers should guard against speculation. To test hypotheses regarding what caused certain findings, managers may find it helpful to interview employees and managers. Select about 50 respondents at random, show them the survey results, and get their opinions about why people answered a particular way. Including supervisors and managers in this process will not only provide additional insight but also enhance the credibility of any proposed changes presented to management as a result of survey findings.

In lieu of conducting an opinion survey, program managers can collect similar information through interviews. Interviews will not provide results as precise as surveys, but, with some commonsense precautions, they can provide reasonably reliable data. To avoid sampling bias, interviewers should talk to employees working in different units, doing different kinds of work, and located in different regions of the country. Using several interviewers who work independently and later combining their notes can help control interviewer bias.

Summary

Anyone working in labor relations knows that analyzing the union-management relationship and determining how it impacts costs and productivity is a big task. The effort runs through the entire fabric of an organization. At the same time, accurate information can have very significant consequences for the accomplishment of organizational goals. In general, failure in labor-management programs typically are caused by two factors:

- a focus on the adversarial aspects of the relationship, and/or
- a failure to do the work necessary to get the right kind of information.

To create and maintain an effective (in terms of meeting the organization's goals) union-management relationship, strategic managers must not allow the labor relations program to become enmeshed in the interpersonal conflicts or the inflexible, ritualistic procedures which accompany the adversarial process.[49] Keeping overall company goals as the highest priority and adopting a problem-solving approach to negotiations and grievance handling has shown itself to be a workable antidote to this tendency.

Failure to obtain accurate, relevant information contributes to program failure in many ways. It can lead to weak bargaining positions and poorly formulated goals for negotiations. Failure to realize the economic implications of a settlement has caused more than one company to go out of business.[50] A lack of information also contributes to poor-quality discussions of issues and promotes competitive posturing over problem solving.[51] Labor-relations staffers can easily get sidetracked by personalities and procedures. Program managers can actively promote a strategic perspective through day-to-day interactions and by requiring the staff to perform the types of information gathering described above.

All this analytical work and information gathering may not seem like labor relations. "Real" labor relations has the excitement of negotiations, strikes, unfair labor practice charges, and grievances. But successful programs are not built on excitement. Successful programs are based on a solid linkage to company strategic goals and a clear understanding of how the union-management relationship impacts organizational results.

Personnel Research

Personnel research is often a support to the HR department. It provides research capabilities and behavioral science expertise to assist the other HR functions. In some organizations, personnel research oversees specific programs, such as selection testing and performance appraisal. Personnel research may also contain the human resources information system.

Identifying Personnel Research Program Goals

The traditional goal of personnel research is to give responsive, good quality assistance on request from client functions. For example, if compensation wants assistance with a salary survey, personnel research would provide timely surveying and analytical help. With a strategically managed personnel research unit, this goal remains the same, but the approach to the goal always emphasizes the organization's strategy. Looking again at compensation as an example, assume that a company goal is to become an industry leader in the production of new computer software. To achieve this organizational goal, the company will have to hire and retain the most talented programmers. The company's salary survey should therefore go beyond mere calculation of average salary levels across a representative sample of software companies. It should focus on what other leading firms have to pay to get their most effective programmers.

A strategically managed personnel research function also has another goal: to provide leadership either through other HR functions or on its own. Personnel research should generate new ideas and research-based information that helps an organization to meet its goals and to discover strategic opportunities. Achieving this ambitious goal will probably require more energy and creativity than any other work the unit has. However, the payoff in organizational results and personal satisfaction easily compensates for the difficulty of the challenge.

Evaluating Personnel Research Programs

Client satisfaction and program impact are two means of assessing the responsiveness and quality of a personnel research function. The following discussion considers ways to obtain information on each of these indices.

Client Satisfaction

This index concerns the perception of clients about the quality of service they received from personnel research. The best place to get this information is from the clients themselves; unfortunately, clients can be reluctant to give unsolicited negative feedback or even to let a program manager know when a job has been done well. Thus, a program manager will need to take the initiative.

Advance preparation can assist the information-gathering process. Personnel research program managers will need to familiarize themselves with the project and the people involved before discussing how the project has been going with the personnel research consultant in charge. Next, interview clients, starting with a few positive, general questions such as, "How could we have been more helpful to you on this project?" This approach will get the client talking and identify some areas in which to ask specific followup questions. During this interview, program managers should maintain the perspective that "the customer is always right." If managers get defensive or start trying to pursuade the client that what he or she sees as a problem really isn't a problem, the client will take the hint and stop talking.

Clients also can offer relevant input for assessing program impact. Ask questions like:

- What did the internal consultant do for you on this project?
- How were you able to use the product or service?
- How helpful was the internal consultant in getting the project done?

Program Impact

Since clients do not always know what impact a program should have had, program managers should have some objective results to examine. The best way to ensure the availability of this information is to have a work planning process which outlines the results desired before work on the project begins. For example, if an internal client requests an attitude survey on some topic, the program manager and personnel research consultant should discuss standards for sampling, return rates, question writing, client relationships, and the resources to be spent. The discussion should keep a perspective on the project's connection with organizational goals and how to best support them. This planning should result in an agreement with the consultant on the project's expected impact, which in turn will provide the assessment criteria. The only work that remains is to keep up with the project's progress, and at the end of the project, to compare actual impact with planned impact.

In assessing the accomplishment of the leadership goal, program managers should look for initiatives that have had a noticeable impact on strategic goals or mission. Specific aspects to examine include the following:

- What ideas have been developed and implemented? What impact did they have?

- What information has been found through research? and, What impact has it had?

As noted earlier, organizational results have multiple causes, making it difficult to isolate the impact of one program or one new idea. However, line managers are a good source of information. For example, ask questions like:

- Has the new appraisal program helped you get better results?

- Is the new selection program bringing in better people?

- Is the new pay plan motivating improved sales performance?

- How have you been using the survey results?

Then, follow up these questions for the specifics that are behind line managers' opinions.

Utility analysis, as discussed in the staffing section, can also be modified and applied to research programs to yield a quantitative estimate of impact. In addition, some organizations are often willing to test a new idea under relatively strict experimental design conditions; this approach will provide excellent data on impact.

Improving Personnel Research Programs

The corrective action required when a personnel research program is not achieving its goals will vary depending on the source of shortcomings. The discussion below examines ways to correct problems with client satisfaction or program impact.

Client Satisfaction

With respect to client satisfaction, the two most common causes of problems are poor interpersonal relations and the lack of responsiveness. Obtaining good information on interpersonal failures can prove difficult because internal clients who feel defensive, put down, or intimidated will likely say nothing and simply avoid personnel research. Another difficulty arises if the program manager is the problem. Personnel research managers may get into competitive relationships with other HR program managers over who controls what program or project. This attitude may spread throughout the personnel research staff and effectively turn clients into adversaries.

If the interpersonal problem appears to be with the staff, and if the research program manager has pretty good relationships with the other program managers, accurate information can be obtained by interviewing other managers. The research manager can also get firsthand information by attending meetings between the internal research consultants and clients. Just listen to the interactions without getting involved in the issues. Then afterwards, meet alone with the client, explain the department's interest in developing interpersonal skills, and ask for some feedback. This discussion should give enough insight into the interaction to start working with subordinates.

Problems associated with a research manager's own interpersonal skills poses more of a challenge. Most people are naturally reluctant to search out bad news about themselves, and clients are equally reluctant about giving negative feedback to someone in person. Asking a supervisor for help may be the best strategy since other program managers will no doubt have conveyed their complaints to a mutual supervisor. Your boss may not be adept at giving candid feedback, but you can make the job easier. Approach him or her from a neutral, self-development perspective: "I've been thinking about self-development, and I'd like to get some feedback from you. Are there things I could do to improve my relationships with the other program managers?" Then keep defensiveness under control and listen as well as possible. The somewhat informal but traditional technique of inviting a peer out for a few drinks after work or to have a coffee at work also can provide feedback.

Problems in responsiveness usually reflect a failure to meet the client's deadline or to provide the help requested. If the research function utilizes a work planning process like the one described above, the program manager should know the deadline and whether it has been missed. When this happens, follow up with the consultant and ask what is going on. Missed deadlines can be caused by anything from a broken computer to fear of asking for help to an obsession with delivering a perfect product. In addition, clients may have underestimated the amount of work involved and unintentionally set impossibly high standards. In such cases, the research manager will need to work with the project consultant to encourage more assertiveness in defining the scope of work or in negotiating deadlines.

At times, a deadline will be met but the product or service is not what the client wanted. A natural temptation is to hold the client partly responsible; they can be amazingly vague about what they want done. However, skilled personnel research consultants will probe until the goals have been reasonably well-defined. It is the consultant's responsibility to define the work, not the client. This shortcoming is a serious problem because it results in an unhappy client and wastes the research unit's resources. One frequent cause is that the research consultant has become so preoccupied with his or her needs (for control, power, prestige, perfection, security, or whatever) that the client's needs go unnoticed. In these cases, a program manager can often adjust the consultant's perspective by forcefully describing the direct relationship between the consultant's tenure and the client's satisfaction.

Program Impact

Regarding program impact, the project planning stages should have led to an agreement on what sort of positive impact personnel research should make. When this impact does not result, and client relationship difficulties are not the cause, three areas deserve a close look. First, a project occasionally is fatally flawed from the start, either through a missed diagnosis of a problem or an error in logic. For example, the research function may be asked to help in a project that initially sounds good, only to learn that the project is part of a senior manager's maneuver to "study an idea to death."

Second, the research consultant's work may not measure up to professional standards. At times, this weakness comes from a failure to keep up with advances in research or methodology; more often, a deficiency in the consultant's graduate training is the cause. Many new personnel researchers have never actually done a job analysis, validated a selection test, or constructed an opinion survey. Others will be unable to analyze data or design a field experiment. A program manager will need to be alert to these possibilities and be ready to pitch in with some on-the-job training.

Third, on occasion, the client and consultant may get along very well on a project that seems well defined and important, but nothing seems to get done. This circumstance arises when clients and consultants are both more relationship-oriented than task-oriented. Neither party will take the leadership role needed to complete the project. When assigning work, take care to try to avoid this type of a match.

Leadership Impact

Leadership can be the most enjoyable and most rewarding role for personnel research. Unfortunately, in traditionally managed personnel research units, this role often gets ignored, particularly if the program manager lacks a desire for leadership. It is very easy to occupy one's time and resources on client projects and have no time left for leadership. However, making time for leadership projects and vigorously pursuing this role can produce remarkable results. As for example, at a national retail chain, personnel research developed a survey for evaluating customer service perceptions. The survey developed into a major marketing tool, and its results led directly to the formation of a new company marketing strategy.

When a program manager finds little or no evidence that the research project has achieved its leadership goal, diagnostic efforts should focus on five areas: program management, choice of project, leadership drive, knowledge, and perseverance.

Program management. Has the program manager provided the research unit the support it needs to tackle the goal? Does the work planning process explicitly require staff members to create leadership projects? Has the research manager provided all the political clout possible to help sell new ideas and projects? Has the research manager been hardnosed enough about demanding concrete results from this area?

Choice of project. Terrific ideas sometimes just cannot be made to work. The idea may have a hidden flaw, the timing may be wrong, a strong organizational tradition or norm may run counter to the direction of the project. These obstacles may be temporary, so don't give up entirely. Flaws can be corrected, or the timing can be changed, or repositioning the project may sidestep the conflicting norm.

Lack of leadership drive. This problem is the most common cause of failure. Some people just do not want to be leaders. For some individuals, a leadership role is too scary, too presumptuous, or too unstructured. However, such individuals often will not express their concerns; they simply will fail to suggest innovative solutions to problems or to get a project off the ground. Unfortunately, a lack of leadership ability or desire is not easy to change; it seems linked to basic parts of a person's personality. These individuals, however, can still contribute effectively if teamed with a leader.

Lack of knowledge. Personnel research consultants tend to be outsiders. Chances are they have come into their current job directly out of school or from another consulting job and, consequently, have little or no other experience in the organization. Furthermore, these individuals tend to have closer affiliation to their profession than their organization. Leadership ideas from these internal consultants sound good and are often theoretically well-developed. The ideas, however, are just not consistent with organizational needs. Fortunately, a lack of organizational perspective can be remedied by temporary assignment to field units and project assignments that require research into organizational performance.

Lack of perseverance. Making an impact on a large organizational usually requires a great deal of perseverance. Research managers will face many obstacles to overcome, some foreseen and some not, to say nothing of normal resistance to change. It often takes four or five years to get a new program going, and those four or five years will contain a lot of frustration. Obviously, if an idea has serious flaws, perseverance is no virtue. However, if the idea has merit, managers should give the project consultant as much time, encouragement, and support as possible. What looks like a failure today may become a winner in six months.

Summary

In conclusion, we have attempted to review above what HR program managers make decisions about. Those decisions were then related to the common HR program areas, with emphases placed on discussing what internal information is typically available for each decision as well as ways for obtaining this information. Although we believe that addressing the above questions and obtaining the noted information with respect to the common HR program areas will assist HR program managers in making informed decisions, good judgement, and creativity must come from the program managers.

◆

Notes

1. Payne and Pugh; Gooding and Wagner. Gooding and Wagner recently integrated 31 published field studies of the size–performance relationship. Their findings, were that subunit size and performance, whether in absolute or relative terms, do not appear to be positively related. However, larger organizations do perform better in absolute terms, but not in relative terms. A rationale offered for this apparent paradox is that the number as well as size of subunits increase along with the size of an organization. As Gooding and Wagner note, as a result, performance invariability or losses incurred through the expansion of existing subunits can be counteracted by additional performance contributions of newer subunits.

2. Payne and Pugh, p. 1168.
3. Townsend.
4. Weisbord.
5. Herbst.
6. Weisbord.
7. Scarpello and Ledvinka.
8. Burke and Pearlman.
9. Kleiman and Clark.
10. See Hawk for a list of specific criteria for measuring short-term results of recruiting efforts. Also, Wanous has discussed more general criteria for evaluating recruiting programs at different stages of organizational entry.
11. Fitz-enz (1984).
12. See Dyer and Holder, and Schuler (1987a) for discussions of the strategic importance of careful employee selection.
13. Schuler and MacMillan provide a discussion of the importance of

careful promotion/selection at Data General, Goldman Sachs, and several other organizations. Hall and Goodale provide a discussion of the importance of careful selection in the success of IBM's PC project.

14. Burke and Frederick. Burke and Pearlman as well as Boudreau also have discussed how HR program managers can transform the results of personnel interventions—such as those obtained from selection procedures—into organizationally relevant outcomes. In particular, Burke and Pearlman discuss how to translate personnel program results into dollars (that is, profits), percentage increase in output, or units of observed performance. The general field of translating HR program results into organizationally relevant outcomes has become known as "utility analysis." For a presentation of new practical procedures in this field which link to economic and accounting theory, the reader is referenced to Raju, Burke, and Normand.

15. See Bemis, Belenky, and Soder, and Ghorpade for surveys of job analysis methods and discussions of the relevance that job analysis methods have in all aspects of HRM. Bemis et al. also provide a good discussion of why variations in job analysis systems are helpful in meeting particular organizational goals.

16. A set of professional guidelines, *Principles for the Use and Validation of Personnel Selection Procedures* (Society for Industrial and Organizational Psychology, 1987), has been developed. This document specifies the principles of good practice in the choice, development, evaluation, and use of personnel selection procedures.

17. Studies by Hunter and Hunter; Hunter; and Schmitt, Gooding, Noe, and Kirsch have examined the generalizability of alternative selection procedure predictions across jobs and organizations. The findings of Hunter are particularly noteworthy. This study of over 12,000 jobs found that general cognitive ability predicts job performance ratings in all lines of work, though predictions were higher for complex jobs than for simple jobs. For recent technical summaries of the validity generalization literature, the reader is referred to Burke and Raju, and Hunter and Schmidt.

18. Cornelius, Schmidt, and Carron have discussed the merits of two job classification approaches which show the appropriateness of using cognitive tests in settings that did not participate in selection procedure validation for a validity generalization analysis.

19. See Arvey and Faley.
20. See Boudreau; Fitz-enz (1984).
21. See Morris, Fitz-Gibbon, and Freeman for a thorough discussion of all aspects of communicating evaluation findings.
22. Hall and Goodale.
23. A common belief today is that urinalysis drug testing produces "false positive" selection errors (that is, individuals are falsely detected as illicit drug users and denied jobs when in fact they do not use illicit drugs). As pointed out by Normand, Salyards, and Mahoney, appropriate confirmation tests can eliminate the error rate for urinalysis drug testing.
24. Hall and Goodale.
25. Fitz-enz (1988).
26. Ibid.
27. Schuler, (1987b) p. 393.
28. Fitz-enz (1988), Godkewitsch.
29. Goldstein and Associates.
30. Mager and Beach.

31. See, for example, Kirkpatrick. Vinton, Clark, and Seybolt have also presented an integrated model for asking successive questions regarding training needs assessments.
32. Burke and Day demonstrate that the effectiveness of behavioral model training as a means of improving managerial job performance trends to generalize across companies.
33. Godkewitsch provides an excellent set of examples of how the job performance outcomes of various types of training (in terms of both the method and content of training) can be translated into financial accounting terms, such as direct profit, present value, discounted cash flow, and payback period. See Robinson and Robinson for discussion of a framework for measuring the operational costs and benefits of training.
34. See Rummler for a guide for troubleshooting performance problems, and Mager and Pipe for a quick-reference checklist for analyzing performance problems.
35. For discussions of rating errors, biases, and other personal tendencies see Berk, and Carroll and Schneier.
36. Kaufman.
37. For discussions of content and process theories of work motivation, see Steers and Porter.
38. Miner and Brewer.
39. Normand and Salyards.
40. See Locke and Latham.
41. Guzzo, Jette, and Katzell.
42. Miner and Brewer.
43. Henderson; Milkovich and Newman.
44. Milkovich and Delaney.
45. See Fitz-enz (1984) for a presentation of indices for assisting in compensation cost control, a discussion of distribution patterns, and an overview of ways to assess payroll costs.
46. Ibid.
47. Barkin discusses employees' perceptions regarding some of the major problems and obstacles with incentive plans which may hinder a program.
48. Miner and Miner.
49. Patten.
50. Miner and Miner.
51. Lawrence and Lorsch.

◆

References

Arvey, R.D., and R.H. Faley. 1988. *Fairness in Selecting Employees*. Reading, MA: Addison-Wesley.

Barkin, S. 1984. "Labor's Attitude Toward Wage Incentive Plans." *Industrial and Labor Relations Review*: 533–572.

Bemis, S.E., A.H. Belenky, and D.A. Soder. 1983. *Job Analysis: An Effective Management Tool*. Washington, D.C.: BNA Books.

Berk, R.A., ed. 1986. *Performance Assessment: Methods and Applications*. Baltimore: John Hopkins University Press.

Boudreau, J.W. 1984. "Decision Theory Contributions to HRM Research and Practice." *Industrial Relations* 23: 198–217.

Burke, M.J., and R.R. Day. 1986. "A Cumulative Study of the Effectiveness of Managerial Training." *Journal of Applied Psychology* 71: 232–245.

Burke, M.J., and J.T. Frederick. 1986. "A Comparison of Economic Utility Estimates for Alternative SDy Estimation Procedures." *Journal of Applied Psychology* 71: 334–339.

Burke, M.J., and K. Pearlman. 1988. "Recruiting, Selecting, and Matching People with Jobs." In *Productivity in Organizations*, ed. J.P. Campbell and R.J. Campbell. San Francisco: Jossey-Bass.

Burke, M.J., and N.S. Raju. 1988. "An Overview of Validity Generalization Models and Procedures." In *Readings in Personnel and Human Resource Management*, eds. R. Schuler, S. Youngblood, and V. Huber. St. Paul: West Publishing Co.

Carroll, S.J., and C.E. Schneier. 1982. *Performance Appraisal and Review Systems*. Glenview, IL: Scott, Foresman and Co.

Cornelius, E.T., F.L. Schmidt, and T.J. Carron. 1984. "Job Classification Approaches and the Implementation of Validity Generalization Results." *Personnel Psychology* 37: 247–260.

Dyer, L., and G.W. Holder. 1988. "A Strategic Perspective of Human Resource Management." In *Human Resource Management: Evolving Roles and Responsibilities*, ASPA/BNA Handbook Series, v. I, ed. L. Dyer and J. Holder. Washington, D.C.: BNA Books.

Fitz-enz, J. 1984. *How to Measure Human Resource Management*. New York: McGraw-Hill.

———. 1988. "Proving the Value of Training." *Personnel* (March): 17, 18, 20, 22, 23.

Ghorpade, J.V. 1988. *Job Analysis: A Handbook for the Human Resource Director*. Englewood Cliffs, NJ: Prentice-Hall.

Gooding, R.Z., and J.A. Wagner. 1985. "A Meta-Analytic Review of the Relationships Between Size and Performance: The Productivity and Efficiency of Organizations and their Subunits." *Administrative Science Quarterly* 30: 462–481.

Godkewitsch, M. 1987. "The Dollars and Sense of Corporate Training." *Training* (May): 79–81.

Goldstein, I.L., and Associates. 1989. *Training and Development in Organizations*. San Francisco: Jossey-Bass.

Guzzo, R.A., R.D. Jette, and R.A. Katzell. 1985. "The Effects of Psychologically Based Intervention Programs on Worker Productivity: A Meta-Analysis." *Personnel Psychology* 38: 275–291.

Hall, D.T. and J.G. Goodale. 1986. *Human Resource Management: Strategy, Design and Implementation*. Glenview, IL: Scott, Foresman and Company.

Hawk, R.H. 1987. *The Recruitment Function*. New York: AMACOM, The American Management Association.

Henderson, R.I. 1989. *Compensation Management: Rewarding Performance*. Englewood Cliffs, NJ: Prentice-Hall.

6-140 Managing HR in the Information Age

Herbst, P.G. 1974. *Socio-Technical Design.* London: Tavistock.

Hunter, J.E. 1983. "Test Validation for 12,000 Jobs: An Application of Job Classification and Validity Generalization Analysis to the General Aptitude Test Battery." *USES Test Research Report 45.* Washington, D.C.: U.S. Department of Labor.

Hunter, J.E., and R.F. Hunter. 1984. "Validity and Utility of Alternative Predictors of Job Performance." *Psychological Bulletin* 96: 72–98.

Hunter, J.E. and F.L. Schmidt. 1990. *Methods of Meta-Analysis.* Beverly Hills, CA: Sage Publications.

Kaufman, G.G. 1987. "Human Resources in the 90s." Address given at The Executive Study Conference.

Kirkpatrick, D. 1985. "Determining Supervision Training Needs and Setting Objectives." In *The Training and Development Sourcebook,* eds. L.S. Baird, C.E. Schneider, and D. Laird. Amherst, MA: Human Resource Development Press.

Kleiman, L.S., and K.J. Clark. 1984. "Recruitment: An Effective Job Posting System." *Personnel Journal* 63: 20, 22, 25.

Lawrence, P.R., and J.W. Lorsch. 1967. *Organization and Environment: Managing Differentiation and Integration.* Boston: Harvard University.

Locke, E.A., and G.P. Latham. 1984. "*Goal Setting: A Motivational Technique That Works.*" Englewood Cliffs, NJ: Prentice-Hall.

Mager, R., and K. Beach, Jr. 1985. "Course Objectives." In *The Training and Development Sourcebook,* eds. L.S. Baird, C.E. Schneider, D. Laird. Amherst, MA: Human Resource Development Press.

Mager, R.F., and P. Pipe. 1985. "Analyzing Performance Problems A Quick-Reference Checklist." In *The Training and Development Sourcebook,* eds. L.S. Baird, C.E. Schneider, and D. Laird. Amherst, MA: Human Resource Development Press.

Milkovich, G.T., and J.M. Newman. 1984. *Compensation.* Plano, TX: Business Publications Inc.

Milkovich, G.T. and M.J. Delaney. 1975. "A Note On Cafeteria Pay Plans." *Industrial Relations* 14: 112–116.

Miner, J.B., and J. Frank Brewer. 1976. "The Management of Ineffective Performance." In *Handbook for Industrial and Organizational Psychology,* ed. Marvin D. Dunnette. Chicago: Rand McNally.

Miner, J.B. and M.G. Miner. 1973. *Personnel and Industrial Relations.* New York: MacMillan Co.

Morris, L.L., C.T. Fitz-Gibbon, and M.E. Freeman. 1987. *How to Communicate Evaluation Findings.* Newbury Park, CA: Sage Publications, Inc.

Normand, J., S. Salyards and J. Mahoney. 1990. "A Preliminary Evaluation of Pre-Employment Drug Testing." *Journal of Applied Psychology* 75: 629–39.

Normand, J., and S. Salyards. 1989. "An Empirical Evaluation of Pre-Employment Drug Testing in the United States Postal Service." In *Drugs In The Work-*

place: *Research and Evaluation Data*, NIDA Research Monograph 91, eds. S.W. Gust and J.M. Walsh, Rockville, MD: NIDA.

Patten, T.H., Jr. 1970. "Collective Bargaining and Consensus: The Potential of a Laboratory Training Input." *Management of Personnel Quarterly* 9:29–37.

Payne, R., and D.S. Pugh. 1976. "Organization Structure and Climate." In *Handbook of Industrial and Organizational Psychology*, ed. Marvin D. Dunnette. Chicago: Rand McNally.

Raju, N.S., M.J. Burke, and J. Normand. 1990. "A New Approach for Utility Analysis." *Journal of Applied Psychology* 75: 3–12.

Robinson, D.G., and J.C. Robinson. 1989. *Training for Impact: How to Link Training to Business Needs and Measure the Results.* San Francisco: Jossey-Bass.

Rummler, G.A. 1985. "Human Performance Problems and Their Solutions." In *The Training and Development Sourcebook*, eds. L.S. Baird, C.E. Schneider, and D. Laird. Amherst, MA: Human Resource Development Press.

Scarpello, V.G., and J. Ledvinka. 1988. *Personnel/Human Resource Management.* Boston: PWS-Kent Publishing Company.

Schmitt, N., R.Z., Gooding, R.D. Noe, and M. Kirsch. 1984. "Meta-Analysis of Validity Studies Published Between 1964 and 1982 and the Investigation of Study Characteristics." *Personnel Psychology* 37: 407–422.

Schuler, R.S., and I.C. MacMillan. 1984. "Gaining Competitive Advantage Through Human Resource Management Practices." *Human Resource Management* 23: 241–255.

Schuler, R.S. 1987a. "Personnel and Human Resource Management Practices." *Human Resource Planning* 10: 1–17.

———. 1987b. *Personnel and Human Resource Management.* St. Paul, MN: West Publishing Co.

Society for Industrial and Organizational Psychology. 1987. *Principles for the Validation and Use of Personnel Selection Procedures.* (Third Edition) College Park, MD: Author.

Steers, R.M., and L.W. Porter. 1987. *Motivation and Work Behavior.* New York: McGraw-Hill.

Townsend, R. 1970. *Up the Organization.* New York: Alfred A. Knopf.

Vinton, K.L., A.O. Clark, and J.W. Seybolt. 1983. "Assessment of Training Needs for Supervisors." *Personnel Administrator* 28: 49.

Wanous, J.P. 1980. *Organizational Entry: Recruitment, Selection and Socialization of Newcomers.* Reading, MA: Addison-Wesley Publishing Company.

Weisbord, M.A. 1987. *Productive Workplace.* San Francisco: Jossey-Bass.

6.4
HR Communication in Times of Change

Richard A. Guzzo
Katherine J. Klein

This chapter analyzes communication processes during times of organizational change. In particular, its focus concerns the effective movement of information to facilitate successful organizational change. The chapter examines three patterns of information flow in organizations—top-down, bottom-up, and lateral—in relation to four types of organizational change: the installation of computer technology, organizational downsizing initiatives, introduction of productivity and quality improvement programs, and implementation of employee ownership. The goals are (1) to develop an understanding of how communication flows can facilitate effective change in these areas and (2) to identify some generally useful principles for managing communication during times of organizational change.

Communication and Organizational Effectiveness

What does communication mean? By 1970, this seemingly simple term had at least 95 different definitions,[1] and new definitions no doubt have been added since. This chapter, however, will focus on organizational communication, that is, the process of transmitting organizationally relevant information.[2] In particular, it will look at communication during periods of organizational change, especially information that bears on HR aspects of that change. It also will examine the direction of communication (top-down, bottom-up, and lateral) during times of change and the relationship between communication and the success of change efforts. As the labels suggest, top-down communication originates in the higher levels of management; lateral communication refers to information exchanged among persons similarly placed in the organizational hierarchy; and bottom-up communication refers to information flowing from lower to higher ranks.

Few dispute the idea that communication impacts organizational effectiveness, although only a few systematic studies exist to support this. Years ago, research showed that effective organizations tended to have greater exchange of information among organizational subunits.[3] Other studies have linked some measures of overall organizational effectiveness to top-down communication and to lateral communication within work groups.[4] One investigation of lateral communication found that the longer R&D groups had been in existence the less their members communicated either with each other or with people outside the group.[5] As a result of this decrease in communication, performance declined as groups aged. Similar findings emerged from a study of Navy teams which found that the openness and accuracy of communication affected team effectiveness.[6] Quite apart from performance, the amount and quality of communication in organizations also relate to employee satisfaction and to job satisfaction.[7] In summary, communication is a key determinant of effective performance and satisfaction with work.

Some analyses of organizational communication concern roles individuals play in transmitting information, such as who is a "gatekeeper" or "boundary spanner." Others seek to map the typical ways in which communication courses through an organization—that is, to chart communication networks. Still other analyses focus on sources of distortion in messages. This chapter's focus examines not only communication flows but also the connection between communication flows during organizational transitions and the effectiveness with which change is implemented.

Organizational Downsizing

A significant type of change that many organizations have experienced is downsizing. Downsizing occurs for a variety of reasons, including: general declines in the economy, the cumulative effects of poor corporate performance, mergers and acquisitions, legal mandates (such as, in the case of AT&T, antitrust rulings), and unexpected catastrophes. As an example of a catastrophic event, Firestone's forced recall of 9 million radial tires in 1979 contributed to the company's decision to close nearly half its production facilities and reduce its work force from 107,000 to 55,000.[8] Whatever the reason behind a specific firm's reduction in size, the effectiveness with which the process is managed greatly depends on the nature of top-down communication within the organization.

Role of Top-Down Communication

Top-down communication during downsizing is important for its substance (what top management says to employees and others) and its symbolic value. It can determine the effectiveness of the actual downsizing activities such as job terminations, closings of plant or office locations, disposing of assets. More importantly, top-down communication also influences the preparedness of the post-downsized organization. How and what top management communicates during downsizing can significantly affect the condition of human resources after the downsizing: Will the work force be poised for an organizational renaissance or distracted and dispirited to the point of endangering the company's competitiveness?

One of the most publicized examples of organizational downsizing is the case of AT&T. During the mid- to late-1980s AT&T eliminated well over 60,000 positions. Early in the process, the company gave little attention to managing communication. As a result, many employees first learned of the cuts through newspapers and periodicals, rather than from any sources inside the company. Those who did hear from sources inside the company often heard rumor and speculation passed off as fact. The grapevine worked overtime, with adverse impacts on morale and productivity.[9]

After seeing these ill effects, top management at AT&T changed its communication practices during the period of transition. A number of very specific tactics were adopted to communicate to employees not only the "facts" of the ongoing changes, but also the new vision of what the company was to become. These tactics involved the highest-ranking members of the organization. For example, the chairman's addresses on the matter were carried closed-circuit within the company or were published and widely disseminated. A videotape of top officers discussing the new vision for AT&T was distributed. A one-week seminar for 800 top executives communicated the envisioned environment and policies of the new company, thus preparing these officers to talk about the changes to groups of employees and field their questions. In-house publications and specially produced documents spread the word about what was happening, what would happen, and where the company would be once it was all over. Other examples of top-down communication during this process included establishing a toll-free number to field employees' questions and using public relations and advertising channels to get the word out to AT&T's various constituencies (including its own employees). By almost all accounts, the transition became much smoother as a result of such communication tactics.

Substantive and Symbolic Messages

The heavy top-down communication used by AT&T had many elements operating to make it effective. One element was content. Getting the facts out so as to quell rumors and suspicions certainly addressed the immediate concerns of employees wondering what (and who) might be next. But the content of communications also concerned the more distant future, the one that would confront remaining employees when all the downsizing ended. The steps taken to prepare people for the "new" organization seemed to have long-term impact.

The symbolic value of AT&T's actions would also seem to have impact. The communications tactics put top management out front and showed them leading and in command during this period of unprecedented change. This strategy not only reassured employees but also may have helped to build enthusiasm for the new organization.

One recent analysis of ways to manage decline and turnarounds in organizations cites the management of information as essential.[10] In addition to its impact on employees, effective communication can enable an organization to retain the trust and support of external stakeholders, such as customers, creditors, and investors. Symbolic information also can have a critical impact during times of change. Contrast the symbolic value of Lee Iacocca's acceptance of a $1.00 salary until his company turned a profit to Atari's top management which, during a period of organizational decline, seemingly refused to share in the reductions and cutbacks that company experienced.[11]

Impact on Employees and Organizational Effectiveness

The transition from larger to smaller size can have profound consequences for the human resources of any firm. Firms engaged in downsizing often provide many services to those displaced, such as lengthy advance notice, extended health care benefits, severance pay, and various forms of outplacement assistance, including resume preparation, retraining, and counseling. Such services undoubtedly communicate a symbolic message to those whose jobs survive the change. Investigations of the effects of layoffs have found that the loss of co-workers can have negative consequences for those who stay, including feelings of exhaustion, worry about one's own career, and decreased self-esteem.[12] Some people seem more prone to experiencing these consequences than others, and the substantive and symbolic top management communication during times of downsizing can influence how survivors react to the process.

The payoff from good top-down communication during times of radical organizational change is difficult to quantify with any certainty. Nonetheless, the payoff can prove significant, judging from the account of one company's experience. In 1987, Bell & Howell lost an estimated $2.1 million in profits due to employees spending their time investigating rumors with each other and commiserating rather than working.[13] Better communication from top management might have averted much of this loss of time and money.

In conclusion, communication plays a key role in the management of downsizing, especially top-down information flows. With a change as profound as a reduction in organizational size, lateral communication channels will be abuzz and bottom-up communication may increase as well. However, top-down communication holds the key to protecting employee morale, maintaining productivity, and positively orienting an organization toward the future. The uncertainty accompanying downsizing seems to heighten the value of information provided by those in charge of the organization. In other words, in times of crisis, people look to their leaders.

Employee Ownership

Employee ownership is an increasingly common innovation on the American scene. In 1976, approximately 1,000 employee ownership companies existed in the United States[14]; a decade later, this number had increased tenfold.[15]

Factors Promoting ESOPs

Employee ownership companies come in a variety of forms: employee stock ownership plans (ESOP) and worker cooperatives; small and large; manufacturing and service; public and private; profitable and unprofitable. Employee ownership companies share at least one common feature: The majority of the employees in the company own some or all of the company.[16] Employees may own as much as 100 percent or as little as one percent of the company. The key fact is that the majority of employees—not just the elite at the top—have a stake in the company's ownership.

The growth of employee ownership in recent years reflects a variety of factors. The Employee Retirement Income Security Act, passed in 1974, provided tax breaks to companies that offered employee stock ownership plans (ESOPs). Subsequent laws have made it even more financially beneficial for companies to share ownership with their employees. For example, the Deficit Reduction Act of 1984 created financial incentives for banks to loan money to ESOP companies, further spurring the growth of employee ownership. As a result, many companies have established ESOPs primarily or even solely for financial reasons—that is, to reap tax savings, to raise capital, to provide a market for the stock of a retiring owner, or to finance a leveraged buyout (as a defense against hostile takeovers).[17]

Besides these direct payoffs, employee ownership has the potential to produce other savings. Managers in many ESOP companies hope that by offering employees stock in the company, they may increase employee productivity, satisfaction, and commitment to the company, and decrease employee turnover.[18] As discussed below, communication—particularly top-down and bottom-up communication—plays a critical role in determining whether employee ownership engenders such increases in employee performance and morale. The discussion focuses on ESOPs, by far the most common form of employee ownership in the United States.

Role of Top-Down Communication

How can communication flows improve implementation of an ESOP? Top-down communication can increase the salience and thus the value of the ESOP to company employees. In the absence of significant top-down communication regarding employee ownership, employees are likely to dismiss the plan as, at best, a trivial aspect of their work life, at worst, a management ploy. All too often, employees in many ESOP companies lack interest in, knowledge about, and enthusiasm for their company's plan. Simply put, ESOPs have very little impact on employees' daily lives. Indeed, the typical employee will find that little changes in his or her company with the onset of an ESOP.

Common Misassumptions About ESOPs

This argument runs counter to common assumptions about ESOPs. One belief, for example, is that ESOPs are highly salient to employees because employees have paid a lot of money for their company stock. But in 96 percent of all ESOP companies, employees have not paid money (or taken wage concessions) for their stock.[19] Instead, the company usually gives employees stock as an employee benefit.

Another mistaken assumption posits that employees gain substantial influence in company decision making as a result of the ESOP. However, no evidence has shown that companies become more participative as a result of establishing an ESOP.[20] In 85 to 95 percent of privately held ESOP companies, employees are not allowed to vote their stock.[21] In publicly held ESOP companies, employees must have the right to vote their ESOP stock, but these voting rights have no more influence on company decision making than the average public (non-employee) stockholder. Of course, some ESOP companies are highly participative, but many, perhaps even most, of these companies may have been highly participative prior to implementation of employee ownership.

One might assume that ESOPs are highly salient because employees experience immediate financial benefits from stock ownership. But this too is not true. In the vast majority of ESOP companies, employees have no access to their stock unless they leave the company.[22] In addition, employees' ESOP accounts vest over time, ensuring that employees will forfeit some percentage of their stock if they leave the company with less than seven years of tenure in the plan. Although some publicly held ESOP companies pay dividends, dividends for the average ESOP participant are typically small.[23] Thus, while ESOPs often offer substantial long-term financial benefits,[24] they offer participants few or no immediate financial benefits.

A final misassumption is that ESOPs have salience because the plan saved the company and employees' jobs. But most ESOP companies didn't need saving. They were profitable, healthy companies, not companies teetering on the brink of disaster that were saved from shutting down by an employee buyout. Employee buyouts to avert shutdowns receive substantial popular media attention,[25] but account for only 4 percent or less of all ESOPs.[26]

In sum, ESOPs typically do not have an immediate, practical, significant, and positive impact on employees' work lives. Instead, the immediate, practical impact of the ESOP on participants is small and neutral. ESOPs may, however, have an immediate, significant, positive, symbolic impact on employees' work lives if a company manages its ESOP communications effectively. Under some circumstances, employees also may respond to the positive symbol of the ESOP and its long-term financial benefits with increased commitment and loyalty to the company.[27]

Substantive and Symbolic Messages

In an ESOP company, top-down communication about the plan can serve three functions. First, top-down communication has educational value. ESOPs are complicated, legalistic benefit plans. Employees need clear, concise explanations of the plan's technical features (such as stock evaluation, vesting, dividends, and so on) in order to understand the structure of the ESOP and its long-term benefits. Without such education, employees are likely to be confused and put off by the plan's legalistic details. Ultimately, employees could become oblivious to the ESOP, suspicious of it, or perhaps even unrealistically optimistic about it. None of these outcomes is a desirable end for the ESOP company.

Second, top-down communication about the ESOP keeps the topic on employees' minds. As already discussed, ESOPs are truly long-term benefit plans. In most ESOP companies, employees experience no financial gain from the ESOP until they leave the company. Top-down communication ensures that employees think about and appreciate the company's ESOP, despite its long-term payoff.

Finally, top-down communication about the ESOP enhances the symbolic value of the ESOP. When top managers refer to the company as employee-owned, when they refer to their subordinates as owners, partners, or associates, they transform the ESOP from a technical, financial plan to a symbol of the company's commitment to and respect for its employees. This symbolic value enhances the plan's potential to enhance employee morale and productivity.

Thus, top-down communication increases the likelihood that employees will view the ESOP with understanding and appreciation. Indeed, research on ESOPs has shown precisely this benefit deriving from effective communication.[28] One study examined the relationship between employee attitudes and ESOP characteristics in 37 ESOP companies. To assess ESOP communications, researchers counted the number of ESOP communications strategies used by each company. The study found that ESOP communications had a significant positive correlation with the average level of employee satisfaction and a significant negative correlation with employee turnover intentions.

Importance of Bottom-Up Communication

Top-down communication alone is no guarantee of a plan's success, however. It will not ensure that employees respond to the ESOP with enthusiasm and commitment. While communication about the ESOP is important, so is the size of the company's contribution to the ESOP (the principal determinant of how lucrative the ESOP is for plan participants).[29] In short, employees are unlikely to be very excited about an ESOP that offers only trivial financial rewards.

Indeed, anecdotal evidence suggests that ESOP communications may even backfire if managers "talk up" an ESOP that employees perceive to be a ruse, or worse, a rip-off." Consider, for example, some of the comments from ESOP participants in one company:[30]

> Although these questions make it sound like I hate my job, this is not true. I do, however, hate the sham being perpetrated on the "little people" via the company's ESOP. While I would not consider my ESOP sufficient to live on, it galls the hell out of me that the company makes such a big deal out of it and then requires a long internment to receive it, knowing full well that most employees will not receive it.
> Our ESOP is set up to benefit the management and/or oldtimers. Technical staff get the contract work done with little pay or "say."
> The ESOP shares are distributed proportionally by salary. Half of the profits are distributed among management outright through corporate development bonuses. The other half is "shared" with the workers through the ESOP. Not a bad scam if you're management!
> It is hard to be enthused about our firm's ESOP plan because the employees do not have voting rights. Our plan is, in effect, a pension plan.

I feel there should be some protection for the employees of this company to prevent upper management from raking off a hog's share of company profits.

As these comments suggest, top-down communication about the ESOP may even damage employee morale and organizational commitment if employees are dissatisfied with the ESOP. Better to improve the features of the ESOP than to heighten the salience of a plan that employees view with dissatisfaction and disdain.

The employee comments listed above also draw attention to the importance of bottom-up communication in an ESOP company. Bottom-up communication provides managers with feedback regarding how employees view the ESOP. Managers need this information to determine the extent to which employees understand the ESOP and value its benefits. The goal is thus not ESOP *communication*, but ESOP *conversation* throughout the organization.

Impact on Organizational Effectiveness

Will such ESOP conversation engender an increase in organizational performance and productivity? Frankly, this outcome appears unlikely. Organizational performance and productivity are influenced by a multitude of factors, only some of which concern human resources. The implementation of an ESOP is but one HR intervention, and it alone should not be expected to yield significant gains in organizational performance. Indeed, the best available evidence suggests that the relationship between ESOP employee ownership and company performance is nonsignificant.[31]

This general conclusion, however, does not apply to all ESOP companies. When employee ownership is accompanied by substantial worker participation, employee ownership appears to lead to improvements in organizational performance.[32] This finding reinforces the point that employee ownership alone may not be enough to enhance organizational performance.[33] It again shows the importance of communication, for at the heart of employee participation is good communication.

Programs for Quality and Productivity

From time to time, organizations initiate systematic change programs to enhance productivity or quality. These programs take many forms. Some have a long history of use while others may appear to be more short-term and faddish. One common feature of these programs, though, is the central role an organization's human resources play in programs for productivity and quality improvements. This section of the chapter examines a variety of programs for improving quality and productivity, with a focus on the role of communication in launching and sustaining those programs.

Incentive Pay Programs

How to pay people for their work is, of course, one of the most crucial HR decisions that organizations must make. The number of considerations are daunting: How much pay is enough to attract and retain people? How much is needed to motivate excellence? How are jobs to be evaluated fairly and accurately in determining pay scales? What role does "merit" play in pay, how should it be assessed, and how are those assessments translated into monetary rewards? The list of questions goes on. However, the concern here is not with the design particulars of compensation systems. Rather, it is with the role of organizational communication in facilitating an effective change from an existing compensation system to a new one.

Changes in organizational pay systems often have major impact. Such changes can be very contentious and they can affect all parts of an organization. Because pay systems in organizations are so crucial, the management of information during times of change is a key ingredient in a successful transition.[34] Top-down communication has been the norm when pay systems change,[35] and the nature of that communication has largely been to "tell" employees what the new system would be. Such a communication style is usually accompanied by very restricted access within the organization to decisions regarding the design and the nature of the new pay scheme. Given the complexities and sensitivities of pay at work, this traditional approach is inherently flawed.[36] A more participative approach is required to make effective transitions from one pay plan to another.

Importance of Multiple Communication Flows

One more participative approach to implementing pay changes is the use of "diagonal slice task forces" to design the new pay plan.[37] A diagonal slice task force mixes people from different levels and functions in the organization. Whether they have final authority to determine all the particulars of a new pay scheme, task force participants still need to be capable (that is, respected and at least somewhat knowledgeable about pay systems), and they must represent important constituencies in the organization. A diagonal slice task force facilitates top-down as well as bottom-up communication because it is populated by people from different levels in the organization. It also enhances lateral communication because it brings together representatives of different functional areas. Other forms of participation in the design of pay plans also exist.

The greatest achievement of participative design is the communication it nurtures.[38] Participation in the process of designing and implementing organizational pay changes results in substantial amounts of information flowing top-down, bottom-up, and laterally. Participation exposes organizational members to facts and considerations that otherwise would have remained hidden. This lack of information potentially would have promoted distrust or resentment toward the new pay scheme and its designers, perceptions of unfairness in pay administration, overestimates by employees of the pay of others in the organization, and dissatisfaction with pay regardless of the absolute amount earned. Because participation *is* communication in the design of pay systems, it overcomes traditional problems associated with lack of information.

Other forms of communication besides participation can be used to sustain the acceptance of a new pay system. Bell Labs, for example, publishes the actual salaries of employees within pay grades—without names attached. Universities, too, often share such information. Ben and Jerry's, the ice cream maker, has well-known rules within the firm for determining the ratio of pay at a higher level to pay at lower levels. In times of transition to a new pay system, an organization can help implement those changes effectively by facilitating all forms of communication. The ongoing effectiveness of the new system also can be maintained by practices designed to communicate relevant information on a continuing basis.

Employee Involvement Programs

When implementing new pay systems, participation is a means to achieving a successful transition, and its value derives from the resulting increase in communication. When implementing programs to promote widespread employee involvement (EI), participation is very much an end state, the goal to be attained.

6-154   Managing HR in the Information Age

Mechanisms to Ensure Multiple Communication Channels

One of the best examples of an organizational change toward increased EI is the Ford Motor Company. The company's underlying goal was to improve quality, and communication played a key role in promoting this change. At the outset, Ford defined EI rather narrowly to include groups of employees meeting with their supervisor to identify and solve quality-related problems.[39] The definition has since expanded to include employee participation in planning, goal setting, and decision making.

The EI program was formally inaugurated in 1979 when Ford and the United Auto Workers signed a letter of agreement about the plan. Shortly thereafter, the company president issued a letter articulating the new policy and guidelines for implementing it.[40] An oversight committee also was established and charged, in part, with the responsibility of disseminating information about EI efforts. Thus, from the outset, top-down communication took place and provisions were made for continued communication about the change effort.

Ford also established other mechanisms of communication. For example, teams of union and management representatives personally visited Ford plants to explain the EI process. Senior management also visited plants to give and get news of employee involvement activities throughout the firm. Newsletters, brochures, handbooks, reference guides, and other printed materials were frequently used vehicles of communication. The company also employed many person-to-person vehicles of communication, such as presentations to and by management, union groups, and ad hoc committees. These person-to-person encounters disseminated information not just from the top to other parts of the organization, but also from the bottom upward. Other person-to-person communication mechanisms ensured lateral communication of information. Such efforts included the creation of many types of teams that brought together employees from different areas of the company. These teams had various designations, such as "interface teams," "opportunity teams," and "launch teams."

As one analyst noted, "A great deal of time and effort were spent in communicating with management, union leaders, and employees."[41] This comment may understate Ford's investment in implementing its change toward increased EI. While the payoff in productivity and quality is quite difficult to assess, Ford's reputation for quality did rise following the implementation of EI practices. In addition, surveys of employees provide evidence that the practices have enjoyed some success.[42] No matter what criterion one uses to measure the success of this planned organizational change, one thing is certain: The extensive top-down, lateral, and bottom-up communication contributed to that success.

Total Quality Management Programs

Employee involvement at Ford is one example of a macro organizational change. Another example of macro organizational change that lately has commanded much interest is "Total Quality Management" (TQM). TQM refers to a family of related practices that aim to modify many facets of organizational functioning in order to improve the quality of goods and services.[43]

Typical elements of TQM include collaboration among functions often separated in organizations; training of employees in quality improvement principles and practices; diffusion of knowledge about statistical quality control methods throughout the organization; revision of selection, training, and reward systems to emphasize increased quality; coordination with suppliers to ensure high-quality parts and resources; and efforts to orient employees toward ever-increasing levels of quality and continuous improvement.[44] Goal setting, new forms of compensation, and employee involvement are all ingredients in TQM programs. TQM is a tall order, indeed.

Role of Top-Down Communication

As with the implementation of employee involvement, the success of TQM practices depends on how communication is managed. Top-down communication at the commencement of a TQM effort is essential to explain the changes in store and to pave the way toward employee acceptance. But top-down communication will not suffice for long in a TQM effort. Mechanisms need to be established for bottom-up communication regarding needed resources and process innovations for enhanced quality. Many TQM programs not only provide the means for employees to communicate their ideas for improvement, but also reward employees for good ideas. These rewards often are monetary but can include various other forms of recognition. Some companies, for example, set aside days for celebration of quality improvements that have been communicated up the organizational hierarchy.

Importance of Lateral Communication

Lateral communication also plays an essential role. For example, TRW has used a team-based approach called "Managing for Reliability" to establish links between different functional areas. An example of such a multi-function team might include sales, product engineering, quality control, purchasing, and others as needed. The required lateral communication in TQM often extends beyond an organization's formal boundaries. For example, one Chrysler plant used daily telephone and in-person meetings between plant representatives and suppliers to identify quality improvement opportunities and rapidly act on them. J.I. Case, a manufacturer of agriculture and construction equipment, forms multi-function teams of employees and sends them out to talk to dealerships and customers. The information brought back by these teams has resulted in changes to productions processes that have raised productivity and quality.

Many elements contribute to the success of TQM programs, including forceful management, training and skill enhancement of employees, participation, and reward systems. A hallmark of TQM, however, is the demand it makes on organizational communication processes. Implementation of TQM practices create very high demands for upward as well as lateral, cross-functional communication, and the success of TQM efforts may depend heavily on the effectiveness of such communication.

The Implementation of Computer Technologies

In the past decade, the "computer revolution" has come to U.S. businesses of all kinds. Manufacturing companies have invested in robots, computerized numerical control systems, computer-aided design systems (CAD), computer-aided manufacturing (CAM), and computer-integrated manufacturing (CIM). Offices have adopted computerized word-processing systems, spreadsheet software packages, FAX systems, and electronic mail systems.[45]

When an organization adopts and implements these new systems, it alters far more than its production processes. Changes also occur in organizational roles,[46] skill requirements,[47] interaction patterns,[48] career paths,[49] organizational bases of power,[50] and even organizational strategies and culture.[51] In short, the imple-

HR Communication in Times of Change   6-157

mentation of major new computerized systems reverberates throughout an organization, affecting numerous features of the company.

To manage this complex and demanding change process, leaders must provide their subordinates with a guiding vision of the future, more technologically advanced organization; top-down communication is thus critical. In addition, employee groups must negotiate to develop computerized systems and coordination routines that are mutually beneficial; lateral communication is thus critical. Finally, computer system users must provide feedback to their supervisors and to the system's developers to ensure adaptations as user needs change; bottom-up communication is thus critical. The following discussion describes ways in which each of these forms of communication can facilitate implementation of complex computerized systems.

Role of Top-Down Communication

The importance of guiding leadership and top-down communication during times of organizational change is well known,[52] and the implementation of computer technology certainly qualifies as a tremendous period of change.[53] Top-down communication about the new technology serves two critical functions. First, its focuses employee attention on the new technology. It communicates that the new technology is indeed a priority of the organization; unlike other management initiatives, it won't just go away. Second, top-down communication explains the technology to employees. Why did the company adopt this particular technology? How will the company benefit? How will the employees benefit? Will employees' jobs change? How? Top-down communication should answer these questions, as well as provide employees with a way to think about the new technology.

These functions of top-down communication seem obvious, even rudimentary. But a surprising number of organizations neglect or mishandle top-down communication during the technology implementation process.[54] For example, one qualitative case study found ample evidence of the neglect of top-down communication during the implementation of a computerized manufacturing resource planning system (MRP II) in a 300-employee, East Coast metal parts manufacturing company.[55] The system in question was a highly sophisticated, computerized planning, production, and inventory control system for manufacturing settings. In this Maryland company, employees complained a great deal about the failure of top management to lead the effort to implement the new MRP II system.[56] The following comment was typical:

> You can't get people to change on that massive a scale with just a memo or a shift meeting or a foreman being called into the president's office. What's needed is a demonstrated commitment from the president on down. The president has to follow up with the plant manager and make tours of the mill all times of the day. It shows people that he's serious.

Apparently as a result of the minimal top-down communication about the new computerized system, employees at the company felt they lacked sufficient understanding of the new system. Thus, employees commented:

> I feel lost. We were told how to use the system but not what it did or what we were doing when we were entering information. It was never explained what exactly is going on. I was explained nothing, not what it will do for the company, not what it'll do for me. Why am I barcoding? If I turn on a TV, I see a picture and I hear a voice and I can understand that. But barcoding ain't changed nothing.

> Whenever you're making a major change, you should assume employees have some pride in what they do. They should have said, "We're doing this and this is how it's going to help our job and this is how it's going to make your job easier." They did just the opposite. Anything they could have done to make people gung-ho, they did just the opposite.

> We've never had a goal that I know of. I'm sure upper management has a goal, but it has never been communicated to me, and if it hasn't been communicated to me and other middle managers, I can't believe that it has been communicated to the operators.

Functions of Lateral Communication

The comment above illustrate the importance of top-down communication during the computer technology implementation process. Lateral communication is no less important. Particularly critical is communication between the users and the in-house developers of a new system.[57] Unless communication between these two groups is frequent and smooth, the new system is unlikely to fit the needs and desires of the actual users. In such cases, of course, employees motivation to learn and to use the new system suffers tremendously.

Another study of a Maryland company that manufactures laminates for flooring and countertops, which also was in the process of implementing a computerized MRP-II system, illustrates the complaints that may arise when communication between system users and developers is poor.[58] Discussing the role of data processing personnel in implementing the new MRP II system, system users commented:

> I learned a while ago not to ask questions. Data processing people say they can't do this or they, or you never get an answer, or they don't want to stop and see.
>
> The people developing the system are extremely defensive. They're unwilling to listen to constructive negative feedback. They aren't listening to suggestions or comments from the people who are using it. If they can't change the system to fit our needs, they ought to stop now. It'll just be an albatross.
>
> Data processing asks us things but it doesn't really matter what we say. Our opinion doesn't really matter. I think they believe they just have to ask. If they think that something's going to work better and we want something else, I don't think our opinion matters at all.

Importance of Bottom-Up Communication

In this case, not only lateral but also bottom-up communication appeared to be lacking. Bottom-up communication about the new computer technology keeps upper-level supervisors and managers informed about the progress of the implementation effort, as well as technology and organization characteristics in need of change. Bottom-up communication thus enhances and expands upon the lateral communication processes described above. It ensures that supervisors and managers, not just technology developers, hear user concerns and complaints. On the basis of such information, managers and supervisors may take steps to adapt the organization to the technology and the technology to the organization.

Consider, as a final example, a recent study of the implementation of computer-aided design and drafting (CADD) in a large construction and engineering firm.[59] Through interviews, the researchers documented numerous issues that would have (and probably should have) been the subject of bottom-up communication, had the organization fostered such communication. These issues include: (1) employees' concerns about the impact of the new CADD system on organizational career paths; (2) supervisors' beliefs that they lacked the necessary expertise to guide and evaluate their now more technically expert subordinates; (3) employee dissatisfaction with the lighting and size of their CADD work stations; and (4) the inadequacy of the computer hardware which rendered the CADD system frustrating slow to operate.

In sum, top-down communication focuses employee attention on the new computer technology and shapes employee interpretation and evaluation of the new system. Lateral and bottom-up communication facilitates the adjustment of the technology to users and the users to the technology. These processes thus greatly increase the likelihood that the new system will prove a success— that is, that employees will accept and use it enthusiastically.

Conclusions

With any type of major organizational change, top-down communication is important. Whether an organizational change is strategic, such as downsizing or a total quality commitment; technological, such as converting to computer-based processes; or of a nature that affects the employer–employee relationship, such as changes in pay or in employee ownership, good top-down communication is imperative.

The mechanisms by which top-down communication can take place are quite numerous. Consider, for example, the variety of ways Ford engaged in top-down communication as part of the change toward increased employee involvement. No matter how information comes down from the top, the important factor is that the information comes.

Impact of Top-Down Communication

Top-down communication in times of change has great symbolic value to organizational members, and this symbolic value can work to the advantage of top management. By being "out front" and by disclosing plans and visions, top management presents itself as in control of a changing world rather than being buffeted by these changes. The symbolic value of top-down communication also can help build work-force commitment to the change that is underway.

But top-down communication serves more than just a symbolic function. The content of what top management tells the work force is essential. One of the most important substantive activities top management can undertake during transitional periods is to communicate goals. Without a clear statement of the organizational goals to be achieved through a major organizational change, organizations can suffer, as in the case of the metal parts manufacturer illustrated. While this communication of goals should occur at the initiation of the change, the AT&T example showed that an organization can recover from a failure to do so. The lesson to be learned is that top-down communication is *always* essential to the success of organizational change, both for its symbolic and substantive functions.

Value of Lateral Communication

The importance of lateral communication varies according to the nature of the change. As in the case of implementing new technologies, changes that affect the working relationships among different functional areas of a company, make good lateral communication indispensable. Ford established many mechanisms of lateral communication when it shifted toward increased employee involvement. Other types of organizational change may benefit from using many of Ford's strategies, such as the creation of temporary cross-functional teams and presentations to update organizational members on the experiences and developments in the change process. Team-based mechanisms of communication also are common in total quality improvement programs.

Need for Bottom-Up Communication

Bottom-up communication is essential to the success of most kinds of organizational change; thus it is incumbent on management to create the opportunities to encourage the upward flow of information. Bottom-up communication does not necessarily require that every employee at the lower ranks is heard. Instead, it involves the creation of opportunities for lower-level employees to communicate upward. Such opportunities can take several different forms. Diagnonal-slice task forces, advocated for use with changes in organizational pay systems, establish a means through which employees at lower ranks can communicate through peer representatives.

Bottom-up communication serves many purposes. One important function is to check on whether an organizational change is going as planned. Employee stock ownership plans, for example, may be regarded with indifference or even seen unfavorably by employees. Such perceptions would come to light through mechanisms of upward communication. Bottom-up communication also is essential to the success of many quality and productivity improvement programs. In general built-in opportunities for upward information flow provides one of the best ways to monitor the change process and detect needed modifications. Like top-down communication, bottom-up channels of communication have considerable symbolic value during times of change. Top management can make a powerful statement simply by providing employees the means to be heard during times of organizational change.

♦

Notes

1. Dance.
2. Farace and MacDonald; Muchinsky.
3. Lawrence and Lorsch.
4. Snyder and Morris.
5. Katz.
6. O'Reilly and Roberts.
7. Muchinsky.
8. Koepp.
9. Fisher.
10. Bedeian and Zammuto.
11. Sutton, Eisenhardt, and Jucker.
12. See, e.g., Brockner.
13. Fisher.
14. Rosen, Klein, and Young.
15. Schwartz; Quarrey, Blasi, and Rosen.
16. Rosen, Klein, and Young; Pierce, Rubenfeld, and Morgan.
17. Rosen, Klein, and Young.
18. Ibid.
19. Ibid.
20. Klein.
21. Rosen, Klein, and Young.
22. Ibid.
23. Rosen.
24. Rosen, Klein, and Young.
25. See, e.g., Labich.
26. U.S. General Accounting Office; Rosen, Klein, and Young.
27. Klein; Rosen, Klein, and Young; Pierce, Rubenfeld, and Morgan.
28. Klein; Klein and Hall; Rosen, Klein, and Young.
29. Klein; Rosen, Klein, and Young.
30. Ibid.
31. U.S. General Accounting Office.
32. U.S. General Accounting Office; Rosen and Quarrey.
33. Rosen and Quarrey.
34. Lawler.
35. Ibid.
36. Ibid.
37. Ibid.
38. Ibid.
39. Banas.
40. Ibid.
41. Ibid., p. 393.
42. Ibid.
43. Crosby; Deming; Juran.
44. Schneider, Guzzo, and Brief.
45. For a general explanation of these technologies, see Office of Technology Assessment (1984 and 1985).
46. See, e.g., Barley; Klein, Hall, and Laliberte.
47. See, e.g., Argote and Goodman; Majchrzak; Majchrzak and Klein; Manufacturing Studies Board; Rousseau.
48. See, e.g., Argote and Goodman; Beatty and Gordon; Schaffitzel and Kersten.
49. See, e.g., Klein, Ralls, and Carter.
50. See, e.g., Markus.
51. See, e.g., Argote and Goodman; Majchrzak; Majchrzak and Klein; Manufacturing Studies Board; Zuboff.

52. See, e.g., Beer; Kilmann and Covin; Nadler and Tushman; Tushman, Newman, and Nadler.
53. Adler and Helleloid; Beatty and Gordon; Leonard-Barton and Krauss.
54. See, e.g., Roitman, Liker, and Roskies.
55. Klein, Ralls, and Carter.
56. Ibid.
57. Leonard-Barton and Krauss; Leonard-Barton.
58. Klein, Carter, and Ralls.
59. Ibid.

◆

References

Adler, P.S., and D.A. Helleloid. 1987. "Effective Implementation of Integrated CAD/CAM: A Model." *IEEE Transactions on Engineering Management* 34: 101–107.

Argote, L., and P.S. Goodman. 1986. "The Organizational Implications of Robotics." In *Managing Technological Innovation*, eds. D.D. Davis and Associates. San Francisco: Jossey-Bass.

Banas, P.B. 1988. "Employee Involvement: A Sustained Labor/Management Intiative at Ford Motor Company." In *Productivity in Organizations*, eds. J.P. Campbell and R.J. Campbell. San Francisco: Jossey-Bass.

Barley, S.R. 1986. "Technology as an Occasion for Structuring: Evidence From Observations of CT Scanners and the Social Order of Radiology Departments." *Administrative Science Quarterly* 31: 78–108.

Beatty, C.A., and J.R.M. Gordon. 1988. "Barriers to the Implementation of CAD/CAM Systems." *Sloan Management Review*, (Summer): 25–33.

Bedeian, A.G., and R.F. Zammuto. 1991. *Organizations*. Chicago: Dryden Press.

Beer, M. 1988. "The Critical Path for Change: Keys to Success and Failure in Six Companies." In *Corporate Transformation*, eds. R.H. Kilmann and T.J. Covin. San Francisco: Jossey-Bass.

Brockner, J. 1988. *Self-Esteem at Work*. Lexington, MA: Lexington Books.

Crosby, P.B. 1984. *Quality Without Tears*. New York: New American Library.

Dance, F.E. 1970. "The 'Concept' of Communication." *Journal of Communication* 20: 201–210.

Deming, W.E. 1986. *Out of the Crisis*. Cambridge, MA: Massachusetts Institute of Technology.

Farace, R.V., and D. MacDonald. 1974. "New Directions in the Study of Organizational Communication." *Personnel Psychology* 27: 1–19.

Fisher, A.B. 1988. "The Downside of Downsizing." *Fortune*, May 23.

Juran, J.M. 1987. *On Quality Leadership*. Wilton, CT: Juran Institute. *Fortune*, 103–107.

Katz, R. 1982. "The Effects of Group Longevity on Project Communication and Performance." *Administrative Science Quarterly* 27: 81–104.

Kilmann, R.H., and T.J. Covin. 1988. "Introduction: Key Themes in Corporate Transformation." In *Corporate Transformation*, eds. R.H. Kilmann and T.J. Covin. San Francisco: Jossey-Bass.

Klein, K.J. 1987. "Employee Stock Ownership and Employee Attitudes: A Test of Three Models." *Journal of Applied Psychology Monograph* 72: 319–332.

Klein, K.J., P.O. Carter, and R.S. Ralls. 1989. *The Implementation of an MRP II System*. Unpublished technical report. University of Maryland, College Park.

Klein, K.J., and R.H. Hall. 1988. "Correlates of Employee Satisfaction with Stock Ownership: Who Likes an ESOP Most?" *Journal of Applied Psychology* 73: 630–638.

Klein, K.J., R.J. Hall, and M. Laliberte. 1990. "Training and the Organizational Consequences of Technological Change: A Case Study of Computer-aided Design and Drafting." In *Technology and End-User Training*, eds. M.E. Gattiker & L. Larwood. New York: Walter de Gruyter.

Klein, K.J., R.S. Ralls, and P.O. Carter. 1989. *The Implementation of A Computerized Inventory Control System*. Unpublished technical report. University of Maryland, College Park.

Koepp, S. 1987. "A Tire Maker Lags." *Time*, February 16.

Labich, K. 1983. "A Steel Town's Bid to Save Itself." *Fortune* (April 18): 103–107.

Lawler, E.E. 1990. *Strategic Pay*. San Francisco: Jossey-Bass.

Lawrence, P.R., and J.W. Lorsch. 1967. *Organization and Environment: Managing Integration and Differentiation*. Boston: Harvard University Graduate School of Business.

Leonard-Barton, D. 1988. "Implementation as Mutual Adaptation of Technology and Organization." *Research Policy* 17: 251–267.

Leonard-Barton, D., and W.A. Krauss. 1985. "Implementing New Technology." *Harvard Business Review* 63:(6): 102–110.

Majchrzak, A. 1988. *The Human Side of Factory Automation*. San Francisco: Jossey-Bass.

Majchrzak A., and K.J. Klein. 1987. "Things Are Always More Complicated than You Think: An Open Systems Approach to the Organizational Effects of Computer-automated Technology." *Journal of Business and Psychology* 2: 27–49.

Manufacturing Studies Board. 1986. *Human Resources Practices for Implementing Advanced Manufacturing Technology*. Washington, D.C.: National Academy Press.

Markus, M.L. 1987. "Power, Politics, and MIS Implementation." In *Readings in Human-Computer Interaction: A Multidisciplinary Approach*, eds. R.M. Baecker and W.A.S. Buxton. Los Altos, CA: Morgan Kaufmann.

HR Communication in Times of Change 6-165

Muchinsky, P.M. 1990. *Psychology Applied to Work* (3rd ed.). Pacific Grove, CA: Brooks/Cole.

Nadler, D.A., and M.L. Tushman. 1989. "Leadership for Organizational Change." In *Large-scale Organizational Change*, eds. A.M. Mohrman, Jr., S.A. Mohrman, G.E. Ledford, Jr., T.G. Cummings, and E.E. Lawler. San Francisco: Jossey-Bass.

O'Reilly, C.A., and K.H. Roberts. 1977. "Task Group Structure, Communication, and Effectiveness in Three Organizations." *Journal of Applied Psychology* 62: 674–681.

Office of Technology Assessment. 1984. *Computerized Manufacturing Automation: Employment, Education and the Workplace*. Washington, DC: U.S. Congress (OTA-CIT-235).

———. 1985. *Automation of America's Offices*. Washington, D.C.: U.S. Congress (OTA-CIT-287).

Pierce, J.L., S.A. Rubenfeld, and S. Morgan. 1991. "Employee Ownership: A Conceptual Model of Process and Effects." *Academy of Management Review* 16: 121–143.

Quarrey M., J. Blasi, and C. Rosen. 1986. *Taking Stock: Employee Ownership at Work*. Cambridge, MA: Ballinger.

Roitman, D.B., J.K. Liker, and E. Roskies. 1988. "Birthing a Factory of the Future: When Is "All at Once" Too Much?" In *Corporate Transformation*, eds. R.H. Kilmann and T.J. Covin. San Francisco: Jossey-Bass.

Rosen, C. 1991. Personal communication.

Rosen, C., K.J. Klein, and K.M. Young. 1986. *Employee Ownership in America*. Lexington, MA: Lexington Books.

Rosen C., and M. Quarrey. 1987. "How Well Is Employee Ownership Working?" *Harvard Business Review* 65(5): 126–128, 132.

Rousseau, D.M. 1989. "Managing the Change to an Automated Office: Lessons from Five Case Studies." *Office: Technology & People* 4: 31–52.

Schaffitzel, W., and U. Kersten. 1985. "Introducing CAD Systems: Problems and the Role of User-Developer Communication in Their Solution." *Behaviour and Information Technology* 4(1): 47–61.

Schneider, B., R.A. Guzzo, and A.P. Brief. In press. "Establishing a Climate for Productivity Improvement." In *Maynard's Industrial Engineering Handbook* (4th ed.), ed. W.K. Hodson. New York: McGraw-Hill.

Schwartz, J. 1989. "Giving Workers a Piece of the Action." *Newsweek* (April 17): 45.

Snyder, R.A., and J.H. Morris. 1984. "Organizational Communication and Performance." *Journal of Applied Psychology* 69: 461–465.

Sutton, R.I., K.M. Eisenhardt, and J.V. Jucker. 1986. "Managing Organizational Decline: Lessons from Atari." *Organization Dynamics* (Spring).

Tushman, M.L., W.H. Newman, and D.A. Nadler. 1989. "Executive Leadership and Organizational Evolution: Managing Incremental and Discontinous Change." In *Corporate Transformation*, eds. R.H. Kilmann and T.J. Covin. San Francisco: Jossey-Bass.

United States General Accounting Office. 1987. *Employee Stock Ownership Plans: Little Evidence of Effects on Corporate Performance*. Washington, DC: GAO.

Zuboff, S. 1988. *In the Age of the Smart Machine*. New York: Basic Books.

6.5
HR Information Systems

Nicholas J. Beutell
Alfred J. Walker

Computer-based human resource information systems have grown in importance over the past two decades to the point where most organizations find it difficult to survive without them. A human resource information system (HRIS) is any computer system used to collect, store, maintain, retrieve, and administer information required by an organization to manage its human resources.[1] The scope of an HRIS is as wide as the need for data on human resources. For most organizations, the functions of such systems extend from the first time information is needed about an employee—usually the recruiting function—to the last time information might be needed—usually the pension payment function. All the intervening personnel functions of staffing, training and development, compensation, benefits, relocation, and work-force planning can be and usually are included within the scope of an HRIS.

The computer has already exerted a major influence on the HR function. This impact has occurred primarily through using internal organizational data to respond to internal needs (such as user requests for information) and external (such as environmental demands and government regulations). As the strategic aspects of HR information are more fully recognized and exploited, the next generation of systems will be much more proactive and place much more emphasis on the external environment. Human resources will be a key player in the strategic planning process in the information-based organization of the future.[2]

This chapter explores the development of HRISs from the 1970s to the present, selection and implementation of an HRIS, concepts behind HRIS, data management and the human resource information center (HRIC), and HRIS applications and modules. It focuses on the ways in which these systems have aided organizations to more effectively handle the acquisition, deployment, and compensation of their human resources. It concludes by presenting some of the factors associated with a successful HRIS.

HRIS Growth From the 1970s to the Present

Most large organizations had implemented or had begun to implement systems projects in the personnel area in the 1970s. Through the use of systems projects, the importance of employee selection and training on the bottom line became apparent, and the personnel department began to grow in number and influence. Management began to ask more questions about employees—their location, work activities, and level of compensation—and information systems offered the means to keep track of these employees.

By the mid-1970s, advances in computer technology (both hardware and software) and reductions in implementation costs made installing systems to handle HR data a top priority for most companies. Software vendors who specialized in personnel systems, with or without payroll, emerged and these systems became best-selling applications. Highly sophisticated mainframe systems, often nationwide in scope, also developed and became available to users through telephone networks. Local terminals in individual plants or in decentralized divisions could be used to input or extract data on employees. Files and programs, as well as applications, were usually centrally developed and maintained, and all users shared the same programs.

Data Base Management

Further breakthroughs in technology in the late 1970s and early 1980s gave additional impetus to the HRIS field. New and powerful software that enabled systems to secure, store, and retrieve information faster became available. These systems, known as data managers or data-base management systems, caused most companies to rethink their systems architecture. With these new systems, data did not have to be kept in each user's file but could be shared and linked as needed by a variety of program applications. Thus, an HR manager interested in performing a base salary study could use a compensation program to access a central data base available to any user linked to the system. Users gained flexibility without having to take responsibility for all the activities associated with a major system project.

Data base management systems also permitted local data bases to be established as a part of the overall set of files. This capability enabled satellite divisions or locations to implement programs which could operate as independent applications, or which when connected, would also represent the entire corporation. From these systems, data base networks developed to fit the needs of many larger companies as they formed divisions or subunits. A large multi-divisional company such as General Motors could allow each division to use the same software and data base to perform all the functions required at the local level, and when corporate-wide statistics and/or studies were needed, the same programs and data bases could be used to yield a corporate overview.

While these systems facilitated the work of HR departments, they also brought to light the need for a data administration function to handle the complexities involved in implementing and maintaining such a network of users. New positions (for example, HR data administrator[3]) and new functions (such as human resource information center—HRIC) arose to handle the growing demands of the HRIS. The HRIC function will be described in more detail in a subsequent section.

The other advance which would completely transform the entire computer industry, and the HRIS world along with it, resulted from the introduction of personal computers (PCs).

Introduction of PCs

Personal computing permitted users to build entire computer applications outside the framework of the data processing organization.[4] Users were finally free to collect, store, retrieve, and analyze information in whatever format they desired on their own timetable. Users were no longer subject to the long waiting periods and high costs of their data processing departments. PCs freed HR users from the bureaucracy and red tape of project request forms and authorizations. As a result, projects which would have taken months or years to finish now could be completed in days or weeks for a fraction of the cost.

Users in most companies became familiar with PC software and began to develop applications on their own. The first software applications for most users were Visicalc or, later, Lotus 1-2-3 models for compensation work. Other uses, such as for budgeting headcount, also became very popular.

The development of communications programs allowed PC users to link up with the HRIS mainframe to access data and move it into the PC for further analysis. For some users, PCs also function as input (or "dumb") terminals, which could be used to update central files.

When permitted by the systems architecture, users could even access the mainframe from remote locations. This capability created a new type of decentralized network, which allowed users not only to have local data bases but to retrieve data from the mainframe and integrate it, if needed, with other data stored on the PC. In this way, HRIS data could be mixed and matched with user software, permitting a wide variety of new applications—such as relocation models, succession planning programs, and pension calculation routines—at vastly reduced costs.

Local area networks were introduced on a wide scale in the mid-1980s.[5] These networks allowed PCs to be linked without a mainframe or minicomputer serving as the host computer. At the same time, software programs for graphics and text-editing were merged into a new series of products called desktop publishing. These new systems shortened the time needed to generate and print written documents and permitted easier (and more aesthetic) integration of HRIS data and other information into a finished report. Although local area networks have tremendous potential, they have not proven that successful for HR work to date because of the complexity of the technology and the nature of HRIS data.

Future Developments

New technology will continue to develop at a steadfast pace. By the year 2000, PCs are expected to be as powerful as today's mainframes.[6] Computer storage capacity will increase dramatically and will be measured in gigabytes (billion words) and terabytes (trillion words) rather than the familiar megabytes (million words).[7] Advances in data base management systems will make HRISs easier to maintain. Systems development also is becoming easier because of software enhancements, screen painting, and data dictionaries. New retrieval programs will allow users to extract and analyze data more quickly and easily. Expert systems[8] and artificial intelligence will enable users to make better decisions and to use HRIS information in more sophisticated ways.[9] Finally, developments in international telecommunications networks (including integrated services digital networks) will facilitate sharing and transporting data on a global basis.[10]

Components of an HRIS

An HRIS consists of hardware, software, data, procedures, and users.[11] Each of these elements is described more fully below.

Hardware

Hardware includes input devices, such as keyboards or scanners; a central processing unit (CPU); communications devices, such as modems; storage devices, such as diskettes; hard-disk drives or tapes; and output devices, such as printers and plotters. Taken together, this equipment performs the input, storage, manipulation, and output of information.

The CPU is the brain of the computer.[12] It is the tool that executes program instructions so that data can be read, stored, written, or otherwise processed. CPUs are grouped into three classes: PCs, minicomputers, and mainframe computers.[13]

PCs, also called "microcomputers" and "desktop computers," are the smallest and least expensive category of computer. They are generally used by one person at a time, although local area networks allow one PC to function as a file server for many users. PCs are typically used to run spreadsheets, word processors, data-base management packages, and HR applications software. PCs are useful for small companies and for "downloading" data from mainframe computers,[14] although the technical barriers for supporting a very large HRIS have not been solved.[15] *Minicomputers* are larger than PCs and generally support multiple users. However, PCs have become so powerful that the distinction between minicomputers and PCs is not very obvious. *Mainframe* computers are the largest and most expensive type of computer. They are multiple-user systems that can support hundreds of cathode ray terminals (CRTs) while simultaneously processing additional work. Until recently, mainframes were generally required to operate a comprehensive HRIS in a large company; many large companies still use a mainframe-based HRIS.

Software

Software is a set of programs that make the computer work. Hardware is the tool; software is the logic for using the tool. An HR computer system needs two types of software: systems software and applications software. Systems software, also called the operating system, serves as both a "housekeeper" and a "traffic cop."[16] Applications software uses the computer and its systems software to solve HR problems. Applications software requires an understanding of personnel problems, not computers. Table 1 shows a listing of HR applications software.

Data

The next component of an HRIS is data. Data are necessary to solve HR problems. Examples of personnel data might include employee name, social security number, date of hire, salary, performance rating, job skills, and education level. Data are input through a keyboard or other input device, processed, and output in the form of personnel reports, statistics, and graphs. Data and data base concepts are critical aspects of an HRIS and will be discussed in more detail below.

Procedures and Personnel

The final two components of an HRIS are procedures and trained personnel. Procedures are instructions for using the system. Procedures tell users what to do if they encounter an error or if the system "crashes." A critical aspect of procedures is complete documentation on the system. Trained personnel include data entry specialists, HR users, and clientele. Data entry personnel input data according to standard procedures. HR users interact with the computer and utilize information to do their jobs. Finally, the clients are the people who benefit from the computerized system. HR specialists, line managers, and top management are typical clients of an HRIS.

Selecting and Implementing an HRIS

Conversion from a manual HR system to a computerized system, or upgrading an existing HRIS, is a significant undertaking that

Table 1

HR Applications Software

- Affirmative action/equal employment opportunity
- Applicant tracking
- Attitude surveys
- Benefits management
- Career planning and assessment
- Employee history and records
- Human resource planning and forecasting
- Job analysis
- Job evaluation
- Labor relations
- Payroll
- Pension administration
- Productivity/work measurement
- Project and event scheduling
- Safety and health
- Salary planning and administration
- Succession planning
- Tuition refund
- Turnover analysis

Source: Reprinted with permission from N.J. Beutell, "Computers and the Management of Human Resources," in *Readings in Personnel and Human Resource Management* 3d ed. R.S. Schuler, S.A. Youngblood, and V.L. Huber (eds.) St. Paul, MN: West, 1988.

requires careful planning.[17] As with other organizational interventions, a decision to computerize involves obtaining valid information about the effects of computerization, allowing free and informed choices on the part of all employees affected by the intervention, and generating internal commitment to those choices.[18] Although top management support is essential, the HR department should take responsibility for the computerization effort. Stated differently, the personnel department—not data processing—should accept ownership of the process.[19]

Development Steps

Justifying an HRIS is the first major step in successful implementation. This step entails a feasibility analysis that evaluates the present system and shows the projected benefits of the new computerized system.[20] A number of questions should be answered: What problems will the automated system solve or reduce? How much will the system (hardware, software, labor) cost? What benefits will accrue from the system? What level of computer expertise exists in the personnel department? Properly analyzing these questions will help to ensure that the computerization effort is properly focused.[21] Such an analysis will also make it easier to secure necessary management commitment to the project.

Needs Analysis

Once the feasibility of the project is determined, the HR department should create a project team to perform a needs analysis and to develop formal recommendations for implementing the project. The team should be headed by a personnel representative and include members from the payroll and data processing departments, among others. The rewards for team participation include (1) a more thorough knowledge of personnel operations; (2) additional knowledge of computers; and (3) the opportunity to participate in an important project.[22] In addition, the personnel representative chairing the team has a unique power position—this person will be perceived as the "expert" in computers.

The project team plays a critically important role since it will develop an overall strategy or blueprint for the intervention. A major aspect of this mission is to perform a needs analysis. The needs analysis should result in a detailed statement that specifies what the computerized system will accomplish.[23] It must address technical aspects of the system: What are the software requirements? Does the software include all of the "must have" modules? What type of hardware will satisfy present as well as anticipated future needs? How much will the system cost? How long will it take to install the system? Is there a backup plan if the system should become inoperative? Can the system generate all of the required reports? What impact will the system have on other departments?

Software Options

The project team should also determine what software options are consistent with the needs analysis. Three basic choices are available when deciding to develop or to enhance an existing HRIS: to design and build it in-house; to purchase a system from a vendor; or to utilize some combination of in-house and vendor systems.

In-House Development

This option relies on internal talent to design and develop the HRIS. The length of time it takes to develop a system internally (often several years) and the quality and depth of resources available for the task are obviously key concerns. These projects can be quite large and highly specialized; a lack of knowledge about such systems is often a drawback. In addition, unless senior management makes the project a top priority, the ability to keep a development team together long enough to finish the project will become an issue. On the other hand, building a customized system normally yields a higher degree of user and company satisfaction than purchased systems. Users receive better training in the system's design and operational characteristics, and the organization also gains a built-in maintenance team.

Vendor Systems

Vendor-supplied systems are an attractive development option since the system is available for purchase immediately. In addition, the vendor would have a track record of similar installations. Vendor software normally costs no more than internally developed systems and may offer features that an internal team has not heard of or would have to develop for the first time.

Larger HRIS vendors have hundreds of installed systems and offer annual maintenance agreements to keep their systems abreast of changes in tax laws, pension and EEO legislation, and the like. Most vendors offer a basic HRIS package that can be augmented with modules to perform various specialized functions. The modular approach is advantageous since it reduces start-up time by concentrating on the most immediate functions while allowing for additional expansion in the future. Figure 1 depicts a modular approach to software implementation.

Although attractive on the surface, highly complex internal HR and/or data processing operations have historically had problems with packaged solutions. Typically, vendor systems have to be modified to fit into the user's environment,[24] and this customizing of the vendor product is at the heart of most vendor evaluation exercises.

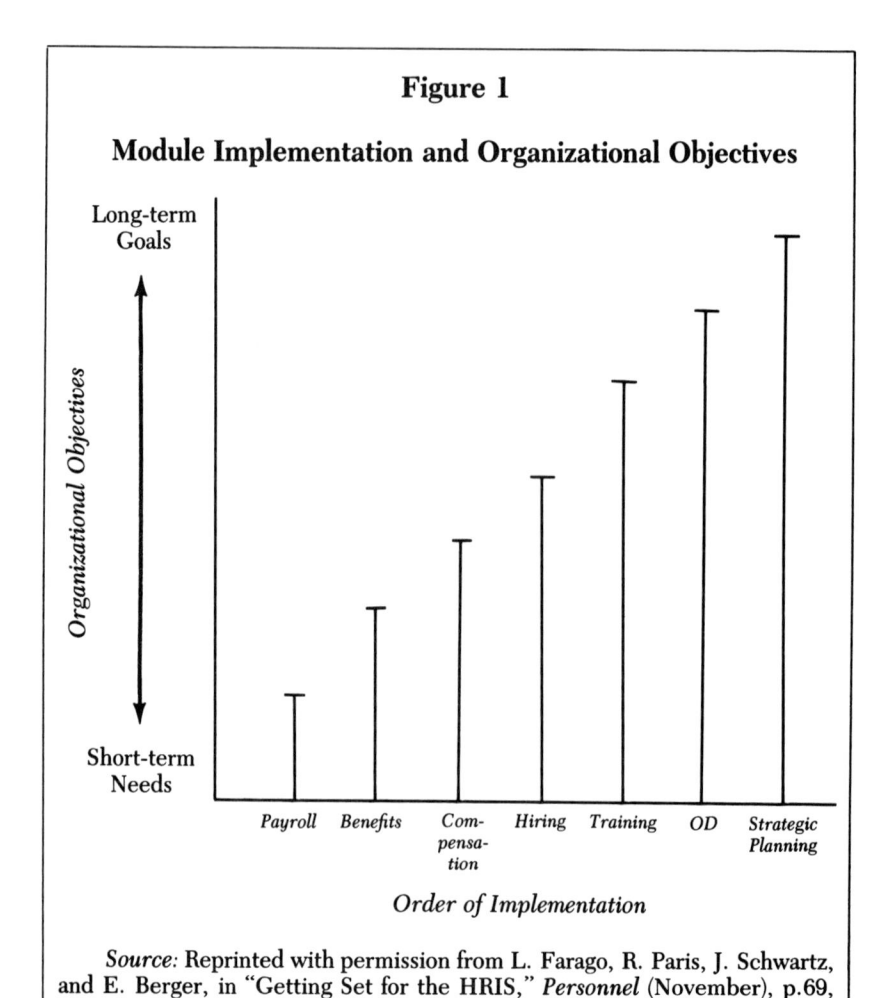

Figure 1

Module Implementation and Organizational Objectives

Organizational Objectives (Short-term Needs ↔ Long-term Goals)

Order of Implementation: Payroll, Benefits, Compensation, Hiring, Training, OD, Strategic Planning

Source: Reprinted with permission from L. Farago, R. Paris, J. Schwartz, and E. Berger, in "Getting Set for the HRIS," *Personnel* (November), p.69, 1988.

Hybrid Approach

A possible solution to the HRIS development dilemma of long in-house development cycles and inadequate off-the-shelf systems is to adopt a joint development approach. Under this scenario, the project team would choose to develop those areas in which it feels most qualified and relegate the rest to a vendor. For example, an organization could maintain a very complex, internally developed staffing program or budget/salary program but purchase a vendor's payroll module. In this way, internal resources are allocated to those company-specific items which would have required a sizable amount of customization anyway. The more straightforward, standard options can be purchased. Integration of the programs may pose problems since as the design may produce a nonuniform data base management environment.

Software Selection and Implementation

The relative pros and cons of each approach must be weighed and outlined during the development evaluation process. Users can easily get presold on a given approach and therefore may not fairly evaluate one or more of the alternatives. Table 2 shows the relative complexity, cost, and "fit" of vendor, hybrid, and in-house approaches. Under the hybrid approach, a middle ground may be reached.

Soliciting requests for proposals is an excellent way to identify appropriate software. Although the HR software is not the system, inappropriate or poor quality software can have disastrous consequences. Formal proposals can help clarify the merits of software offerings under each approach; however, it does favor vendor and hybrid approaches. A request for proposals helps to determine which vendors offer the software best suited to the company's requirements. The request should include the following information to assist vendors in developing proposals:[25]

- *Introduction.* This section should provide descriptive information about the company.

- *Functional requirements.* The request should specify how and where the system performs its functions and on what equipment.

Table 2

Relative Complexity/Cost and Fit for Three HRIS Approaches[1]

	Complexity/Cost	Degree of "Fit"
Vendor (unmodified)	1	60%
Hybrid	2X	70%
In-house	4X	95%

[1]The unmodified vendor system serves as a baseline for the costs of the other approaches.

- *Technical criteria.* Relevant information includes file structures, program design and modification, hardware, software, telecommunications, security, and controls.

- *Vendor information.* The organization should determine how long the vendor has been in business, how many systems the vendor has installed, and so on.

- *Costs, maintenance, and support.* Proposals should supply specifics on direct and indirect costs of the software purchase, including support and service contracts.

The proposals can help narrow the list of vendors down to serious contenders. Once a vendor is chosen, the organization should draw up a contract detailing payment and installation deadlines. Once the system is installed and the staff is trained to use it, the final step is to audit system outputs against pre-installation data to assure accuracy.

Staff Resistance

The above discussion presents a somewhat idealized analysis of the development and implementation process. Besides evaluating hardware and software issues, the development phase should address staff resistance to computerization. Not all employees are ready for the "computer age," and the success of an HRIS depends on the people who use the system.

Employees' reactions to new technology range from mild anxiety to full-blown phobias.[26] Fear of computers, or cyberphobia, is

Table 3

Employee Concerns and Fears Regarding Computers

- Little personal knowledge about computers and worry that they will not be able to learn how to use them
- Having to abandon familiar activities and acquired expertise to take on new duties as a virtual novice
- Concern over computer-induced health hazards or physical ailments
- Worry that they will be tied to a computer all day, isolated, paced by it, and monitored for productivity
- Fear that they can damage the machine or destroy all its contents by entering improper commands
- A perception that they will have to be more rigid, with less opportunity to be creative and use different approaches to issues
- Human fear of change and the unknown
- Apprehension that they could lose their jobs
- Not being consulted during the planning for the computer acquisition and implementation
- A perception of less personal importance to the department
- Previous disappointing experiences with computers with residual skepticism as to their value
- Frustration because they must continue to do their normal duties and also learn to use the computer (a feeling of overload)
- A general uneasiness about computers and their potential misuse

Source: Reprinted with permission from G.J. Meyer, "Automating Personnel Operations" in *Business and Legal Reports*, Madison, CT, 1984.

an increasingly important problem for employees in an information-based economy. Employees at all levels, from clerical employees to professionals and executives, have shown evidence of computer anxiety. Some employees may fear that they will be displaced by computers; others worry about breaking the computer, losing control over work output, changing the routine or usual way of doing things, and looking stupid.[27] Table 3 lists some employees' fears regarding computers. In order to minimize these fears, employees at all levels of the personnel department should be involved in the project. Showing employees the benefits of the computerized system and making it clear the intent is not to displace staff should make the process less difficult.

HRIS Data Base Concepts

The essential ingredient in an HRIS is the data. This information is captured and stored in a logical fashion on the HRIS data base. Data are used to produce a display, report, or analysis on one or more data subjects, or they can be transferred to another program for further analysis. The data base contains all of the information that is relevant, lawful, and needed by an organization to support its goals and mission. This information could concern employees, former employees, organizational structure, positions, locations, plans and programs, or almost any other aspect of the HR function.

A major task during the design and development stages of an HRIS project is to determine the size and extent of the data base. This analysis should identify both overall needs (that is, which populations and groups of data are necessary to have in the system) and specific requirements (that is, the attributes needed for each of the various population types).[28] Other issues to settle include data retention, access, and functional usage.

Data Update and Entry

The data base should have a set method for entering, calculating, and changing every item contained in the system. Data-entry requirements should identify the proper source of particular data. Since information can emanate from more than one user, the standard procedure is to assign an item "owner" to each piece of input. This person or group becomes responsible for inputting and editing data and for defining an item's meaning, code structure, and ultimate usage. Other requirements should specify the input vehicle (such as through a company form or record, voice, or screen) and the proper edits and controls for each item.

Data update is one of the most complex areas as it often results in debates about organizational roles and responsibilities. For example, in a multi-divisional, highly decentralized company, how does an employee's salary get entered into the HRIS? Should the line manager input it directly, or should the local personnel depart-

HR Information Systems   6-181

ment? Should the authorizing document be sent to corporate? With today's technology, does an authorizing document have to be on file, or can the change be made without a signature?

Certain items may not always need a direct external input mechanism, but a method should be developed to update these items. The procedure must spell out the required frequency of updates, the triggering events, and the result of the calculation which will take place as one of the items is changed.

Changes in the data base could also occur as associated items in tables or other such internal look-ups and conversions are changed. For instance, if a table with salary ranges is updated, the system software may automatically revise an employee's salary range and comp-ratio. In a similar fashion, a program could automatically calculate vesting in a pension plan once an employee attains five years of service with the firm.

The most typical method of entering or changing data elements is via screen entry. A user would access the appropriate screen and input the necessary changes. If the revisions are accepted (that is, no editing rules are violated), then the changes replace old information, which is retained in a backup file.

Data Access, Retrieval, and Analysis

The primary reason for installing an HRIS is that it allows quick and easy access to data—whether a record or a group of records—contained in the system, and it allows users to perform a function regarding the record(s). Therefore, information access and retrieval is one of the most critical areas of the HRIS.

Single-Subject Retrieval

Finding all the pertinent data about a single subject—be it an employee, applicant, training program, or benefit claim—is usually the simplest form of data access. A user typically would inquire about the status of the subject via a computer terminal, and visually scan the data. The user should then be able to answer most questions that might arise, such as: Where does an employee work? What happened to the claim I submitted? When is a course offered, and where is it taught? What is the status of an application for employment?

Data Analysis

Data for more complex questions or for detailed administrative functions normally is generated for reports or analyses. Information in these reports can range from data needed to audit the system itself, to statistics required for government reports, to calculations needed to produce the payroll for thousands of employees. To generate such reports, the HRIS must contain sufficient information regarding hours worked, work locations, job functions, wages and salaries, and similar details. It also must have the capacity to retain the information that was generated. Accomplishing this task involves highly complex historical recordkeeping and processing.

Sophisticated ad-hoc retrieval programs enable users to either browse through the data base or construct queries to satisfy management requests. Knowledgeable and authorized users can almost instantaneously find data that meet specific criteria. For example, a user may wish to identify all employees who have received a compensation increase greater than 10 percent, or the number of expatriates currently assigned to Singapore, or how many employees signed up for the Kaiser-Permanente HMO plan in Phoenix, AZ. The access and retrieval capability of the HRIS therefore must allow users both to look up individual data subjects and to perform complex processing of grouped data, such as payroll runs.

Modeling Programs

An organization also may need a system that can handle more advanced queries involving "what if" calculations. "What if" scenarios allow a user to solve one or more problems involving a combination of data elements, all of which can be varied to generate a vast number of possible outcomes. These programs present a screen display from which users can select an option to model. The HRIS then computes the effect of the change or set of events and presents the results to the user. Data are accessed but not actually changed. Examples of this type of "what if" modeling might include computing the effect of a 6 percent increase in pay for a certain group of employees, or the effect of a 50 percent premium decrease in health insurance. The HRIS could compute the results of these changes based on either the current population or a combination of current demographics and future projections of the population two or three years from present.

Artificial Intelligence

Another form of access and retrieval involves a series of pre-programmed references to answer often-asked questions or perform other routine administrative tasks and policy interpretations. These questions usually are repetitive in nature and can be answered with access to the employee data base. These systems fit into the emerging category of "artificial intelligence" or "expert" systems. Functions of these early forms of expert systems may include tracking annual sign-ups for the flexible benefits program, answering questions regarding access to 401(k) balances for loans, and determining the acceptable number of vacation days to carry over from one year to another.

Data Administration: The Human Resource Information Center (HRIC)

Because of the complexity of the technical environment and the need to control the data base, an organization often will need to set up and oversee data collection, maintenance, and use. The management of an HRIC includes several functions: 1) ensuring accurate, consistent, and timely HRIS information; 2) coordinating the HRIS operation, update cycles, processing flows, and interface with other systems and users; 3) ensuring security and privacy of files maintained in the HRIS; 4) planning for future information needs; and 5) supporting and training the system's users.

Ensuring Accuracy, Consistency, and Timeliness

Keeping data accurate, consistent, and timely involves establishing standards for the items of information, determining needed accuracy levels, and measuring the quality of the information contained in the HRIS.

The accuracy of information in the data base can be achieved through a good systems design and procedures to ensure user understanding and commitment. Editing and filtering incorrect information will catch only some errors. Having data input by those closest to the source and knowing where the data expertise lies will help, as will a desire on the part of users to keep the data base accurate. Redesigning input forms, having clearly understood instructions, building in "help" commands, and interrelating some edit checks also facilitate accurate input and upkeep of information.

Achieving consistency in data reporting and usage depends on several factors. First, the definition and meaning of the information must remain constant over time. For example, when inputting information on "marketing representatives," or "clerical workers," the definitions and coding of the job titles and/or functions must not change over time. This requirement is often difficult to achieve in a geographically decentralized organization or where turnover has occurred among reporters of data. Second, the retrieval tools used to access the data must be applied consistently. For example, including secretaries in a clerical grouping for one analysis but excluding them from a subsequent analysis would yield inconsistent results. Data analyses also should use the same base populations (such as the same departments or subsidiaries). Lastly, analyses should have similar reporting cycles and time periods. Inconsistencies will result if, for example, a report for the month of April covers a four-week time span one year but five weeks the next year. The calendar should be preset and days or weeks should be handled in a standard manner, whenever possible.

To ensure timeliness, HRIS programs should be set up to capture information as soon as the data have been approved. The programs should allow the HRIS to store or "pend" certain data until the effective date or processing cycle becomes current. This method is the most expedient way to handle data and should be used whenever possible. Data held at the user level until needed could be forgotten, or the person responsible for entering the data may be out sick or on leave when information should be input. As an example of timeliness, a salary increase, approved in advance, can be entered into the HRIS as a pending file. Prior to the payroll processor run, the system accesses this file, and if the effective date matches the date of the next payroll run, the HRIS makes the change and automatically updates the data base. The result is a more timely and efficient operation.

Timeliness also depends on the accessibility of the reports and retrieval mechanisms. Making the system available to the ultimate end user helps in this regard. Line managers, personnel users, or others in the field will find it easier to input changes directly on data in the system, rather than request such information, wait for it to be delivered, and then make corrections to it. Extending the scope and reach of the system to include everyone responsible for the data helps increase timeliness as well as accuracy.

Coordinating Operations

Handling the day-to-day operation of an HRIS entails making sure the system remains functional, has the proper level of technical and user support, keeps current with the calendar, and interfaces with the proper external data sources and files.

A major portion of the operations function involves ensuring that the data base is accurate and that the proper inputs and changes have been posted. In organizations with highly decentralized business units and perhaps a global network, ascertaining whether the current data base is fully up to date can prove extremely difficult.

Scheduling is another critical component of operations. The timing of major processing runs, such as end-of-month auditing reports, quarterly runs, payrolls, insurance premium bills, and budget reports, requires coordination to maintain efficiency.

The operations function also handles the task of receiving information from and/or supplying data to other systems with data. In large companies, the operations function can easily have more than 100 interfaced systems to plan and schedule on an ongoing basis. These systems and files can be internal or external. Examples of internal systems are the general ledger systems, labor distribution, budgeting systems, training, and pension systems. External systems include banks, third-party administrators, insurance companies, and actuaries.

Ensuring Security and Privacy

Since an HRIS maintains identifiable data regarding individual employees, as well as other sensitive organizational information, properly safeguarding the information is imperative. A number of different privacy and security issues must be addressed in the establishment and operation of an HRIS.

Security Safeguards

First, an HRIS must prevent access to unauthorized users both inside and outside the organization.[29] Access granted to individual users should be limited in terms of scope, time, and functions; that is, not all records in the system need to be accessible to all users. For instance, users in subsidiary "A" probably should have access only to records for individuals in subsidiary "A," and denied access to records in subsidiaries "B" and "C."

The time element can be used to further security goals. A good policy is to limit access to current employees or current payroll records, unless specific privileges have been granted that include access to all historical records.

Finally, an organization should limit information access according to function. Recruiters, for example, should be restricted to the applicant component of the HRIS, while payroll staffers should not typically have access to succession planning information. User access can be further limited to "read data" only or "read and write" (change) data.

The HRIS should have proper backup and recovery procedures to protect against data base loss or computer failure in the event of power interruptions or disasters. Copies of master files and all data base programs should be made periodically (for example, monthly for small systems, quarterly for very large systems,) and stored off-site. These precautions should extend to user-developed programs, which have been proliferating with the use of PCs. Documentation for user-developed programs or applications should be dated and stored with the backup.

Access to internal files and programs by external users should be very carefully restricted and monitored. Dial-up access to data bases should have stringent controls and undergo regular reviews. Passwords should change periodically (such as monthly or whenever a group experiences turnover) and limits to files should be very narrowly defined. Contractors and other temporary employees should be placed under the same restrictions as employees, but they should not be given any exemptions in handling data. Use of data by noncompany employees should generally be denied to everyone other than plan administrators.

Privacy Protections

Privacy concerns center primarily around use of and access to information. First, employers should collect only information which serves valid business or legal purposes. Any proposal to collect sensitive information should receive careful scrutiny, and if collected, the information should not be used for purposes other than the original intent. For instance, medical background or benefits claims data is valid information to collect and process via the HRIS but access to files should be limited to only benefit and medical plan participants and their agents, such as the insurance carrier and benefits consultants. Such information should not normally be "mixed and matched" or supplied to other users.

Other aspects of privacy regulate the access that individuals have to view their own files and to require changes if any data are incorrected or disputed. Many states and federal agencies require employers to grant such rights of review to workers. Therefore, an HRIS must print or be able to print a profile or data background sheet on the individuals in the data base.

Supporting and Training HRIS Users

Working with employees to define new or user group needs, to specify and alter design screens and reports, and to teach them how to use the HRIS are all aspects of the data administration function.[30]

One major activity in meeting the changing needs of HRIS users is to develop "front-end" awareness capability. This task starts with selecting the data elements to be included in the HRIS. The next step is to develop the technical specifications, documentation, and training for each data element by identifying its characteristics, determining the data source and edits, and defining the use of the data.[31] Combining this information with the processing components yields the system specifications and a final support program for users. Training programs in data usage can then be developed or updated with these new elements included. More traditional training programs on retrieving data, maintaining data quality, interpreting legal requirements, handling interactive sessions, and using PCs also can prove useful.

Other support activities can assist users in such matters as detailed analyses of problems, preparation of data, support for litigation, issuance of annual filings, training of new employees, responses to senior management requests, and consultations about possible mergers and acquisitions. In short, an HRIC should be prepared to support users on a wide variety of practical issues.

Planning for Future Needs

An HRIS is a system that will continually expand in scope, undergo alterations and refinements, and require modification in the edits, screens, data base, and reports. An organization should plan for such alterations because the number and complexity of changes can increase dramatically. Organizations with large systems have learned to limit the number of changes over the course of a year and to schedule the release of new modules so that users may plan for and more easily accommodate the changes. Revisions often will influence reports, interfaces with other systems, the data base, and screen design—in short, all of the components of an HRIS. Documentation and training usually need to be revised whenever any major change occurs.[32]

Planning for changes to all aspects of the HRIS from the very start makes good sense. Changes in the system can result from new legal requirements, plan changes, organizational changes, and technological advancements. Coding techniques, open screen design, as well as advanced data base management systems and other flexible approaches to design and development, will help to lessen the negative impact of change.

New Roles for an HRIC

A strategic approach will cause a shift from the current *data-oriented* HRIC activities toward *information management* responsibilities (see Figure 2).[33] Information management involves working with collections of data elements to meet the needs of the system's users. Information management enhances the contribution of HRICs to strategic planning. As a result, the HRIS will gain new users, and the HRIC will need to increase the time spent on training and documentation, as well as increase its presence as an internal consultant to clients.[34] Taken together, these factors reflect the "customerization" of the HRIC function.[35]

Despite shifting responsibilities, organizations will still need a centralized HRIC function.[36] As one analysis of new HRIC roles points out[37]:

> We are seeing a move toward powerful, integrated payroll and human resources systems that are built and maintained centrally but administered by local business units. That means that companies are moving beyond distributed processing to distributed control: local screens, local table structures, etc. The HRIC, however, is still the link between the system and its users. In fact, this linkage function becomes more significant as our user base broadens. What the HRIC manager must understand in order to succeed is that, more and more, our users are a cross-section of corporate managers and top executives, who need data on the demographics and costs related to employees and potential employees in order to make sound business decisions. No longer are our users just HR functional executives.

HR Information Systems 6-189

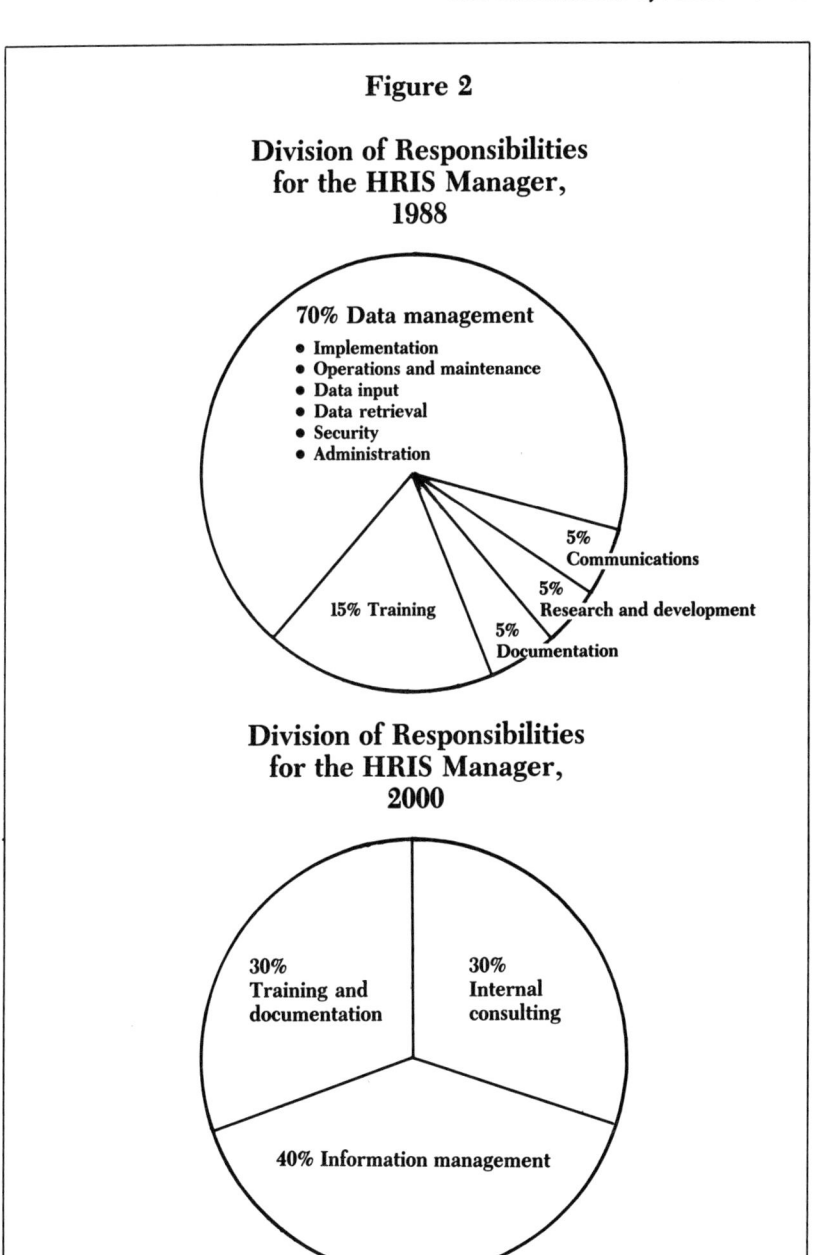

Figure 2

Division of Responsibilities
for the HRIS Manager,
1988

- 70% Data management
  - Implementation
  - Operations and maintenance
  - Data input
  - Data retrieval
  - Security
  - Administration
- 15% Training
- 5% Communications
- 5% Research and development
- 5% Documentation

Division of Responsibilities
for the HRIS Manager,
2000

- 30% Training and documentation
- 30% Internal consulting
- 40% Information management

Source: Reprinted with permission from M.S. Miller and A.S. Heller, "Attention HRIS Professionals!", Personnel (December), p.21, 1988.

HRIS Applications and Modules

From a user's perspective, an HRIS is simply one or more components that assist with or are tailored to a series of special applications. Users in the employment function may desire the system to help with as many of the selection activities as possible, but they will care little about the system's ability to produce a payroll or compute a pension. The functionality of an HRIS always depends on the user's needs. The module(s) should help users to generate calculations or reports that help in the administration of one or more functional areas. This section describes some of the major HRIS modules.

Applicant Tracking and Recruiting

An applicant tracking and recruiting module maintains needed information and produces reports and displays regarding open jobs and candidates for those jobs. This HRIS module tracks applicants and their resumes, prepares logs and EEO statistics on candidates and job offers, and produces interview and recruiter schedules. Information can be stored on departmental visits, pre-employment exams and physicals and open requisition status.

Based on the information stored, the module can match candidates on file to the prerequisites for open jobs and send lists of potentially qualified applicants to the vacancy manager. The program also can generate lists of applicants by source, thereby tracking schools, employment agencies, and executive recruiting referrals. By comparing dates internally, the HRIS can compute the length of time jobs remain vacant, and compute visit-to-offer and offer-to-acceptance ratios (that is, yield ratios).

Staffing

A staffing module permits an efficient and complete method of listing available positions and it allows an impartial consideration of eligible employees to be made across all (or a set of) business units and locations.

The staffing process typically begins with authorization for a new position or notice of a vacancy in a current position. In either case, a requisition is created containing job specifications. These specifications describe the duties, title, department, salary level

HR Information Systems   6-191

and range, location, supervisor, and other pertinent facts about the job. These data, along with the more subjective qualifications which job candidates should possess, are stored in the HRIS and used to evaluate candidates.

Inclusion of subjective data differentiates good from bad staffing modules, but most HRIS managers have difficulty quantifying subjective job qualifications because of the vagueness of such criteria. For example, a requisition might indicate that a successful candidate should have five years of marketing experience in the particular consumer product area, work well in a fast-changing business environment, and have the ability to get along with people at all levels in the organization. Quantifying such requirements requires an HRIS module that incorporates competency test scores, ratings on skills inventories, and/or evaluations by the staffing group and line managers. Skills systems, in particular, have been used successfully in highly technical areas where engineering, medical, data processing, and similar needs exist.

The selection process must be evaluated in light of equal employment laws and other criteria to ensure fairness. Like other personnel processes, storage of selection data usually does not violate any law; rather, the difficulty may arise in using the data. To ensure against discrimination in selection decisions based on race, sex, age or any other variable, the HRIS should have built-in statistics or audits to alert management of a potential problem.

Like recruitment modules, staffing programs can generate listings of potential candidates for the requesting manager to review. The manager can then select likely candidates from the list for interviews or further screening.

Since an HRIS contains historical data on employee movement, career-pathing data can be analyzed to show employee flows and job progression.[38] Transition matrices can then be generated. Such data are very useful for hiring forecasts, recruiting, employee development, and counseling. Some organizations have given employees' access to such historical data, as well as to mechanized job briefs, so that they can make more intelligent and realistic career choices.

Employee Statistics

An employee statistics module maintains basic information on employees. Data on hires, terminations, and transfers are stored within the HRIS and are available for reporting. The module also records movement between employee categories and groups, thereby supplying the basis for budget information, head-count tracking, benefits, and compensation reporting. Employee data can be reported by location, job type, part-time and full-time status, race, sex, and other demographic characteristics. The employee statistics module serves for the entire HRIS, thereby alleviating each component from having to collect, maintain, and produce similar data.

The EEO-1 report, head-count reports, employee profiles, and turn-around documents would be produced by this module. Inherent functions include basic audit reports, transactions accepted or rejected, as well as the computation and retention of employee history. Maintaining turnover analyses, telephone and location codes, data for employment verification, and personnel records activities are other typical uses of an employee statistics module.

Training and Development

A training and development module compares an individual's training and development needs with the training and development options available. Both employee's and manager's evaluations of training needs can be entered. Based on the target job concept, the module can be set up to identify and track along with needed training on other developmental activities.

The training component of the module, by itself, can be quite extensive. An HRIS is capable of carrying complete training course information on thousands of internal and external courses, instructors, costs, room assignments, students scheduled to participate, classroom assignments, billing systems, and grade computations—in other words, a complete registry and training delivery and administration subsystem.

Another aspect of training delivery is to build a computer-based training course into the HRIS. The system can store instructional material as well as automatically update trainees' files as they complete a course module and/or take the test required for completion of the course.

Developmental experiences can be tracked as they are completed. This data could entail job rotations, supervising jobs, task force assignments, transfers, promotions, project team participation—whatever management wishes to track regarding employee development.

Payroll

This application produces the employee or retiree payroll transactions, including paychecks, electronic-fund transfers, pay advances, and registers. The input could be based on employee salary, salary plus bonus, hours of work, or some combination of these earnings. The module also could handle multiple sets of payroll data, various categories of incentives and commissions, as well as multiple levels of employee deductions.

A payroll module must also calculate all needed earnings, hours, and taxes on a pay period, month-to-date, quarter-to-date, and year-to-date basis. Earnings limits based on taxable amounts (such as FICA wage limits) must be accommodated by the module. The complexities of the tax laws and changes in the accounting systems of many companies make this module quite complex. New benefits plans, such as flexible benefits and 401(k) programs, have caused quite a number of revisions in these modules, and contending with the auditing and control features can prove very difficult. Obviously, in an on-line environment, security has to be very stringent.

Other areas of the payroll module include: sick day and vacation accruals; production of W-2 (W-2p) and 1099 forms; output to recordkeepers in the benefits area; and employee loans and savings plans.

A payroll module usually is directly linked with other modules in an HRIS, such as compensation and defined contribution, to ensure consistency and coordination of functions.

Compensation

In the compensation area, an HRIS handles several major applications: administering salary plans; tracking and controlling various incentive, bonus, and commission plans; participating in outside salary surveys; and handling stock purchase and/or stock option plans.

The foundation of many firms' compensation programs is the salary plan, most of which can be computerized. The program usually begins by establishing salary grades, a job classification system, or both, and it typically contains salary ranges. Salary ranges allow base salaries to be varied according to job performance and length of time in the grade or on the job. The salary values in the ranges would be adjusted periodically, depending on market conditions and plan objectives. Variations in salary (namely, differentials) are permitted according to geographic location.

Bonuses, commissions, and other incentive plans have become more popular in recent years as companies seek to increase the effectiveness of their pay plans and put more salary "at risk." An HRIS can set aside pools of money for a group of people and distribute funds based on individual performance, group performance, sales, or other factors. The system also can apply these incentives to selected periods of time (such as the past year or the current quarter), but these incentives must be maintained separately in the HRIS. Levels of incentives can rise or fall by sales or over time, and recipients of such awards may transfer to other units within the organization or leave the company altogether but still remain eligible for the funds. As a result, the HRIS design must be flexible enough to permit these variations. All or some of this money may also be counted as compensation in the HRIS pension and other benefit programs. The HRIS data base structure should specify which payments are to be included in the various plans and under what conditions.

Companies participate in salary surveys in order to compare their wages and compensation programs with those of other firms. An HRIS facilitates such comparisons by providing job titles and brief job descriptions along with wages paid. An analyst can easily select comparable job titles and geographic areas using data provided by the HRIS based on the selected parameters.

With the wide variety of compensation programs available, line managers have increasingly turned to the HRIS and the models associated with it, to facilitate plan administration. Many firms have developed complex salary modeling programs and made them available to supervisors and managers. With such systems, users can directly access the HRIS and, on an interactive basis, model the salary or incentive plan for their group by adjusting rates of pay, bonuses, payment dates, and similar factors. The results can then be stored for review by senior management or the salary analyst. If approved, the models can be put into the "active" payroll module or stored for implementation on the effective date.

Pension Calculation

The pension calculation module is applicable to those organizations which have a defined benefits plan. A defined benefits plan is one in which the benefits that a retiree will receive upon retirement have been predefined by a formula and related rules of the plan. Benefits thus do not directly depend on plan performance but rather on service and compensation.

This module maintains the history of service, earnings, and plan participation and together with the basic employee demographic information maintained in other HRIS modules, the program calculates benefits due to members. At the time of retirement, the employee provides additional information such as beneficiary name, payment option selection, and monthly payment amounts, which is entered into the HRIS module.

Many pension calculation modules have the ability to model the benefits a retiree would receive based on various combinations of retirement dates, earnings, interest rates, and changes in pension formulas. An employee, manager, or benefits analyst can enter the desired date of retirement and the HRIS modeling program would permit the user to alter basic information such as future salary levels or formulas, or the user can accept benefit calculation the HRIS module currently projects. Data could be altered if, for example, an employee is expecting either a 10 percent increase in salary or a job transfer that would entail a pay cut. If the company is considering a new pension formula, the benefits analyst could determine the effects of such changes on selected groups. Following input of any data revisions, the model would display the amount of benefits the employee could receive based on the new data. The program also displays the earnings, payment options, and interest rates that were assumed in the calculation. Changing the date of retirement, as well as any of the factors involved, would produce a different payable amount.

Along with the staffing module, the pension module is generally considered the most difficult to build and keep up to date since pension calculations are normally integrated with the Social Security Administration's payout of benefits. Thus, calculating the Primary Insurance Amount (PIA) benefit is a complex but integral step in the process.

Detailed information on compensation, length of service, eligibility and vesting, and prior formulas are needed in this module. Further, the definition of compensation and service used in the calculation changes from employer to employer, and standard software programs cannot be purchased off the shelf for this application. In addition, legislative changes and regulatory updates come out continually in this area, making it difficult to maintain the currency and accuracy of this module.

The major outputs from this module typically provide participants' investments, federal filings, individual statements of benefits to participants, data to help with actuarial valuation of the plan, and other needed financial reports for auditors.

Defined Contribution and Savings Plans

The use of defined contribution and savings plans has grown tremendously in the past several years because of changes in tax laws and the desire of organizations to have employees participate in planning and saving for their retirement. Contributions to these plans are usually permitted on both a pre- and post-tax basis, within established upper limits. An HRIS must be able to determine eligibility for participation in the various plans, accept contributions or set percentage-of-pay allocations, establish directions, keep track of plan values, allow for loans and withdrawals, and handle all plan filings, tax payments, and inquiries by plan participants and administrators. Administration of these plans is often handled by a third party since the financial nature and tax implications of these plans have become quite complex.

Group Insurance

The rising cost of insurance, particularly in the medical area, has prompted many organizations to install or enhance an HRIS. A group insurance module maintains information on the type of insurance plan in which the employee is enrolled, the effective date of the coverage, premiums due for the insurance (split between the employee and the employer when co-payments are required), dependent information, and levels of coverage desired for each individual. Since calculation of premiums is one of the primary functions of this module, accurate data is critical.

Another important use of this module is claims verification. The program can certify that an individual is covered by insurance and produce lists of participants for the carriers, HMOs, and other health-care providers. For companies which self-administer health-care programs, this module proves essential for keeping records of claims and historical data. The HRIS can also store information regarding actual claims experience. Data on the results of certain medical or dental procedures can include details on the procedure, costs involved, hospital, length of stay, and the like. This data is extremely useful for controlling costs as well as for establishing the insurance rate structure when the plan comes up for renewal.

Successful HRIS Installations

The past 25 years of experience provides some important lessons with regard to computerized personnel systems. In some instances, the installation of an HRIS met with success, while in others, the system did not live up to expectations or failed outright. An analysis of many of these systems, including the environment in which they were developed and implemented produces a clearer picture of the successful system. In order to succeed in the long-term, an HRIS must meet three conditions: It must support the strategies of both the HR function *and* the organization; it must be architecturally and technically sound; and it must be administered well.

Strategic Support

When the HR department and its users get the major benefit from an HRIS, senior management may express dissatisfaction with HR systems and services. Systems which are inwardly focused on the HR user, rather than outwardly focused on the line manager, must be realigned to provide better support of corporate strategies.

To ensure the system furthers organizational strategy, the HRIS management should seek ways of helping the firm generate profit. The HRIS should focus on generating reports, assisting internal projects, developing output models, and supplying other information which can enhance sales, sales support, information on markets, market share, and product costs. To accomplish this goal, the HRIS should give top priority to the needs of line management. In dealing with day-to-day issues, such as product sales and delivery, customer satisfaction, quality control, and competition, line managers have urgent needs for HRM staff support and services, including those available through the HRIS.

In addition to generating profit for the firm, an HRIS can help reduce costs and expenses. It can save time in obtaining resources and filling jobs, cut the need for clerical employees in support functions, eliminate redundant operations, produce information and deliver it more quickly and easily, and maintain information for billing, salary surveys, and the like. In short, the implementation of computer-based personnel systems presents an opportunity to save money while gaining more information.

The HRIS management also might consider rerouting data flows and integrating HR information so as to permit users to share previously unavailable data while streamlining operations at the same time. Early attempts at computerization often just automated manual operations without redirecting flows or improving operations. Rerouting and integration facilitates decentralization and provides access to new information which may lead to new ways of handling jobs. New sets of users emerge, including customers, suppliers, and others who have a stake in the organization. Integrating data and redesigning the overall information stream also presents opportunities to eliminate costly functions.

Another way in which HRIS can back corporate strategies is through early awareness and involvement in HR plan design and administration. The HRIS manager should seek out ways to support new training and development initiatives, succession planning programs, flexible benefits plans, and new compensation plans. In many companies, the HRIS is needed to deliver these new plans and therefore it is a vital component of the plans themselves.

Although the HRIS is and should be involved in personnel recordkeeping, it can do much more. Through artificial intelligence and data integration, the HRIS and related technologies can not only automate records, but also handle much of the current policy interpretation, HR program delivery, and communication with employees and management. As a result, the HRIS can eliminate costly HR staffing for these activities.

An HRIS can serve the primary vehicle for most HR program administration and technology. As such, the system should be at the core of all planning and enable the company to achieve its strategic objectives.

Architectures

Architectural design for an HRIS also play an important role in determining the success of the system. A key ingredient in this plan is the right choice of technical programming languages, file design, programming approaches, and, especially, data base management systems. Although some languages and data base management systems are similar, individual variations in technical approaches can make a big difference in terms of user satisfaction. For example, some data base management systems are easier to use for making programming changes and are more oriented toward data-processing activities; others facilitate users' ability to extract data and generate reports. Systems also differ in their approach to security: Some permit users to be locked out of certain files and/or functions, while others do not afford this measure of protection. This last scenario creates a risk which could cause user dissatisfaction.

A second aspect of architectural design concerns the ability of the data base management system to adapt to changes in the HRIS. These changes could range from simply changing an existing code, editing or modifying a table of values, and expanding or contracting the size of a field, to more complex activities such as designing input or display screens, adding new sets of data attributes, or developing entire new modules or applications.

A third architectural design issue which can "make or break" a system's success is the extent of work displacement and enhanced functional power which can result through the use of the HRIS. The system, as stated earlier, should do more than keep records and track data. For example, in calculating a benefit under a retirement plan, the HRIS should prepare earnings and service verification steps and compute the gross pension, Social Security offset, and payment options. If systems do not go the "extra 10 yards" but stop short of producing the calculation, users will not benefit fully and will feel that the HRIS has limited success. In short, technology should save costs and users' time, thereby displacing the tedium of repetitive or low value-added activities.

Another key area in the architectural design of an HRIS is the extent of user support and user involvement in the system. Users are eager for value, and in today's PC-literate environment, the HRIS must permit users to access the data base, enter data, produce computations and modeling applications, and perform similar tasks at their work locations. This access is especially important in a decentralized environment. In other words, users must feel they have a full-function system at their fingertips, a system that is responsive to their needs.

A related objective is to employ as many new technologies in the design as practical. These technologies would include expert systems, artificial intelligence, desk-top publishing, downloading, scanners, video disk, image processing, touch screens, and windows. Not all these technologies need to be present at each user site, but an HRIS manager should be familiar with these newer technical features and be willing to incorporate them into the design where appropriate. A forward-thinking HRIS manager stands a greater chance of success over the long run than a conservative one.

Finally, the architectural design should permit changes in the system as laws and other plan features change. Although this feature of data base management systems was discussed above, other components of the HRIS also will need to be altered. A design which can easily keep abreast of all changes must be addressed early in the HRIS development process and dealt with on a continuing basis.

Administration

As noted earlier, an HRIS operation which has managers and staff who are well-trained in systems administration will succeed, even when the systems are less than state of the art. Keeping in touch with users, training and supporting them, communicating with management, and maintaining an ongoing enhancement strategy will often spell success. While these activities cannot make up for a deficient system or one which is not directed to support needed strategies, good administration is vital. Without it, good systems, even superior systems, will often fail.

Conclusion

This chapter has presented a broad view of HRIS, including historical developments, system components, and data base management concepts, human resource information centers, HRIS modules and applications, and factors associated with successful HRIS implementation. The HRIS field continues to grow and develop at a rapid pace. Keeping pace with such changes requires a well-designed and well-administered system. In the future, HRIS operations will shift to a proactive position in organizations and line managers and top managers becoming more involved in the system as HR information becomes a major source of competitive advantage in the information age.

Notes

1. Walker (1982a).
2. Jenkins and Gayle.
3. Walker (1982b).
4. See Meyer (1985) for a thorough treatment of PCs in personnel prior to the development of local area networks.
5. See Kustoff for a discussion of network structures.
6. Johnson and Packer.
7. Ibid.
8. Ford and McAlister; O'Leary and Turban.
9. Blair; Edwards.
10. Mathys and LaVan.
11. See Kroenke, McElroy, Shuman, and Willliams.
12. See Meyer (1984).
13. Beutell.
14. Keough.
15. Perry.
16. Meyer (1984).
17. See Walker (1982a) for a more complete description.
18. Argyris.
19. See Nardoni.
20. Lederer.
21. Simon.
22. Meyer (1985).
23. Munn.
24. See Leote for a discussion of software modification needs.
25. Platamura.
26. Brod.
27. Bloom; Brod; Landry.
28. Walker (1982a).
29. See Bland-Acosta regarding privacy policies.
30. See MacAdam.
31. See MacAdam for a discussion of the relationship between effective HRIS documentation and training.
32. Leote.
33. Miller and Heller.
34. Ibid.
35. See Witkin.
36. Spirig.
37. Miller and Heller, p. 21.
38. Miner.

References

Argyris, C. 1970. *Intervention Theory and Method: A Behavioral Science View.* Reading, MA: Addison-Wesley.

Beutell, N.J. 1988. "Computers and the Management of Human Resources." In *Personnel and Human Resource Management*, 4th ed., eds. R.S. Schuler, S.A. Youngblood, and V.L. Huber. St. Paul, MN: West Publishing Company.

Blair, E. 1988. "Decision Support Systems are Personal Tools." *Personnel Journal* (December): 100–108.

Bland-Acosta, B.A. 1988. "Developing an HRIS Privacy Policy." *Personnel Administrator* (July): 52–59.

Bloom, A.J. 1985. "An Anxiety Management Approach to Computerphobia." *Training and Development Journal* (January): 90–94.

Brod, C. 1985. *Technostress: The Human Cost of the Computer Revolution.* Reading, MA: Addison-Wesley.

6-202 Managing HR in the Information Age

Edwards, M.R. 1988. "An Expert System for Equitable Career Decisions." *Computers in Personnel* (Fall): 40–47.

Ford, R.C. and M.K. McAlister. 1989. "Tapping into Expert Systems." *Personnel Administrator* (January): 26–32.

Jenkins, K., and L. Gayle. 1985. "How Corporate Philosophy and Strategy Shape the Use of HR Information Systems." *Personnel* (May): 28–38.

Johnson, W.B. and A.H. Packer. 1987. *Workforce 2000*. Indianapolis, IN: Hudson Institute.

Keough, L. 1985. "Managing Personnel the Micro Way." *Computer Decisions* (March): 76–82.

Kroenke, D.M., M.L. McElroy, J.E. Shuman, and M.C. Williams. 1986. *Business Computer Systems: Using Application Software*. Santa Cruz, CA: Mitchell Publishing.

Kustoff, M. 1988. "Battle of the HR Network Stars and Rings." *Computers in Personnel* (Spring): 37–41.

Landry, R.M. 1988. "Countering HR Computerphobia?" *Computers in Personnel* (Summer): 16–19.

Lederer, A.L. 1984. "Planning and Developing a Human Resource Information System." *Personnel Administrator* (August): 27–39.

Leote, D.M. 1987. "Evaluating the Need for Software Modification." *Personnel Journal* (July): 85–90.

MacAdam, M. 1987. "HRIS Training: Keep Documentation on Track." *Personnel Journal* (October): 45–51.

Mathys, N.J., and H. LaVan. 1988. "HRISs That Cover the Earth." *Computers in Personnel* (Spring): 58–59.

Meyer, G.J. 1984. *Automating Personnel Operations*. Madison, CT: Business and Legal Reports.

———. 1985. *PCs in Personnel*. Madison, CT: Business and Legal Reports.

Miller, M.S. and A.S. Heller. 1988. "Attention, HRIS Professionals! You, Too, Can Earn a Six-Figure Salary!" *Personnel* (December): 19–26.

Miner, F.J. 1986. "Computer Applications in Career Development Planning." In *Career Development in Organizations*, eds. D.T. Hall and Associates. San Francisco: Jossey-Bass.

Munn, R.W. 1985. "HRIS: Towards an Effective Requirements Analysis." *Personnel Administrator* (August): 14–15.

Nardoni, R. 1985. "Piecing Together a Micro-Based HRIS." *Personnel Journal* (February): 38–43.

O'Leary, D.E. and E. Turban. 1987. "The Organizational Impact of Expert Systems." *Human Systems Management* 7: 11–19.

Perry, S.G. 1988. "The PC-based HRIS." *Personnel Administrator* (February): 60–63.

Platamura, L.M. 1985. "Choosing an HRIS Vendor." *Personnel Administrator* (November): 18–22.

Simon, S.H. 1988. "Mainframe Versus Microcomputer Solutions." *HR/PC* (October 1–November 15): 1–4.

Spirig, J.E. 1988. "Selling the HRIS." *Personnel* (October): 26–34.

Walker, A.J. 1982a. *HRIS Development*. New York: Van Nostrand Reinhold Company.

———. 1982b. "The Newest Job in Personnel: Human Resources Data Administrator." *Personnel Journal* (December): 924–928.

Witkin, E. 1988. "The HRIS Business: Making the Customer Happy." *Personnel* (February): 18–26.

———— ♦ ————

6.6
New HRM Roles, Responsibilities, and Structures

Stephen J. Carroll

The HRM function and HRM units, like all organizational components, exist to perform certain roles and responsibilities required by the larger system or organization of which they are a part. It is apparent from reading the various chapters in this Handbook that the HRM function's roles and responsibilities have expanded significantly over the years. It is obvious also that the nature of the roles and responsibilities of the HRM function has important implications for the type of persons needed to perform well in HRM work and also for the type of education and experiences needed by HRM professionals. This has important implications for all those organizations that are associated with the education and advancement of such HRM personnel such as universities and HRM professional associations as well as for the organizations that employ HRM personnel.

When discussing HRM roles and responsibilities some obvious questions come to mind. These would include such issues as what these roles are and how have they changed over time, how well are these roles being performed by HRM units and personnel, what are the primary facilitators or barriers to effective HRM role performance, how should HRM units be structured to best perform these roles, and, in general, what might be done to improve the performance of these roles by HRM professionals? This chapter will attempt to respond to these questions on the basis of research and written reports existing on these topics. Since this is a Handbook designed to improve practice, the chapter will attempt to make some suggestions based on this review.

Evolution of HRM Roles

The word evolution implies a response to an environmental demand. The environments of the HRM function, as most HRM textbooks indicate, are the organization itself and the environments of this organization. As changes in the economic, technological, social, or political-legal environments occur, organizations must adjust in a functional way if they are to survive. In the case of many such environmental pressures, especially those relating to the employment of people and to performance needs of the organization, the HRM function and its personnel are delegated these change responsibilities. Various company concerns and expectations for employees have changed over time giving rise to HRM responsibilities for managing programs and systems involving employee discipline, safety and health, motion and time study, psychological testing, employee counseling, employee communication, pension plans, foremen training, management by objectives, job enrichment, and outplacement programs among the hundreds of other activities presently overburdening HRM units and the HRM profession to an almost impossible degree.[1]

Perhaps the most significant recent development impacting on HRM roles and responsibilities is the new economic competitiveness. The significant market losses experienced by many U.S. industries between the 1970s and the 1980s due to foreign competititon and other developments such as deregulation have greatly increased competitiveness in many other industries.[2] These new competitive pressures have forced organizations to make sure that all resources including personel are used in such a way as to generate the maximum value to the organization in terms of contributions in return for the inducements provided. Increases in the diversity of the labor force and in new protections for employees have also been widely discussed in terms of their implications for the HRM profession.

New Focus for Traditional HRM Roles

Most prognisticators agree that that future will bring an ongoing need for the traditional HRM service and advisory functions. These roles relate largely to the acquisition, motivation, and retention of employees. Traditional HR units focus on staffing, training, and compensation programs, as well as the impact of these programs on performance, job satisfaction, and turnover.[1] Other traditional HRM services that will continue to be in demand include activities related to labor relations, legal compliance, record keeping, and morale enhancement. Of course new techniques as described in this handbook represent continuous improvements in the effectiveness of how these traditional HRM roles are performed.

Emphasis on Organizational Effectiveness

In the future, greater emphasis will go toward designing and implementing HR practices within these traditional areas to improve overall organizational effectiveness. In fact, evidence is mounting that organizations can significantly improve their overall performance simply by implementing more effective HRM practices in these areas. For example, a study of declining industries found differences between high and low performers in all the major HRM areas: staffing, training, performance appraisal, and compensation.[3] Other studies of specific HRM activities also have demonstrated a strong relationship between effective HRM practices and organizational performance:

- Effective selection can produce an employee body worth tens of thousands of dollars more than other employees.[4] Studies examining staffing sophistication[5] and executive staffing policies[6] likewise have shown a relationship between hiring practices and organizational performance.

- Certain performance appraisal systems, such as those based on objectives, can significantly boost both individual and organizational performance.[7]

- At one company, implementation of gainsharing at a test plant increased its productivity by 31 percent, reduced variable costs by 14 percent, and lowered absenteeism by 26 percent.[8]

- In another case, a new HRM manager implemented practices that greatly reduced employee turnover and almost doubled their productivity over a few years.[9]

Linkages Between HRM and Business Needs

Effectiveness in these traditional HR areas will depend on selecting practices that can best meet emerging business needs. A good illustration involves the ways in which recent changes in the basic employment relationship have affected the traditional HR activities of training and compensation.[10] The trends of the past decade—plant closing, mergers, downsizing, and elimination of middle management—have eliminated the notions of long-term employee tenure and loyalty to a particular employer. As a result, HR managers can expect diminished returns on training activities and an increased demand for compensation systems that emphasize short-term rewards.

In terms of staffing, this shift in the basic employment relationship means more employers will look toward implementing the dual work-force model used by many Asian companies.[11] Under this model, one group of highly competent employees receives high pay, benefits, and special employment guarantees, while the rest of the work force is viewed as temporary employees. In this fashion, employers can continue to fulfill their need for a stable body of employees who are knowledgeable about the industry, skilled in their job, and capable of transmitting organizational culture and norms.

A related trend that will impact traditional HRM activities concerns the move toward team, rather than individual, work assignments.[12] This shift has enormous implications for staffing, performance appraisal, training, and compensation programs. Selection, for example, will have to focus on identifying individuals who can work together, while training programs will need to emphasize team-building, group appraisal, and feedback procedures.

In short, the demand for particular HRM activities to improve overall effectiveness will change as the competitive environment evolves. One study which examined the relationship between organizational effectiveness and HRM has conceptualized seven activities in which effective HR managers of the future will have to take part:[13]

- Input provision. As always, the HRM unit will act to supply an organization with workers who possess appropriate abilities and motivations.

- Behavior management. HR managers will design and implement behavior-influencing systems (such as compensation and performance appraisal) to ensure people behave and perform appropriately once hired.

- Environmental scanning. This function would monitor outside changes and developments that might impact the organization.
- Policy formulation. In this role, the HR unit would advise top management on the compatibility of HR availabilities with organizational goals or plans.
- Conflict resolution. This function reflects the HR unit's expertise in the people and behavioral skills necessary for effective problem solving.
- Audits. This role would involve investigations of employee satisfaction, quality of work life, and similar issues.
- Behavioral consulting/problem-solving. HR mangers will act as consultants to line managers seeking ways to correct problems with particular employees.

HR Managers as Change Agents

Given the linkage between organizational performance and HRM, familiarity with the most effective practices in these traditional HR areas clearly will rank as an important asset for HR managers in the future. However, even in today's environment, the pressure is on HR managers to expand beyond these traditional HRM roles.

One recent analysis examined a number of trends, such as the growing costs of employing human resources, the productivity crisis, the amount of outside change itself, employee discontent, and new HRM information technologies.[14] The conclusion reached in this analysis identified at least five roles essential for effective HRM. Two roles, policy formulator and provider of personnel services, resemble the traditional HR activities already described. The other three functions include the following:

- Delegator. This role enables line management to serve as primary implementors of HRM systems.
- Technical expert. This function encompasses a number of highly specific HR-related skills.
- Innovator. As innovators, HR managers recommend new approaches to solving HRM-related problems, such as pro-

ductivity. For example, pension and benefits, traditionally treated as entitlements, could become rewards for effective performance.

This last role, of innovator, will become an increasingly important aspect of HRM in the future. More and more, HR managers will be called upon to serve in a proactive capacity, helping top management to formulate and implement business strategy. They also will have closer involvement with line managers, acting as consultants to resolve current problems and to carry out new business thrusts. Finally, HRM managers will serve as change agents, encouraging their organizations to adopt new ways of operating that will enhance overall competitiveness.

Examples of HRM Units as Change Agents

Some of the most spectacular documented HRM successes in recent years have resulted from HR intiatives that significantly changed organizational work processes to boost overall performance. The following examples of Kiethley Instruments and Swiss Bank Corporation illustrate the ways in which an HRM unit can act as a change agent to promote organizational development.

At Kiethley Instruments, an Ohio company, the HRM unit utilized an action research approach to identify needed changes in how work was performed.[15] Working through a management task force, the company redefined supervisors' roles and placed greater responsibility on employees for the quality of their performance. In addition, Kiethley reassigned work to teams rather than individuals, and provided training so that work groups could set their own goals and solve any problems they encountered.

As a result of these changes, Kiethley increased its productivity by over 90 percent in four years, with only a 28 percent increase in the number of employees. Warranty repairs dropped by 15 percent during the same period, and decreases also took place in inventories and employee turnover. The switch from a traditional role to a change agent role also boosted the credibility and esteem of the HRM unit, which line management had previously viewed unfavorably.

At Swiss Bank Corporation in New York City, the HRM unit's vice president shifted the department's emphasis to a more active, behavioral science orientation.[16] This approach attempted to bring HRM activities and responsibilities into closer alignment with the organizational culture, the employees, the needs of other functional units, as well as new trends in the company's environment.[17]

The changes implemented at Swiss Bank followed a sequence similar to the stages of an overall organization development effort. The first stage, information gathering, surveyed everyone in the company as to problems, deficiencies, opportunities, and other perceptions. Based on this information, change priorities and agendas were developed and implemented. Finally, the company monitored outcomes related to these changes, revising the program as needed.

This approach has resulted in better selection and utilization of personnel, lower turnover, and higher organizational effectiveness. In addition, the HRM unit, in its new facilitative and customer-oriented role, has gained higher credibility within the company.

Barriers to Change

Change is a difficult process that typically provokes much resistance. Along with the natural human desire for consistency and order,[18] the sheer size of some organizations and the competing needs and agendas of different organizational subgroups can create considerable barriers. In addition, change efforts tend to garner support only if top management or charismatic leaders push the initiative;[19] otherwise, people must believe that the change will prevent or alleviate a crisis.[20]

Some of the research on HRM innovation has targeted a number of key areas that can thwart acceptance of new initiatives.[21] Union opposition, lack of resources, unfamiliarity with the proposed innovation, and lack of rewards all can act as detriments. The most critical factors in gaining acceptance, however, relate to the HR unit's track record in implementing other changes and to its ability to convince top management that the change will produce benefits that exceed associated costs.

In general, a gradual, step-by-step model for implementing change, such as the approach used by Swiss Bank, will facilitate acceptance of HRM innovations. This service-oriented HRM model assumes continual change is necessary to meet new customer needs.[22] In a similar fashion, the total quality management system introduced in many U.S. firms, such as Xerox and Ford, emphasizes boosting value through ongoing incremental improvements.[23] The key is to ensure change takes place in small enough steps to create what one author has called "the boiled frog phenomenon."[24] This phenomenon arises when a frog sitting in a cooking pot fails to notice his own demise because the changes in water temperature occur so slowly.

Greater Emphasis on Strategic HRM

When the original ASPA handbook came out a dozen years ago, George Odiorne was among the first in the HRM field to call for a more strategic HR function.[25] His comments regarding the need for HRM units to go beyond addressing immediate problems to anticipate future changes have finally garnered widespread attention. In recent years, numerous authors have addressed the need to align HRM policies and practices with corporate and business strategies.[26] Many of these writings give prescriptive advice, identifying compatible HRM systems and policies for certain competitive strategies, based upon actual company practices which have received publicity.

For example, one analysis discusses the HRM implications of "defender" vs. "prospector" business strategies.[27] Defenders are companies that desire stability and wish to protect their turf or market share. These companies tend to use HR strategies to build their own needed work-force competencies. Prospectors, on the other hand, pursue an aggressive business strategy, and tend to meet their human resource needs by acquiring them from outside. Either strategy has implications for an organization's selection, training, performance appraisal, and compensation systems.

Another set of authors have examined the relationship between HR policy choices and three popular business strategies: quality enhancement, innovation, and cost reduction.[28] They have found evidence that companies do follow different HRM practices under certain strategies. However, these HRM practices tend to vary among the different levels in these companies. Other writers have linked various HRM practices to stages in the product life cycle.[29] Still others have linked very specific HRM practices, such as staffing or compensation, to some of the more popular business strategies.[30] All of these writings support a contingency theory of management which indicates that no particular HRM system will suit all conditions; rather the system must fit what is needed to implement a certain strategy or to meet various demands imposed on the firm by its environment.[31]

The extent to which companies actually use HRM units in developing and implementing strategies remains uncertain, however. While some reviewers have cited IBM, General Electric, Hewlett-Packard, Eli Lilly, and United Parcel as companies that use strategic HRM,[32] these companies may be exceptions to typical practice. One survey of 168 large U.S. firms indicated that only 20 percent gave significant consideration to HR issues when developing and implementing strategic plans.[33] Another study of compensation managers likewise indicated little interest in tying compensation policies to organization profit goals.[34] While both these studies took place in the early 1980s, a more recent survey of 281 personnel professionals indicated only 14 percent of them planned to emphasize their unit's role in strategic planning during the next year.[35]

Strategic HRM in Action

In companies that do include HRM in the development and implementation of strategic plans, HRM participation takes a number of forms. A study of 16 Cleveland (OH) companies found that while most agreed that HRM should be involved in strategic planning, not all companies had actually done this.[36] Of the nine companies using HRM strategically, four asked their HRM units to design appropriate programs after the strategic plan had been developed. While four other firms asked the HR department for input during development of the strategic plan, only one company actually included the top HRM person on the strategic management team.

Two interesting approaches to strategic HRM are demonstrated by two Minnesota companies, 3M, and Honeywell. At 3M, the corporation not only works to get HR managers to adopt a more business-oriented approach, but also encourages line managers to incorporate more HRM into their thoughts and actions.[37] The company makes line managers responsible for conducting employee surveys and for analyzing deficiencies in how they manage their department's human resources.

At Honeywell, human resources gets at least equal priority with technical and financial considerations in all strategic decisions.[38] To obtain this emphasis, every HR professional sits with the general manager and the GM's planning staff during the formulation of business plans. These plans then become the basis for developing operational HR plans that identify three to four key HR functions essential to the success of the strategic business plan. Honeywell's planning process seems to be a version of comprehensive management by objectives in which unit goals are directly derived from strategic goals and plans set by top management.[39]

New Orientation Toward HRM Clientele

Beside business strategy, the exact nature of an HR function often reflects the demands of the more powerful groups within an organization. HR managers must serve various constituencies who frequently have different beliefs regarding the HRM role. Not surprisingly, these constituencies express differing satisfaction with the HR unit, depending on whether its orientation suits their needs.

Top executives, for example, seem to agree on the importance of HRM, but many of them express dissatisfaction with how the HRM function operates in their companies. One survey of 71 CEOs found significant gaps between what top management wanted from HRM and what the function actually delivered:[40]

> Many indicated that human resources is increasingly valuable in differentiating a company competitively. They cited quality of talent, flexibility and innovation, superior performance or productivity, and customer service as key factors in accomplishing this. The executives also said that they want human resource managers to understand the changing needs of the business and act as strong leaders. . . . Yet in contrast to this kind of leadership, many CEOs see their human resource department as administratively oriented—concentrating on recordkeeping and day-to-day problem solving. The function's staff, however eager to respond to management requests, are seen as taking insufficient initiative and viewing their roles narrowly, focusing on employee concerns rather than business issues, and lacking business understanding and judgment.

Revamping the HR function to suit top management, however, can create unfulfilled expectations among others in an organization. A recent study, which surveyed HR professionals, academics in the HRM field, top executives, and line managers, illustrates this point.[41] While top management emphasized the strategic HRM function, line managers expressed a preference for HR service activities. Thus, perceptions regarding the appropriate role of an HRM unit can vary considerably within an organization.

As a result, the effectiveness of an HRM unit will depend on its ability to balance these conflicting constituencies. At Honeywell's

Aerospace and Defense division, for example, HRM functions and roles reflect an effort "to serve our customers, employees, vendors, shareholders, and our communities," according to the division's general manager.[42] To manage this balancing act, HR managers will have to become adept at identifying key stakeholder interests and situational factors that affect these interests.

Using this perspective of stakeholder interests, several Harvard Business School professors have delineated four policy areas in which future HR managers will have to develop expertise to function effectively.[43] This analysis expanded the definition of stakeholders to include not only organizational constituents, but also external stakeholders—consumers, regulator agencies, communities, and so on. The four policy areas identified would involve the HR unit in designing and managing the following:

- Employee-influence systems. These systems address employee participation, union-related concerns, and similar issues.
- HR flow management. Employee selection, development, career management, retirement systems fall into this policy area.
- Reward systems. These systems govern policies and programs related to compensation, incentives, and benefits.
- Work systems. Duties in this area include task analysis, job design, and performance standards.

Behavioral Requirements of Future HR Managers

After investigating the HRM function in leading U.S. companies, one researcher delineated two types of HR managers: Type As and type Bs.[44] Type A managers have gained a great deal of influence, credibility, and respect within their organizations, and accordingly, these managers earn higher compensation than their more numerous counterparts, Type B managers.

Type B managers fit the traditional HR mold. They tend to focus only on their function, and take little interest in the business side of their organizations. In general, Type B managers are reactive rather than innovative; they wait for someone to hand them an assignment or ask for input on a problem. These individuals view themselves as functional specialists and take pride in pleasing other specialists instead of gaining credit with top management.

Type A managers, in contrast, eschew traditional HRM roles, viewing themselves first and foremost as business managers and strategic partners to top management. These managers develop a broad understanding of the entire business in all its functional aspects and take a deep interest in the firm's overall strategy and goals. They actively search out problems that their HR knowledge and skills can address. They adopt an internal marketing orientation, viewing other functional areas as key clients whose needs must be met. In companies with Type A managers, HRM activities integrate business strategies with the needs of key clients.

While the demand for Type A managers appears likely to increase, most firms will continue to need some Type B managers as well. Type B managers are, to some degree, quite expert in particular types of HRM systems and programs, and many large companies require such experts. The correct proportion of Type A and Type B managers to hire will depend on the behavioral requirements of various HRM roles with a particular organization.

Another analysis that looked at the HRM behavioral requirements predicted that future HRM professionals will serve in the following six roles:[45]

- Business person. This strategic function would involve HR managers in major business problems affecting every organizational department. Knowledge of business functions and business analysis methods would become necessary skills for HR professionals.

- Shaper of change. This role would require familiarity with the skill in implementing behavioral change approaches throughout an organization.

- Organization consultant. HR managers will need consulting skills to serve in a capacity similar to outside organizational development consultants.

- Strategy formulator and implementor. Environmental scanning skills and strategic planning abilities would rank among the necessary attributes of HR managers acting in this role.

- Talent manager. This role would involve knowledge of effective approaches to managing people, plus the communication skills to enable line managers to assume responsibility for implementing these approaches.

- Asset manager and cost controller. Effective HR managers will need compentencies in financial management not only to control departmental costs but also to stay abreast of economic issues affecting the entire organization.

All these roles call for a significant change in the perspective of HR managers. HRM professionals will have to have a broader, more strategic, business-oriented focus to serve effectively in many of these future roles. However, evidence suggests that many HR managers will find it difficult to meet these new behavioral requirements.

Shortcomings of Current HR Professionals in Fulfilling the New Roles

One study compared the managerial values and personal orientations of HR managers to those of other types of managers.[46] The underlying goal of this study attempted to test out the assertion that HRM professionals lack the will to manage and, as a result, fail to achieve their full potential as contributors to the management systems of most companies.[47] A sample of 101 HRM managers was administered a "motivation to manage" scale, and their scores were compared to those of managers in other functional areas from previous samples.

In summarizing the study's results, the researcher reported that the HRM field seemed to attract individuals who are relatively low in motivation to manage:[48]

> The data support the hypothesis that motivation to manage is relatively low among personnel and industrial relations managers. At the maximum, middle managers in the field appear to be at the same level as the average first-line supervisor in other functional areas. Top managers appear to fall at a point roughly intermediate between lower- and middle-level managers in other areas of the business.

Another recent survey by the Bureau of National Affairs, Inc., further documents the limited perspectives of many HRM professionals.[49] The survey, which encompassed 281 personnel and HR executives, asked them to prioritize 14 broad HRM issues and to identify the three areas they planned to emphasize during the next year. The five areas receiving the most votes, in order of priority, were: employee benefits, training and development, recruitment and selection, compensation, and employee/labor relations. Only 14 percent of these HR professionals planned to expand their department's role in strategic planning, and only 13 percent intended to target productivity improvements. These data certainly will be disappointing to those who hope the present HRM professionals are willing and able to jump in and perform the new needed roles and responsibilities.

Implications for HRM Units

This lack of strategic orientation among the HRM function can have adverse consequences for HR departments and the individuals who staff these units. The trend in recent surveys indicates that top management is committed to the importance of strategic HRM. Rather than abandon this approach when the HR unit lacks a strategic perspective, management may look elsewhere for qualified individuals to implement appropriate programs:[50]

> In recent years, some companies have replaced key human resource managers, hiring executives from outside or transferring line managers to transform the function. Others have trimmed the staff of Human Resources and its budget from program. And many others have decentralized the human resource function to put staff close to line departments and increase business contracts and accountability.

Some firms have gone even further and eliminated the HRM function, delegating its responsibilities to line mangement. Robert Townsend, a former company president and author of the popular book *Up the Organization*, has long advocated just such an initiative,[51] and some companies have begun to take this advice. According to the CEO of Preston Trucking, his company abolished its HR function because "HRM is too important to be left to the HRM department."[52]

New HRM Structures

Organizational structures can vary along several dimensions. They can emphasize formal hierarchies or take a more fluid, organic form. The organizational structure can centralize all decision-making responsibility at the top or delegate numerous decisions to lower levels. Finally, the type of organizational structure determines whether specialists or generalists will predominate among a unit's staff. Each of these alternatives offers certain advantages and disadvantages that have implications for the HRM function.

In general, most of the writings on new HRM roles call for less formal HRM systems, less specialized HR managers, and greater decentralization and delegation of HRM responsibilities to lower HRM levels and to operating units.

Less Formalized HR Structures

Formal, hierarchical structures offer advantages of speed, consistency in execution, ease of learning, ability to use lower-quality personnel, and so on. However, formalized methods work only when tasks or problems are stable and require little flexibility or creativity. The demands for innovation and responsiveness to changing environments make it likely that HR departments in the future will have more organic, fluid structures.

Diminished bureaucratization can promote a number of HR initiatives, such as a contingency approach to HRM. Using this approach, an organization would tailor selection, training, and compensation policies to suit the unique strategic orientations of different organizational entities. However, any shift to a more organic HRM structure will have implications for staffing of the HR function, since some research indicates that organic structures demand higher-quality managers.[53]

Smaller Corporate HR Functions

Along with more fluid organizational structures, the responsibility for HR activities appears likely to become less centralized. For example, a recent survey of CEOs and top executives at 71 U.S. corporations found most wanted to reduce the size of the corporate HRM staff and its functions.[54] This shift is consistent with the emphasis on zero-based budgeting and accountability. As one CEO expressed it, "If a staff function adds value, we should have it; it doesn't, it should be eliminated."

In general, many of the companies surveyed believed that the corporate HRM unit should act to set policy and advise top management on issues critical to the entire corporation; all other HR activities should be decentralized. In addition, the responses indicated that executives increasingly believe that they themselves should retain responsibility for new HR thrusts and programs.

Consistent with other studies, this survey found a perception among top management that HR professionals are too bureaucratic and lack sufficient initiative and creativity and therefore, they must perform these new required roles themselves. Likewise, another recent survey found that executives ranked their need for skill in HRM issues second in priority only to financial management skills.[55]

Decentralization of HR Responsibilities

Along with this reduction in corporate HRM responsibilities, most surveys predict that day-to-day HR activities will become increasingly a line function. Organizational structures will no longer have specialists who exclusively handle HR functions; instead, line managers will perform these duties.

Implementing this shift in responsibility, however, will necessitate considerable training. Current evidence indicates that line managers have generally performed poorly when assigned responsibility for such things as conducting performance appraisals, training programs, and selection interviews.[56] Changes in MBA program requirements may alleviate this problem. In fact, Harvard Business School and the University of Maryland already have begun to require that all MBA students take a HRM course, and other universities may follow suit.[57]

More Complex HRM Structures

Despite the trend toward generalist orientation and decentralization, organizations will likely need some HR specialists and some centralized control over certain HR activities, such as equal employment opportunity issues.[58] As a result, HRM structures will have to become more complex so as to allow some specialization while adopting a more generalist and decentralized approach.

One method for achieving this balance is a matrix approach to HRM. Under this approach, a generalist manager would oversee a particular plant or group of employees and coordinate the different specialists who handle specific HRM functions (staffing, training, and so on) for that unit. In a sense, the generalist HR manager would function much as the product manager in other organizational units. Atlantic-Richfield already has implemented a system similar to this one.[59] This combination approach permits tailoring of HR policies to suit particular units, while providing the integration of diverse HRM functions to ensure consistent and effective implementation of overall strategy.

Another way to combine specialists and generalists could involve setting up entirely different HRM units, each staffed by quite different types of people, to handle certain HR activities. For example, a more bureaucratic unit could manage traditional activities—records, compensation plans, formal selection procedures, and formal training programs—while a different unit would act in the business partner or change agent role. A third unit would handle long-range strategic planning forecasts and develop creative and innovative ways to implement current thrusts.

This last approach would create a structure congruent with present organization theory.[60] In general, current theory indicates that if an organization simultaneously needs stability and creativity/change, it should have two separate units to perform these roles. Some companies have already adopted a similar system, hiring outside consultants to perform organizational development activities while leaving traditional HR functions to the HRM department.

HRM Structures and Organizational Strategy

Despite these general trends, actual HRM structures and roles will continue to reflect the nature of the firm itself—the industry in which it operates, its particular business strategy,[61] as well as its philosophy and culture. The examples of Merck & Company and TRW illustrate how these unique factors permit companies to succeed using very different HRM structures.[62]

At Merck, the HRM structure is highly centralized. A large specialized corporate HRM staff formulates and designs HRM strategies and activities, which are then communicated to the smaller HRM staffs in operating units for implementation. This structure ensures that HR policy attains high consistency and congruence with corporate goals, a strategy that works for Merck's stable competitive focus.

At TRW, in contrast, the HRM function is highly decentralized. Its small corporate staff handles the HRM systems for executives and serves to advise operating units, which manage HRM for other employees. This strategy leads to wider divergence in HRM practices and can pose greater risks for legal and other problems. However, TRW, a high technology company with many divergent businesses and a competitive environment, requires this flexibility to succeed.

New Staffing Requirements for HR Professionals

Structures are made up of people, so any shift in structural design has implications for staffing. General Electric has explicitly recognized this fact, calling its HR function "Organization and Human Resources," so as to reflect the inseparability of the company and its employees.[63] At times, an organizational structure or management system may change to better suit a job incumbent.[64] More often than not, however, changes in organizational structures may call for hiring new types of people or retraining of current personnel.

All of the predicted changes in HRM roles and structures appear likely to create a demand for new types of HR personnel. As noted earlier, some companies have already shifted to hiring more generally trained MBAs to handle HRM activities. These companies feel that MBAs have the quantitative and general business knowledge to perform the more strategic HRM role.

Along with an increased focus on generalists,[65] organizations have begun to hire new types of HR specialists. The new HRM roles require individuals who are experts in total quality management, new service technologies, behavioral performance improvement systems, and organizational development. Indeed, unless these new specialties become subfunctions of HR departments, few of the predicted HRM innovations will meet much success.

Despite the demand for more business-oriented HR professionals, it appears unlikely that MBAs will flock to the field. For example, in a class of 59 MBA students at the University of Maryland, only six indicated an interest in an HRM career; the remaining responses clearly indicated a negative perception of HRM.[66] Another study surveyed business graduate students as to the desirability of an HRM career.[67] Most students viewed HRM as a dull field that is overly concerned with minor issues and has little status either in business schools or industry. Ph.D. students in particular viewed HR studies as overemphasizing techniques and procedures with too little attention on theory. Likewise, at Harvard Business

School, fewer than 150 of its 39,000 graduates have entered the field of personnel or industrial relations.[68]

Instead, university HR training programs will have to change to reflect the evolving needs of organizations and HR roles. For example, the University of Maryland already has adopted masters-level courses that focus primarily on line HRM activities, rather than HR specialist or staff functions. Universities also will have to require more business and finance courses for HRM degrees. In a similar fashion, HRM professional organizations, such as SHRM, will have to support these new initiatives through educational activities, accreditation policies, publications, and other services.

Conclusion

Organizations' attitudes toward human resources have undergone a profound shift. Once viewed as a cost to be minimized, employees are now seen as a real competitive resource when invested in appropriately. In a similar fashion, many employers now recognize that the HR systems used to manage employees rank among the most important competitive assets an organization possesses.[69]

This growing realization has created pressures on HR professionals to assume new roles, and for HR units to evolve into different types of structures. The traditional HR service and advisory functions will continue, but new demands are arising for strategic, proactive, and customer-oriented HRM activities.[70] Organizations in which HR professionals successfully handle these new roles will likely gain a significant competitive edge, and will reward their HR managers accordingly.

Our review indicated that middle management in-line units prefer that the HRM function should emphasize the old service and advisory functions. However, top management seem to prefer HRM units to perform the newer roles emphasizing strategic design, strategy implementation, and organizational improvement roles. Also, HRM professionals themselves seem to want to emphasize the older roles rather than the new ones. The review indicated that the new roles require a different type of HRM person than the older roles. The HRM function as it is presently structured is not likely to be able to attract this more bottom line-oriented and generalist type of person. The solution would seem to lie in creating two different types of HRM units within the organization as some organizations have already done. One type of unit would perform the traditional roles while the other would perform the new roles. New educational programs at universities could produce the type of HRM personnel that are required to staff and manage the new HRM units that have been set up to perform the new roles. However, only a few universities seem to have recognized the need for these new HRM roles and the importance of HRM as a knowledge base for *all* managers, not just HRM specialists.

We might close with a reminder that improving HRM practices can raise organizational productivity and bottom line performance. There is evidence that this is the case.[71] This is important not only because it is good for particular companies, but also because it helps the nation as a whole. There is now also good evidence that a real productivity decline has taken place in the United States in the majority of industries and the situation does not appear to be improving.[72] Acceptance of the new HRM roles by the HRM profession and HRM units in organizations could make a real contribution to the economy. However, as this review has indicated, there are many barriers to be overcome before this can occur.

◆

Notes

1. Carroll and Schuler.
2. Carroll (1989).
3. Cook and Ferris.
4. Hunter and Schmidt.
5. Dimick and Murray.
6. Peery and Shetty.
7. Carroll (1986).
8. Magnus.
9. Frohman.
10. Tornow.
11. Carroll (1987b).
12. Tosi, Rizzo, and Carroll (1990).
13. Carroll and Schuler.
14. Schuler and Youngblood.
15. Frohman.
16. Halcrow.
17. Schuler (1988).
18. Farquhar, Evans, and Tawadey.
19. Farquhar, Evans, and Tawadey.
20. Schein.
21. Kossek.
22. Schuler (1988).
23. Carr; Kearns.
24. Tichy.
25. Odiorne.
26. See, for example, Fombrun, Tichy, and Devanna; Carroll (1987a); Schuler and Jackson (1987).
27. Miles and Snow.
28. Schuler and Jackson (1988).
29. Kellerher and Cotter; Kerr.
30. Olian and Rynes; Carroll (1987a).
31. See Galbraith and Kazanjian for a discussion of this theory.
32. Dyer and Holder.
33. Devanna, Fombrun, and Tichy.
34. Freedman, Keller, and Montanari.
35. The Bureau of National Affairs, Inc.
36. Golden and Ramanujam.
37. Angle, Manz, and Van de Ven.

38. "Interview with Warde F. Wheaton and Larry M. Smith."
39. See Carroll and Tosi for a description of how this can be done.
40. Walker and Moorhead.
41. Tsui.
42. "Interview with Warde F. Wheaton and Larry M. Smith."
43. Beer, Spector, Lawrence, Mills, and Dalton.
44. Holder; see also, "Becoming a Business Partner First."
45. Schuler (1990).
46. Miner (1976).
47. Patten.
48. Miner (1976).
49. Bureau of National Affairs, Inc.
50. Walker and Moorhead.
51. Townsend.
52. Personal communication with the author.
53. Gillen and Carroll.
54. Cresap, McCormick, and Paget.
55. Hambrick, Frederickson, Korn, and Ferry.
56. Carroll and Schneier.
57. Beer, Spector, Lawrence, Mills, and Dalton.
58. Schuler (1990).
59. Miner (1988).
60. Kanter.
61. Carroll (1987a); Dyer and Holder.
62. Milkovich and Boudreau.
63. Sears.
64. Griffin.
65. Walker and Moorhead.
66. Informal survey conducted by author.
67. Carroll (1969).
68. Russ.
69. Solomon.
70. Schuler and MacMillan, Schuler (1990).
71. Kravetz.
72. Ullmann.

♦

References

Angle, H.L., C.C. Manz, A.H. Van de Ven. 1985. "Integrating Human Resource Management and Corporate Strategy: A Preview of the 3M Story." *Human Resource Management* 24: 51–68.

"Becoming a Business Partner First." 1986. *Personnel Administrator* (June): 61–65, 118.

Beer, M., B. Spector, P.R. Lawrence, D.Q. Mills, and R.E. Dalton. 1984. *Managing Human Assets*. New York: The Free Press.

Bureau of National Affairs, Inc. 1990. "Goals and Challenges in Human Resource Management: A BNA Policy and Practice Series Survey." *Bulletin to Management* 41, 4: 1–12.

Carr, C. 1987. "Injecting Quality into Personnel Management." *Personnel Journal* 80: 43–51.

Carroll, S.J. 1969. "Student Interest in Manpower Management Topics." Symposium paper presented at Academy of Management annual meeting.

―――. 1986. "Management by Objectives: Three Decades of Research and Experience." In *The Human Resources Management Reader*, eds. S.L. Rynes and G.T. Milkovich. Plano, TX: Business Publications, Inc.

―――. 1987a. "Strategic Planning and Compensation Systems." In *New Perspectives on Compensation*, eds. D.B. Balkin and L. Gomez-Mejia. Englewood Cliffs, NJ: Prentice Hall.

———. 1987b. "What Can HRM Do to Help U.S. Industrial Enterprises Cope with Current Change Pressures? Some Ideas from the Pacific Basin Nations." *Human Resources Planning* 3: 115–124.

———. 1989. "Multiple Management, Corporate Innovation, and U.S. Competitiveness." In *Perspectives in Human Resources*, American Society for Personnel Administration: 133–141.

Carroll, S.J., and C.E. Schneier. 1982. *Performance Appraisal and Review Systems*. Glenview, IL: Scott, Foresman & Co.

Carroll, S.J., and R.S. Schuler. 1983. "Professional HRM: Changing Functions and Problems." In *Readings in Human Resource Management*, ed. R.S. Schuler. St. Paul, MN: West Publishing Co.

Carroll, S.I., and H.L. Tosi. 1977. *Organizational Behavior*. Chicago: St. Clair Press.

Cook, D.S., and G.R. Ferris. 1986. "Management and Firm Effectiveness in Industries Experiencing Decline." *Human Resource Management* 25: 441–458.

Cresap, McCormick, and Paget. 1986. *Positioning Corporate Staff for the 1990s: A Survey of Top Executives of U.S. Corporations*. New York: Cresap, McCormick, and Paget.

Devanna, M.A., C. Fombrun, and N.M. Tichy. 1981. "Human Resources Management: A Strategic Perspective." *Organizational Dynamics* Winter: 51–67.

Dimick, D., and V.V. Murray. 1978. "Correlates of Substantive Policy Decisions in Organizations: The Case of Human Resource Management." *Academy of Management Journal* 21: 61–613.

Dyer, L., and G.W. Holder. 1987. "A Strategic Perspective of Human Resource Management." In *Human Resource Management: Evolving Roles and Responsibilities*, ed. L. Dyer.

Farquhar, A., P. Evans, and K. Tawadey. 1989. "Lessons from Practice in Managing Organizational Change." In *Human Resource Management in International Firms*, eds. P. Evans, Y. Doz, and A. Laurent. London: The Macmillan Press.

Fombrun, C., N.M. Tichy, and M.A. Devanna. 1984. *Strategic Human Resource Management*. New York: John Wiley and Sons.

Freedman, S.M., R.T. Keller, and R. Montanari. 1982. "The Compensation Program: Balancing Organizational and Employee Needs." *Compensation Review* 2: 47–53.

Frohman, M.A. 1984. "Human Resource Management and the Bottom Line." *Human Resource Management* 23: 315–337.

Galbraith, J., and R.K. Kazanjian. 1986. *Strategy Implementation: Structure, Systems, and Process*, 2nd ed. Reading, MA: Addison, Wesley.

Gillen, D.A., and S.J. Carroll. 1985. "Relationship of Managerial Ability to Unit Effectiveness in Organic Versus Mechanistic Units." *Journal of Management Studies* 22: 351–359.

Golden, K.A., and V. Ramanujam. 1985. "Between a Dream and a Nightmare: On the Integration of the Human Resource Management and Strategic Business Planning Processes." *Human Resource Management* 24: 429–454.

Griffin, R.J. 1982. *Task Design*. Glenview, IL: Scott, Foresman.

Halcrow, A. 1987. "Operation Phoenix: The Business of Human Resources." *Personnel Journal* 66: 92–101.

Hambrick, D.C., J.W. Frederickson, L.B. Korn, and R.M. Ferry. 1989. "Preparing Today's Leaders for Tomorrow's Realities." *Personnel* 66: 23–26.

Holder, G. 1986. "Human Resource Professionals: Adaptations to Changes in Function." Paper presented at the 18th annual meeting of the Personnel section of the Personnel Management Association, Key Biscayne, FL, Feb. 10.

Hunter, J.E., and F.L. Schmidt. 1984. "Validity and Utility of Alternative Predictors of Job Performance." *Psychological Bulletin* 96: 72–95.

"Interview with Warde F. Wheaton and Larry M. Smith." 1984. *Human Resource Management* 23: 161–186.

Kanter, R.M. 1983. *The Change Masters*. New York: Simon & Schuster.

Kearns, D. 1990. "Leadership through Quality." *The Executive* 4: 86–89.

Kellerher, E.J., and K.L. Cotter. 1982. "An Integrative Model for Human Resource Planning and Management." *Human Resource Management* 5: 15–27.

Kerr, J.L. 1982. "Assigning Managers on the Basis of the Life Cycle." *Journal of Business Strategy* 2: 58–65.

Kossek, E.E. 1987. "Human Resources Management Innovation." *Human Resource Management* 26: 71–92.

Kravetz, D.J. 1991. "Increase Finances through Progressive Management." *HR Magazine* 362: 57–62.

Magnus, M. 1987. "Personnel Policies in Partnership with Profit." *Personnel Journal* 66: 102–109.

Miles, R.E., and C.C. Snow, 1984. "Designing Strategic Human Resource Systems." *Organizational Dynamics* 12: 36–52.

Milkovich, G.T., and J.W. Boudreau. 1988. *Personnel/Human Resource Management*. Plano, TX: Business Publications, Inc.

Miner, J.B. 1976. "Levels of Motivation to Manage among Personnel and Industrial Relations Managers." *Journal of Applied Psychology* 61: 419–427.

―――. 1988. *Organizational Behavior*. New York: Random House.

Odiorne, G.S. 1978. "Personnel Management in the 1980s." In *PAIR Policy and Program Management, ASPA Handbook of Personnel and Industrial Relations, vol. VII*, eds. D. Yoder and H.G. Heneman Jr. Washington, DC: Bureau of National Affairs, Inc.

Olian, J.D., and S.L. Rynes. 1984. "Organizational Staffing: Integrating Practice with Strategy." *Industrial Relations* 23: 170–183.

Patten, T.H. 1972. "Personnel Administration and the Will to Manage." *Human Resource Management* 11, 3: 4–9.

Peery, N.S., and Y.K. Shetty. 1976. "An Empirical Study of Executive Transferability and Organizational Performance." *Academy of Management Proceedings*, Kansas City, MO.

Russ, C.F., Jr. 1985. "Should the Personnel Department Be Abolished?" *Personnel Journal* 64: 78–81.

Schein, E.H. 1989. "Organizational Culture: What It Is and How to Change It." In *Human Resource Management in International Firms*, eds. P. Evans, Y. Doz, and A. Laurent. New York: Macmillan.

Schuler, R.S. 1988. "A Case Study of the HR Department at Swiss Bank Corporation." *Human Resource Planning* 27: 242–254.

———. 1990. "Repositioning the Human Resource Function: Transformation or Demise?" *Academy of Management Executive* 4,3: 49–60.

Schuler, R.S., and S.E. Jackson. 1987. "Linking Competitive Strategies with Human Resource Management Practices." *Academy of Management Executive* (August) 2: 207–219.

———. 1988. "Organizational Strategy and Organization Level as Determinants of Human Resource Management Practices." *Human Resource Planning* 10: 125–141.

Schuler, R.S., and I.C. MacMillan. 1984. "Gaining Competitive Advantage through HRM Practices." *Human Resource Management* 23: 240–252.

Schuler, R.S., and S.A. Youngblood. 1986. *Effective Personnel Management*. St. Paul, MN: West Publishing Co.

Sears, L.N., Jr. 1984. "Organization and Human Resource Professionals in Transition." *Human Resource Management* 23:409–421.

Solomon, J. 1990. "People Power: Corporations Are Beginning to See Personnel Professionals as Strategic Managers of a Major Asset: Human Beings." *Wall Street Journal* (March 9).

Tichy, N. 1983. *Managing Strategic Change*. New York: Wiley.

Tornow, W.W. 1988. "Contract Redesign." *Personnel Administrator* 97: 101.

Tosi, H.L., J.R. Rizzo, and S.J. Carroll. 1990. *Managing Organizational Behavior*. New York: Harper & Row.

Townsend, R. 1970. *Up the Organization*. New York: Alfred Knopf.

Tsui, A.S. 1987. "Defining the Activities and Effectiveness of the Human Resource Department: A Multiple Constituency Approach." *Human Resource Management* 26: 35–70.

Ullmann, J.E. 1986. *The Anatomy of Industrial Decline: Productivity Investment and Location in U.S. Manufacturing*. Westport, CT: Quorum Books.

Walker, J.W., and G. Moorhead. 1987. "CEOs: What They Want from HRM." *Personnel Administrator* 32: 50–59.

Author Index

Authors appearing in this Index appear in the Notes and References at the end of each chapter. The individual authors of the chapters appear here also. Anyone referenced in the body of the text will appear in the Subject Index.

Adler, P.S. 6–163n, 6–163
Anderson, R.W. 6–45
Angle, H.L. 6–80n, 6–81, 6–223n, 6–224
Ann Arbor Business to Business 6–44n, 6–47
Applebaum, E. 6–80n, 6–81
Argote, L. 6–162n, 6–163
Argyris, C. 6–201n, 6–201
Armstrong, J.S. 6–44
Arvey, R.D. 6–137n, 6–138
Ascher, W. 6–44
Axel, H. 6–44n, 6–47
Ayres, R.V. 6–44

Bacon, K.H. 6–44n, 6–47
Bakshian, A., Jr. 6–45
Banas, P.B. 6–162n, 6–163
Barkin, S. 6–138n, 6–138
Barley, S.R. 6–162n, 6–163
Barrett, N.S. 6–80n, 6–81
Beach, K., Jr. 6–137n, 6–140
Beatty, C.A. 6–162n, 6–163, 6–163n
Bedeian, A.G. 6–162n, 6–163
Beer, M. 6–163, 6–163n, 6–224, 6–224n
Belenky, A.H. 6–137n, 6–138
Bemis, S.E. 6–137n, 6–138
Bergen Record 6–45
Berk, R.A. 6–138n, 6–138
Bernstein, A. 6–45
Berry, J.M. 6–80n, 6–81
Beutell, N.J. 6–45, 6–80n, 6–83, 6–167—6–200, 6–201n, 6–201
Bird, C. 6–80n, 6–81
Blair, E. 6–201n, 6–201
Blair, S.N. 6–80n, 6–81
Bland-Acosta, B.A. 6–201n, 6–201
Blasi, J. 6–162n, 6–165
Bloom, A.J. 6–201n, 6–201

Boucher, W.I. 6–45
Boudreau, J.W. 6–137n, 6–138, 6–224n, 6–226
Bower, C.D. 6–43n, 6–47
Bremmer, B. 6–46
Brewer, J. Frank 6–138n, 6–140
Brief, A.P. 6–162n, 6–165
Briscoe, D.E. 6–80n, 6–81
Britt, L.P., III 6–80n, 6–81
Brockner, J. 6–162n, 6–163
Brod, C. 6–201n, 6–201
Brown, J.K. 6–45, 6–46
Bulletin to Management 6–44n, 6–47
Bureau of National Affairs, Inc. 6–223n, 6–224n, 6–224
Bureau of the Census. *See* U.S. Bureau of the Census
Burke, E. 6–80n, 6–83, 6–136n, 6–137n, 6–138n
Burke, M.J. 6–84—6–136, 6–138, 6–139, 6–141
Business Week 6–44n, 6–47

Caldwell, P. 6–80n, 6–81
Carr, C. 6–223n, 6–224
Carroll, S.J. 6–138n, 6–139, 6–204—6–223, 6–223n, 6–224, 6–224n, 6–225, 6–227
Carron, T.J. 6–137n, 6–139
Carter, P.O. 6–162n, 6–163n, 6–164
Chapman, B.L. 6–46
Chase, W.H. 6–45
Clark, A.O. 6–136n, 6–138n, 6–141
Clark, K.J. 6–136n, 6–140
Coates, J.F. 6–43n, 6–44n, 6–47
Cook, D.S. 6–223n, 6–225
Copeland, L. 6–44n, 6–47
Cornelius, E.T. 6–137n, 6–139
Cotter, K.L. 6–223n, 6–226
Covin, T.J. 6–163n, 6–163, 6–164
Cresap 6–224n, 6–225

Crosby, P.B.   6-162n, 6-163
Crowder, J.H.   6-80n, 6-81

Dalton, R.E.   6-224n, 6-224
Dance, F.E.   6-162n, 6-163
David, F.R.   6-46
Davis, K.   6-80n, 6-81
Davis, S.M.   6-45
Day, R.R.   6-138n, 6-138
Delaney, M.J.   6-138n, 6-140
Deming, W.E.   6-162n, 6-163
DePree, H.   6-45
Devanna, M.A.   6-44n, 6-49, 6-223n, 6-225
Didsbury, H.F., Jr.   6-45
Dimick, D.   6-223n, 6-225
Doering, M.   6-43n, 6-47
Dreyfuss, J.   6-44n, 6-47
Dyer, L.   6-45, 6-80n, 6-81, 6-136n, 6-139, 6-223n, 6-224n, 6-225

Edwards, M.R.   6-201n, 6-202
Ehrlich, E.   6-44n, 6-47
Eisenhardt, K.M.   6-162n, 6-165
Eurich, N.P.   6-80n, 6-81
Evans, P.   6-223n, 6-225
Evans, P.A.L.   6-80n, 6-81

Fair Employment Practices   6-44n, 6-47
Fairbairn, U.   6-50—6-80
Faley, R.H.   6-137n, 6-138
Farace, R.V.   6-162n, 6-163
Farquhar   6-223n, 6-225
Ferris, G.R.   6-223n, 6-225
Ferry, R.M.   6-224n, 6-226
Fierman, J.   6-44n, 6-48
Fisher, A.B.   6-162n, 6-163
Fitz-enz, J.   6-136n, 6-137n, 6-139
Fitz-Gibbon, C.T.   6-137n, 6-140
Fombrun, C.   6-223n, 6-225
Ford, R.C.   6-201n, 6-202
Fossum, J.A.   6-80n, 6-81
Foster, B.P.   6-44n, 6-48
Fowler, E.   6-44n, 6-48
Fraze, J.   6-44n, 6-48
Frederick, J.T.   6-137n, 6-139
Frederick, W.C.   6-80n, 6-81
Frederickson, J.W.   6-224n, 6-226

Freedman, S.M.   6-223n, 6-225
Freeman, M.E.   6-137n, 6-140
Friedman, D.A.   6-80n, 6-81
Frohman, M.A.   6-223n, 6-225

Galbraith, J.   6-223n, 6-225
Gallup, G., Jr.   6-43n, 6-48
Garland, S.B.   6-44n, 6-47
Garvin, C.C., Jr.   6-46
Gayle, L.   6-201n, 6-202
Gelford, S.M.   6-46
General Accounting Office. See U.S. General Accounting Office
Gerson, H.E.   6-80n, 6-81
Ghorpade, J.V.   6-137n, 6-139
Gillen, D.A.   6-224n, 6-225
Godiwalla, Y.   6-46
Godkewitsch, M.   6-137n, 6-138n, 6-139
Golden, K.A.   6-223n, 6-226
Goldstein and Associates   6-137n, 6-139
Goodale, J.G.   6-137n, 6-139
Gooding, R.Z.   6-136n, 6-137n, 6-139, 6-141
Goodman, P.S.   6-162n, 6-163
Goodstein, M.L.   6-46
Gordon, J.R.M.   6-162n, 6-163n, 6-163
Granrose, C.S.   6-80n, 6-81
Grayson, T.   6-44n, 6-48
Griffin, R.J.   6-224n, 6-226
Guzzo, R.A.   6-138n, 6-139, 6-142—6-162, 6-162n, 6-165

Halcrow, A.   6-223n, 6-226
Hall, D.T.   6-137n, 6-139
Hall, R.H.   6-162n, 6-164
Hallet, J.J.   6-43n, 6-47
Hambrick, D.C.   6-224n, 6-226
Harris, D.L.   6-46
Harris, P.R.   6-46
Hawk, R.H.   6-136n, 6-139
Hegarty, W.H.   6-46
Heilbroner, R.L.   6-80n, 6-81
Helleloid, D.A.   6-163n, 6-163
Heller, A.S.   6-201n, 6-202
Henderson, R.I.   6-138n, 6-139
Heneman, H.G., III   6-80n, 6-81
Herbst, P.G.   6-136n, 6-140

Hickman, C.R. 6–45
Hoffman, C.C. 6–80n, 6–82
Holder, G. 6–136n, 6–139, 6–223n, 6–224n, 6–225, 6–226
Horton, S.G. 6–80n, 6–82
Howard, J.S. 6–80n, 6–82
HR Reporter 6–44n, 6–48
Hunt, V.D. 6–45
Hunter, J.E. 6–137n, 6–140, 6–223n, 6–226
Hunter, R.F. 6–137n, 6–140

Irion, M.S. 6–80n, 6–82

Jackson, S.E. 6–44n, 6–49, 6–223n, 6–227
Jain, C. 6–46
Jenkins, K. 6–201n, 6–202
Jette, R.D. 6–138n, 6–139
Johnston, W.B. 6–43n, 6–44n, 6–48, 6–201n, 6–202
Joyce, M.M. 6–50—6–80
Jucker, J.V. 6–162n, 6–165
Juran, J.M. 6–162n, 6–163

Kahn, H. 6–45
Kanabayashi, M. 6–44n, 6–48
Kanter, R.M. 6–44n, 6–48, 6–224n, 6–226
Katz, R. 6–162n, 6–164
Katzell, R.A. 6–138n, 6–139
Kaufman, G. 6–84—6–136, 6–138n, 6–140
Kazanjian, R.K. 6–223n, 6–225
Kearns, D.T. 6–80n, 6–82, 6–223n, 6–226
Keller, R.T. 6–223n, 6–225
Kellerher, E.J. 6–223n, 6–226
Keough, L. 6–201n, 6–202
Kerr, J.L. 6–223n, 6–226
Kersten, U. 6–162n, 6–165
Kilmann, R.H. 6–163n, 6–163, 6–164
Kirkland, R.I., Jr. 6–44n, 6–48
Kirkpatrick, D. 6–138n, 6–140
Kirsch, M. 6–137n, 6–141
Kleiman, L.S. 6–136n, 6–140
Klein, H.E. 6–46
Klein, K.J. 6–142—6–162, 6–162n, 6–163n, 6–164, 6–165

Koepp, S. 6–44n, 6–48, 6–162n, 6–164
Koretz, G. 6–44n, 6–48
Korn, L.B. 6–224n, 6–226
Kossek, E.E. 6–223n, 6–226
Koxlowski, S. 6–45
Krauss, W.A. 6–163n, 6–164
Kravetz, D.J. 6–224n, 6–226
Kroenke, D.M. 6–201n, 6–202
Kupfer, A. 6–44n, 6–48
Kustoff, M. 6–201n, 6–202
Kutscher, R.E. 6–46

Labich, K. 6–46, 6–162n, 6–164
Laliberte, M. 6–162n, 6–164
Landry, R.M. 6–201n, 6–202
Latham, G.P. 6–138n, 6–140
LaVan, H. 6–201n, 6–202
Lawler, E.E. 6–162n, 6–164
Lawrence, P.R. 6–138n, 6–140, 6–162n, 6–164, 6–224, 6–224n
Lederer, A.L. 6–201n, 6–202
Ledvinka, J. 6–136n, 6–141
Leonard-Barton, D. 6–163n, 6–164
Leote, D.M. 6–201n, 6–202
Levine, J. 6–44n, 6–48
Liker, J.K. 6–163n, 6–165
Ling, C.C. 6–80n, 6–82
Linneman, R.E. 6–46
Locke, E.A. 6–138n, 6–140
Lodge, G.C. 6–80n, 6–82
Lorsch, J.W. 6–138n, 6–140, 6–162n, 6–164

MacAdam, M. 6–201n, 6–202
Maccoby, M. 6–45
MacDonald, D. 6–162n, 6–163
MacMillan, I. 6–46, 6–80n, 6–83, 6–136n, 6–141, 6–224n, 6–227
Mager, R. 6–137n, 6–138n, 6–140
Magnus, M. 6–223n, 6–226
Mahoney, J. 6–137n, 6–140
Main, J. 6–44n, 6–48
Majchrzak, A. 6–162n, 6–164
Manufacturing Studies Board 6–162n, 6–164
Manz, C.C. 6–80n, 6–81, 6–223n, 6–224

Marcus, A.A. 6–80n, 6–82
Markus, M.L. 6–162n, 6–164
Masi, D.A. 6–80n, 6–82
Mathys, N.J. 6–201n, 6–202
McAlister, M.K. 6–201n, 6–202
McComas, M. 6–44n, 6–48
McCormick 6–224n, 6–225
McElroy, M.L. 6–201n, 6–202
Mellor, E.F. 6–80n, 6–82
Meyer, G.J. 6–201n, 6–202
Miles, R.E. 6–223n, 6–226
Milkovich, G.T. 6–138n, 6–140, 6–224n, 6–226
Miller, M.S. 6–201n, 6–202
Miller, W.H. 6–44n, 6–48
Mills, D.Q. 6–224n, 6–224
Miner, F.J. 6–201n, 6–202
Miner, J.B. 6–80n, 6–82, 6–138n, 6–140, 6–224n, 6–226
Miner, M.G. 6–80n, 6–82, 6–138n, 6–140
Mitroff, I.I. 6–45
Montanari, R. 6–223n, 6–225
Moorhead, G. 6–224n, 6–227
Morgan, S. 6–162n, 6–165
Morris, J.H. 6–162n, 6–165
Morris, L.L. 6–137n, 6–140
Morrison, J.L. 6–45
Muchinsky, P.M. 6–162n, 6–165
Munn, R.W. 6–201n, 6–202
Murray, V.V. 6–223n, 6–225

Nadler, D.A. 6–163n, 6–165, 6–166
Nanus, B. 6–46
Nardone, T.J. 6–80n, 6–82
Nardoni, R. 6–201n, 6–202
Narod, S. 6–80n, 6–82
Nasar, S. 6–46
Nash, A.N. 6–80n, 6–82
Nelson-Horchler, J. 6–44n, 6–48
Nelton, S. 6–46
Nemirow, M. 6–80n, 6–82
Newman, J.M. 6–138n, 6–140
Newman, W.H. 6–46, 6–163n, 6–166
Noe, R.D. 6–137n, 6–141
Normand, J. 6–137n, 6–138n, 6–140, 6–141
Nussbaum, B. 6–44n, 6–48

O'Dell, C. 6–44n, 6–48
Odiorne, G.S. 6–223n, 6–226
Office of Technology Assessment. *See* U.S. Office of Technology Assessment
O'Leary, D.E. 6–201n, 6–202
Olian, J.D. 6–223n, 6–227
O'Reilly, C.A. 6–162n, 6–165
Owens, E.L. 6–46

Packer, A.H. 6–201n, 6–202
Paget 6–224n, 6–225
Pake, G.E. 6–80n, 6–82
Patten, T.H., Jr. 6–138n, 6–141, 6–224n, 6–227
Payne, R. 6–136n, 6–141
Pearce, J.A., II 6–46
Pearlman, K. 6–136n, 6–137n, 6–139
Peery, N.S. 6–223n, 6–227
Perkins, D.S. 6–80n, 6–82
Perry, N. 6–44n, 6–48
Perry, S.G. 6–201n, 6–202
Perryman, W. 6–80n, 6–82
Peters, T. 6–44n, 6–49
Petersen, D.J. 6–80n, 6–82
Pierce, J.L. 6–162n, 6–165
Pipe, P. 6–138n, 6–140
Piserchia, P.V. 6–80n, 6–81
Platamura, L.M. 6–201n, 6–203
Porter, L.W. 6–138n, 6–141
Prokesch, S.E. 6–44n, 6–49
Pugh, D.S. 6–136n, 6–141

Quarrey, M. 6–162n, 6–165

Raju, N.S. 6–137n, 6–139, 6–141
Ralls, R.S. 6–162n, 6–163n, 6–164
Ramanujam, V. 6–223n, 6–226
Ramirez, A. 6–44n, 6–49
Rappaport, M. 6–80n, 6–82
Reich, R.B. 6–45
Rendero, T. 6–44n, 6–49
Renfro, W.L. 6–45
Rhodes, S.R. 6–43n, 6–47
Rice, M.F. 6–46
Rizzo, J.R. 6–223n, 6–227
Roberts, K.H. 6–162n, 6–165
Robinson, D.G. 6–138n, 6–141
Robinson, J.C. 6–138n, 6–141
Roitman, D.B. 6–163n, 6–165

Rosen, C.   6-162n, 6-165
Roskies, E.   6-163n, 6-165
Rousseau, D.M.   6-162n, 6-165
Rubenfeld, S.A.   6-162n, 6-165
Rummler, G.A.   6-138n, 6-141
Russ, C.F., Jr.   6-224n, 6-227
Rynes, S.L.   6-223n, 6-226

Salyards, S.   6-137n, 6-138n, 6-140
Saseen, S.   6-80n, 6-82
Scarpello, V.G.   6-136n, 6-141
Schaffitzel, W.   6-162n, 6-165
Schein, E.H.   6-223n, 6-227
Schmidt, F.L.   6-137n, 6-139, 6-140, 6-223n, 6-226
Schmitt, N.   6-137n, 6-141
Schneider, B.   6-162n, 6-165
Schneier, C.E.   6-138n, 6-139, 6-224n, 6-225
Schodt, F.L.   6-45
Schrenk, L.P.   6-43n, 6-49
Schuler, R.S.   6-1—6-43, 6-44n, 6-46, 6-49, 6-80n, 6-83, 6-136n, 6-137n, 6-141, 6-223n, 6-224n, 6-225, 6-227
Schuster, M.   6-43n, 6-47
Schwab, D.P.   6-80n, 6-81
Schwartz, J.   6-162n, 6-165
Sears, L.N., Jr.   6-224n, 6-227
Seybolt, J.W.   6-138n, 6-141
Shank, S.E.   6-43n, 6-49
Sherwood, J.J.   6-46
Shetty, Y.K.   6-223n, 6-227
Shuman, J.E.   6-201n, 6-202
Silva, M.A.   6-45
Simon, S.H.   6-201n, 6-203
Slater, R.   6-80n, 6-83
Smith, Larry M.   6-224n, 6-226
Snow, C.C.   6-223n, 6-226
Snyder, R.A.   6-162n, 6-165
Society for Industrial and
    Organizational
    Psychology   6-137n, 6-141
Soder, D.A.   6-137n, 6-138
Solomon, J.   6-224n, 6-227
Sovereign, K.L.   6-80n, 6-83
Spector, B.   6-224n, 6-224
Spirig, J.E.   6-201n, 6-203
Stackel, L.   6-80n, 6-83

Steers, R.M.   6-138n, 6-141
Susser, P.A.   6-80n, 6-83
Sutton, R.I.   6-162n, 6-165

Tarbania, D.L.   6-44n, 6-49
Tawadey, K.   6-223n, 6-225
Teltsch, K.   6-44n, 6-49
Thorne, D.R.   6-80n, 6-83
Thurow, L.C.   6-80n, 6-81, 6-83
Tichy, N.M.   6-44n, 6-49, 6-225, 6-227
Tornow, W.W.   6-223n, 6-227
Tosi, H.L.   6-223n, 6-224n, 6-225, 6-227
Townsend, R.   6-136n, 6-141, 6-224n, 6-227
Tsui, A.S.   6-224n, 6-227
Turban, E.   6-201n, 6-202
Tushman, M.L.   6-163n, 6-165, 6-166

Ullmann, J.E.   6-224n, 6-227
U.S. Bureau of the Census   6-45, 6-80n, 6-83
U.S. General Accounting
    Office   6-162n, 6-166
U.S. Office of Technology
    Assessment   6-162n, 6-165

Van de Ven, A.H.   6-80n, 6-81, 6-223n, 6-224
Verespej, M.A.   6-80n, 6-83
Vernon-Gerstenfeld, S.   6-80n, 6-83
Vinton, K.L.   6-138n, 6-141

Wagel, W.H.   6-80n, 6-83
Wagner, J.A.   6-136n, 6-139
Walker, A.J.   6-167—6-200, 6-201n, 6-203
Walker, J.W.   6-44n, 6-49, 6-224n, 6-227
Wall Street Journal   6-43n, 6-49
Wanous, J.P.   6-136n, 6-141
Weiner, D.   6-46
Weisbord, M.A.   6-136n, 6-141
Wheaton, Warde F.   6-224n, 6-226
Wiener, A.   6-45
Wilbur, C.S.   6-80n, 6-81, 6-83
Williams, M.C.   6-201n, 6-202
Witkin, E.   6-201n, 6-203

Young, K.M. 6–162n, 6–165
Youngblood, S.A. 6–80n, 6–83, 6–223n, 6–227

Zammuto, R.F. 6–162n, 6–163
Zellner, W. 6–45
Zentner, R.D. 6–47
Zuboff, S. 6–45, 6–162n, 6–166

Subject Index

Academy of Finance 6–15
Accidents 6–74
Acquisitions and mergers 6–32, 6–65
Action Technologies 6–38
ADP (company) 6–31
AETNA 6–61—6–62
Age Discrimination in Employment Act (1967) 6–72
Aging of the work force 6–4—6–6, 6–51, 6–56—6–57
AIDS in the workplace 6–13, 6–75—6–77
Alcohol abuse. *See* Substance and drug abuse in the workplace
Allocation systems 6–93
American Express 6–15
American Foundation for AIDS Research 6–77
American Institute for Managing Diversity 6–17
Ameritech 6–33, 6–34
Applicant drug screening programs 6–77—6–78
Appraisals. *See* Performance evaluation programs
Architectural design for HRIS 6–198—6–200
Arizona State University 6–14
Armco Inc. 6–98
Arthur D. Little, Inc. 6–63—6–64
Artificial intelligence 6–170, 6–183
Assessment centers 6–96
Atari 6–145
Atlantic-Richfield 6–219
AT&T
   AIDS education programs 6–75
   downsizing 6–143, 6–144, 6–145
   innovation programs 6–33
   personnel selection 6–96
   training/development 6–14
Automation
   applications 6–31—6–32, 6–39—6–40
   organizational structure 6–40—6–42

Automobile industry 6–66—6–67. *See also* Ford Motor Company
Avon Products Inc. 6–16

Baby boomers 6–12, 6–66
Balance of payments 6–21
Bank of America 6–19
Banks and banking 6–19
Bell & Howell 6–146
Bell Labs 6–153
BellSouth Corporation 6–64
Ben and Jerry's 6–153
Benefits. *See* Compensation and benefits
Black workers 6–8—6–9, 6–10, 6–27
Booz Allen & Hamilton 6–39
Boston Compact 6–14
Bottom-up communication 6–143, 6–150—6–151, 6–159—6–160, 6–161—6–162
Bridgestone 6–21
Brunswick Mercury Marine Division 6–34
Bureau of Labor Statistics. *See* U.S. Bureau of Labor Statistics
Bureau of National Affairs, Inc. 6–216
Bureau of the Census. *See* U.S. Bureau of the Census

CADD. *See* Computer-aided design and drafting
Cafeteria plans 6–119
California Medical Center (Los Angeles) 6–53
Change. *See* Organizational change; Resistance to change
Chase (bank) 6–19
Chemical Bank 6–11, 6–75
Chicago and Northwestern Railroad 6–96
Child care programs 6–4, 6–52—6–55

6-235

China
  economic conditions 6–18
Chrysler 6–156
CIA 6–98
Citibank 6–19
Citicorp 6–65
Citizens Commission on AIDS (NY) 6–75
Civil Rights Act (1964) 6–72
Client satisfaction and personnel research 6–130, 6–132—6–133
Comerce Clearing House 6–35
Commonwealth v. Hunt 6–121
Communication and organizational change
  computer technology implementation and 6–156—6–160
  downsizing and 6–143—6–146
  employee ownership and 6–146—6–151
  overview 6–142—6–143, 6–160—6–162
  quality/productivity programs and 6–151—6–156
Compensation and benefits programs. *See also* Wages and salaries
  establishment/evaluation/improvement 6–116—6–121, 6–123
  HRIS and 6–193—6–197
  incentive pay 6–152—6–153
  pay equity 6–7—6–8
Competition, international 6–17—6–25, 6–25—6–36
Computer-aided design and drafting (CADD) 6–159, 6–160
Computer phobia 6–178—6–180
Computer technology implementation 6–156—6–160, 6–178—6–180
Conference Board 6–28
Consumer Credit Protection Act (1970) 6–72
Contingent workers 6–28, 6–29, 6–31, 6–41
Coordination Technology 6–38
Coordinator (computer program) 6–38
Copeland-Griggs Productions (San Francisco, CA) 6–17

Corning Glass 6–34
Corporate Education Center 6–60
Cyberphobia 6–178—6–180

Dai-Ichi Kangyo Bank (Japan) 6–19
Data base management systems 6–168—6–169, 6–180—6–183
Data General 6–95
Davis, Donald 6–11
Decentralization 6–29, 6–32
Decision-making processes in HRM 6–84
Decker, Hans W. 6–21
"Defender" business strategies 6–211
Deficit Reduction Act (1984) 6–147
Defined benefits plan 6–194
Defined contribution and savings plans 6–196
Department of Health and Human Services. *See* U.S. Department of Health and Human Services
Desktop computers 6–171
Diagonal slice task forces 6–152, 6–153
Digital Equipment Corp. 6–16
Disney 6–31
Diversity in the work force 6–15—6–17
Dow Chemical Company 6–23, 6–34
Downsizing 6–29—6–31, 6–143—6–146
Drug abuse. *See* Substance and drug abuse in the workplace
Dual-income families 6–4, 6–7, 6–51, 6–55
Dual work-force staffing model 6–207
DuPont Company 6–75

EAPs. *See* Employee assistance programs
Economic conditions. *See* International economic conditions
Educational Testing Service 6–119
Education and business needs 6–13—6–15, 6–51, 6–59—6–64

Subject Index   6-237

EI. *See* Employee involvement programs
Elder care programs   6-53—6-55
Elder Services of Merrimack Valley, Inc.   6-53—6-54
Electronic Sweatshop, The   6-41
Eli Lilly   6-212
Employee assistance programs (EAPs)   6-57—6-58, 6-112
Employee Development Program   6-68
Employee involvement programs (EI)   6-67—6-68, 6-153—6-156
Employee ownership   6-146—6-151
Employee Polygraph Protection Act (1988)   6-13
Employee referral programs   6-94—6-95
Employee relations   6-122
Employee Retirement Income Security Act of 1974 (ERISA)   6-72, 6-147
Employee statistics   6-191—6-192
Employee stock ownership plans (ESOP)   6-147—6-151
Employee values   6-11—6-13
Employment Service. *See* U.S. Employment Service
"Enter-Prize" program   6-34
Environment. *See* External environment
Equal opportunity programs   6-73—6-74
Equal Pay Act (1963)   6-72
Equitable Life Assurance Society   6-16
ERISA. *See* Employee Retirement Income Security Act of 1974
ESOP. *See* Employee stock ownership plans
Evaluations. *See* Performance evaluation programs
Expert systems   6-170, 6-183
External environment and HRM
  economic/competitive trends   6-65—6-71
  economic/organizational trends   6-25—6-35
  international conditions   6-17—6-25
  legal/regulatory conditions   6-71—6-78
  overview   6-1—6-2, 6-42—6-43, 6-50—6-51, 6-78—6-80, 6-205, 6-207
  social/demographic changes   6-2—6-16, 6-51—6-64
  technological trends/developments   6-36—6-42
Exxon   6-65, 6-68

Fear of computers   6-178—6-180
Federal Aviation Administration. *See* U.S. Federal Aviation Administration
Firestone   6-21, 6-144
Flexible benefits plans   6-119
Flexible work schedules   6-55—6-57
Ford Motor Company
  employee involvement   6-67—6-68, 6-154
  international competition   6-23
  labor relations   6-122
  organizational change   6-210
  quality management programs   6-31, 6-155
Freedman, Audrey   6-28, 6-29

Galvin, Robert   6-43
Galvin Center (Chicago, IL)   6-60
Garson, Barbara   6-41
General Accounting Office. *See* U.S. General Accounting Office
General Electric
  HRM function   6-212, 6-221
  organizational change   6-32
  training/development   6-14, 6-103
General Motors   6-21, 6-31, 6-68—6-69, 6-169
Germany
  economic conditions   6-19, 6-66
GNP
  international comparisons   6-18—6-19
Goldman Sachs   6-95
Goodyear   6-71
Graying of the work force. *See* Aging of the work force
Grievances   6-123

Group insurance 6-196—6-197
Gyllenhammar, Pehr G. 6-21

Hackman, J. Richard 6-12
Hardware for HRIS 6-171
Harvard Business School 6-214, 6-219, 6-221—6-222
Health and safety programs 6-74—6-78
Herman Miller (company) 6-70—6-71
Hershey 6-101
Hewlett-Packard 6-16, 6-73—6-74, 6-212
Hispanic workers 6-8—6-9, 6-10—6-11, 6-27
Honeywell Inc.
 diversity programs 6-16
 employee ownership 6-13
 HRM function 6-212, 6-213—6-214
 training/development 6-14
Hong Kong
 economic conditions 6-18
Human resouce information center (HRIC)
 applications and modules 6-190—6-197
 data administration 6-183—6-185
 installations 6-197—6-200
 overview 6-167, 6-169
 security/privacy and 6-185—6-187
 support/training/future roles for 6-187—6-189
Human resource information systems (HRIS)
 applications and models 6-190—6-197
 components of 6-171—6-172
 data base management 6-168—6-169, 6-180—6-189
 installations 6-197—6-200
 overview/history 6-167—6-168, 6-170—6-171, 6-200
 personal computers and 6-169—6-170
 selection/implementation 6-172—6-180

Human resource managers
 behavioral requirements 6-214—6-217
 education 6-219, 6-221—6-222
Human resources management. *See also* External environment and HRM; Internal information and HRM; Training and development
 allocation systems 6-93
 program goals 6-85—6-87
 roles/responsibilities/structures 6-204—6-223

Iacocca, Lee 6-145
IBM Corp.
 AIDS education program 6-75, 6-76—6-77
 child/elder care program 6-54—6-55
 drug screening program 6-77—6-78
 education programs 6-59—6-60, 6-62—6-63
 HRM function 6-212
 international competition 6-23
 promotion/selection 6-95
 restructuring 6-30—6-31
 training/development 6-11, 6-70, 6-101
"I Have a Dream Foundation" 6-14
Illiteracy 6-10—6-11, 6-13—6-15, 6-59, 6-62
Immigrants in the work force 6-9—6-10
Imperial Oil of Canada 6-103
Incentive pay programs 6-152—6-153
Industrial accidents 6-74
Information management. *See* Communication and organizational change; Internal information and HRM
In-house development of HRIS software 6-175, 6-177
In-house educational programs 6-59—6-64
Innovation and productivity 6-32, 6-33—6-34

Subject Index 6-239

Institute for Corporate Education 6-61—6-62
Institute for Research on Learning 6-64
Insurance 6-196—6-197
Internal information and HRM. *See also* Human resource information systems
  compensation and benefits 6-116—6-121
  establishing program goals 6-85—6-87
  labor relations 6-121—6-129
  organizational design and position management 6-87—6-92
  overview 6-84, 6-188
  performance evaluation/appraisal 6-106—6-116
  personnel research programs 6-129—6-136
  staffing/internal recruitment 6-92—6-100
  training/development 6-100—6-106
Internal recruitment programs
  establishment/evaluation/improvement 6-93—6-100
Internal Revenue Service. *See* U.S. Internal Revenue Service
International economic conditions 6-17—6-23, 6-65—6-66
In the Age of the Smart Machine 6-41
Intrapreneurship 6-33—6-34
Investments, Japanese
  United States 6-19—6-22
Investments, US
  international 6-18—6-23

Jannotta, Bray, and Associates 6-69
Japan
  economic conditions 6-18—6-19, 6-19—6-22, 6-65, 6-66
Japanese Educational Challenge, The 6-11
J.C. Penney Co. 6-115
J.I. Case 6-156
Job Opportunity Bank 6-68
Job posting systems 6-94—6-95

Job projections 6-25, 6-27
Job security programs 6-68—6-69
Job sharing 6-56
JOBS Pension Program 6-68
Johnson & Johnson 6-58, 6-75
Joseph Schlitz Brewing Company 6-69
Junkins, Jerry 6-24

Kearns, David 6-11
Kiethley Instruments 6-209
Knowledge, skills and abilities 6-10—6-11, 6-25—6-27, 6-59, 6-100
Korea, South. *See* South Korea

Labor force. *See* Work force
Labor law and legislation 6-71—6-78
Labor relations programs
  establishment/evaluation/improvement 6-121—6-129
Labor unions 6-121. *See also* United Auto Workers
Lateral communication 6-143, 6-156, 6-158—6-159, 6-161
Layoffs 6-68—6-70, 6-146
Leadership 6-129, 6-134—6-136
Literacy volunteers 6-13
"Little Tigers" 6-18
Live for Life program 6-58
L.L. Bean 6-31, 6-32, 6-34
Local area networks 6-170
Lockheed-Georgia Company 6-39
Lotus 1-2-3 6-169

Macro organizational change 6-155
Mainframe computers 6-171
Management by objectives 6-90
Management Education Institute 6-63—6-64
Managerial assessment centers 6-96
Managers 6-109—6-110, 6-114—6-115. *See also* Human resource managers
Manufacturer's Hanover 6-19
Manufacturing industry 6-156

Manufacturing resource planning system (MRP II) 6–157, 6–158
MBA programs 6–219, 6–221
McDonalds 6–31
Medical care programs 6–57—6–59
Medical insurance 6–196—6–197
Merck & Company 6–220
Merck Corporation 6–52—6–53
Mergers. *See* Acquisitions and mergers
Merit pay 6–152
Microcomputers and minicomputers 6–171
Minnesota Mining & Manufacturing. *See* 3M
Minorities in the work force 6–8—6–9, 6–14—6–15, 6–73
Modeling programs 6–182
Modular development of HRIS software 6–175, 6–176
Morehouse College (GA) 6–17
Morgan (bank) 6–19
Motivation 6–12—6–13, 6–108—6–109, 6–112—6–114
Motorola 6–43, 6–60—6–61
MRP II. *See* Manufacturing resource planning system

NASA-Manned Spacecraft Center 6–103
National Institute for Occupational Safety and Health 6–74
National Institute of Drug Abuse 6–77
Needs analysis for HRIS implementation 6–174—6–175
Need theories of motivation 6–108
Negotiations 6–123
Nissan 6–23
Nordstroms 6–31
NUMMI plant (Fremont, CA) 6–21, 6–32

Occupational Safety and Health Act (1970) 6–72, 6–74
Occupational Safety and Health Administration. *See* U.S. Occupational Safety and Health Administration

Odiorne, George 6–211
Ohio Bell 6–34
Older Americans Program 6–56
On-the-job performance 6–106—6–116
Organizational change. *See also* Communication and organizational change; Computer technology implementation; Downsizing
external environment and 6–25, 6–27, 6–32, 6–34—6–35
HRIS and 6–187—6–188
HRM and 6–208—6–211
Organizational design and position management programs establishment/evaluation/improvement 6–87—6–92
Organizational structure anticipated trends/changes 6–25—6–35
automation and 6–40—6–42
implications for HRM structure 6–23—6–25, 6–217—6–221
OSHA. *See* U.S. Occupational Safety and Health Administration
Ownership as employee motivation 6–12—6–13

Pacific Intermountain Express 6–38
Part-time workers 6–51, 6–55—6–66
Pay equity 6–7—6–8
Payroll and HRIS 6–193
Pension calculation and HRIS 6–194—6–196
Performance evaluation programs establishment/evaluation/improvement 6–106—6–116
Personal computers (PCs) 6–169—6–170
Personal Safety Program 6–75
Personnel research programs identification/evaluation/improvement 6–129—6–136
Pillsbury Company 6–103
Pitney Bowes 6–31
Pizza Hut 6–5

Subject Index   6-241

Poor performers
  identification/rehabilitation/
    removal   6–110—6–112,
    6–115—6–116
Popoff, Frank P.   6–34
Population rate statistics   6–2—6–4,
  6–17—6–18, 6–51
Postal Service. See U.S. Postal Service
Pregnancy Discrimination Act
  (1978)   6–72
Preston Trucking   6–217
Primary Insurance Amount
  (PIA)   6–195
Privacy safeguards in HRIS   6–186—
  6–187
Private Industry Council (Boston,
  MA)   6–14
Process theories of motivation   6–109
Procter & Gamble   6–16
Productivity
  enhancement programs and
    communication   6–151—
    6–156
  impact of labor relations
    6–124—6–125, 6–126
  international comparisons
    6–20—6–22, 6–66
  motivation and   6–109
Program goals
  establishment/evaluation/
    improvement   6–85—6–87
Promotion programs   6–99—6–100,
  6–114—6–115
"Prospector" business
  strategies   6–211
Protectionism   6–22

Quality enhancement programs
  6–31—6–32, 6–151—6–156

Recruitment   6–93—6–100, 6–190
Reichmann family (Canada)   6–20
Reorganization and restructuring
  6–23—6–25, 6–40—6–42
Resistance to change   6–178—6–180,
  6–210—6–211
Retiree Job Bank   6–56—6–57
Retirement Equity Act (1984)   6–72
Retraining   6–13, 6–70
Robots and robotics   6–39
Rochester Products   6–12

Safety programs See Health and safety
  programs
Savings plans   6–196—6–197
Schools. See Education and business
  needs
Screening programs   6–77—6–78
Sears-Roebuck   6–98
Security (JOBS) programs   6–68
Security safeguards in HRIS   6–185—
  6–186
SEED. See Student Employment and
  Educational Development
  program
SEI Corp.   6–13
Selection programs   6–95—6–99,
  6–191
Shearson Lehman Hutton   6–15
Siemens   6–21
Singapore
  economic conditions   6–18
Single-subject data retrieval   6–181
Skills   6–10—6–11, 6–25, 6–27, 6–59,
  6–100
Social Security Administration. See
  U.S. Social Security
  Administration
Society for Human Resource
  Management   6–35, 6–222
Software for HRIS   6–172, 6–173,
  6–175—6–178
South Korea
  economic conditions   6–18
St. Luke's-Roosevelt Hospital
  (NY)   6–77
Staffing programs   6–207
  establishment/evaluation/
    improvement   6–92—6–100
  HRIS and   6–190—6–191
Stanley Works   6–11
Strategic planning and HRM   6–85,
  6–90, 6–188, 6–197—6–198,
  6–206—6–208, 6–211—6–212
Stroh   6–69
Student Employment and Educational
  Development (SEED)
  program   6–73—6–74
Subcontracting   6–31, 6–41
Substance and drug abuse in the
  workplace   6–13, 6–57—
  6–58, 6–77—6–78
Supercare for Kids program   6–53

Surgeon General. *See* U.S. Surgeon General
Surveys 6–110, 6–126—6–128, 6–129
Swiss Bank Corporation 6–209, 6–210

Taiwan
  economic conditions 6–18
Takeovers 6–70—6–71
Tax Reform Act (1986) 6–72
Taylor, Frederick 6–41
Teacher Academy 6–14
Technical Academic Career Program 6–62—6–63
Technology 6–65. *See also* Computer technology implementation; Telematics technologies
Telematics technologies
  automation and 6–31—6–32, 6–39—6–42
  customer service/quality and 6–38
  overview 6–30, 6–36—6–38
Termination transition services 6–68—6–70
Texas Air 6–122
Texas Instruments 6–24
The Job Bank 6–56
The Limited 6–38
3M 6–13, 6–33, 6–212
Time Inc. 6–13—6–14
Top-down communication
  computer technology implementation and 6–157—6–158, 6–160—6–161
  definition 6–143
  downsizing and 6–144—6–145
  ESOPs and 6–147—6–150
  total quality management and 6–155
Total Quality Management (TQM) 6–155—6–156
Townsend, Robert 6–217
Toyota 6–21
TQM. *See* Total Quality Management
Training and development programs
  demographic implications 6–13—6–15

  establishment/evaluation/improvement 6–100—6–106
  HRIS and 6–187, 6–192
Training and Education Center (MTEC) 6–60—6–61
Transamerica Life Company 6–53, 6–76
Transition services 6–68—6–70
Travelers Companies 6–56—6–57
TRW 6–119, 6–156, 6–220, 6–221
Tulkoff, Joseph 6–39
Turnover 6–109, 6–110, 6–111
Tuskegee Institute 6–14
Two-income families. *See* Dual-income families
Type A and Type B HR managers 6–214—6–215

Unions 6–121
United Auto Workers (UAW) 6–67, 6–68—6–69, 6–122, 6–154
United Parcel 6–212
United States
  economic conditions 6–18—6–23, 6–66
U.S. Bureau of Labor Statistics 6–3
U.S. Bureau of the Census 6–3
U.S. Department of Health and Human Services 6–54
U.S. Employment Service 6–96, 6–98
U.S. Federal Aviation Administration 6–122
U.S. General Accounting Office 6–56
U.S. Internal Revenue Service 6–115
U.S. Occupational Safety and Health Administration (OSHA) 6–74
U.S. Postal Service 6–112
U.S. Social Security Administration 6–195
U.S. Surgeon General 6–76
University of California Graduate School of Education (Berkeley) 6–64
University of Maryland 6–219, 6–222